Cognitive Behavioral Therapy for Preventing Suicide Attempts

Cognitive Behavioral Therapy for Preventing Suicide Attempts consolidates the accumulated knowledge and efforts of leading suicide researchers and describes how a common, cognitive behavioral model of suicide has resulted in 50% or greater reductions in suicide attempts across clinical settings. Simple and straightforward descriptions of these techniques are provided, along with clear explanations of the interventions' rationale and scientific support. Critically, specific adaptations of these interventions designed to meet the demands and needs of diverse settings and populations are explained. The result is a practical, clinician-friendly, how-to guide that demonstrates how to effectively reduce the risk for suicide attempts in any setting.

Craig J. Bryan, PsyD, ABPP, is a board-certified clinical psychologist in cognitive behavioral psychology and is currently the executive director of the National Center for Veterans Studies and an assistant professor in the department of psychology at the University of Utah.

Clinical Topics in Psychology and Psychiatry
Bret A. Moore, PsyD, Series Editor

Cognitive Behavioral Therapy for Preventing Suicide Attempts

A Guide to Brief Treatments Across Clinical Settings

EDITED BY CRAIG J. BRYAN

Routledge
Taylor & Francis Group

NEW YORK AND LONDON

First published 2015
by Routledge
711 Third Avenue, New York, NY 10017

and by Routledge
27 Church Road, Hove, East Sussex BN3 2FA

Routledge is an imprint of the Taylor & Francis Group, an informa business

© 2015 Taylor & Francis

Library of Congress Cataloging-in-Publication Data
Cognitive behavioral therapy for preventing suicide attempts : a guide to brief treatments across clinical settings / edited by Craig J. Bryan.
    pages cm. — (Clinical topics in psychology and psychiatry)
    Includes bibliographical references and index.
  1. Suicide—Prevention. 2. Suicidal behavior—Treatment. 3. Cognitive therapy. I. Bryan, Craig J., editor.
  RC569.C64 2015
  616.85'8445—dc23
  2014032412

ISBN: 978-0-415-85716-1 (hbk)
ISBN: 978-0-415-85717-8 (pbk)
ISBN: 978-0-203-79851-5 (ebk)

Typeset in Minion
by Apex CoVantage, LLC

Dedicated to Robert, whom I never met

Contents

Contributors

Michael D. Anestis, PhD, is the Nina Bell Suggs Professor of Psychology and the Director of the Suicide and Emotion Dysregulation Laboratory at the University of Southern Mississippi.

Emily Biggs, MA, is a project coordinator at the New York State Psychiatric Institute.

Lisa A. Brenner, PhD, ABPP, is the Director of the VA Rocky Mountain Mental Illness Research Education and Clinical Center in Denver, Colorado, and associate professor in the Departments of Psychiatry, Neurology, and Physical Medicine and Rehabilitation at the University of Colorado, Denver School of Medicine, Anschutz Medical Campus.

Peter C. Britton, PhD, is a research psychologist at the VA VISN 2 Center of Excellence for Suicide Prevention at the Canandaigua VA Medical Center and an assistant professor in the Department of Psychiatry at the University of Rochester School of Medicine and Dentistry.

Gregory K. Brown, PhD, is the Director of the Center for the Prevention of Suicide and a research associate professor of Clinical Psychology in the Department of Psychiatry at the University of Pennsylvania.

Craig J. Bryan, PsyD, ABPP, is the Executive Director of the National Center for Veterans Studies and an assistant professor in the Department of Psychology at the University of Utah.

Tracy A. Clemans, PsyD, is a research fellow at the National Center for Veterans Studies at the University of Utah.

Samantha A. Farro, PhD, is the Director of Evaluation and Research at Judi's House in Denver, Colorado.

Marjan Ghahramanlou-Holloway, PhD, is an associate professor of Medical and Clinical Psychology and the clinical internship coordinator at the Uniformed Services University of the Health Sciences.

Kelly L. Green, PhD, is a research associate in the Department of Psychiatry at the University of Pennsylvania.

Ann Marie Hernandez, PhD, is an assistant professor in the Department of Psychiatry at the University of Texas Health Science Center at San Antonio.

Beeta Y. Homaifar, PhD, is the Training Director of the Psychology Fellowship Program and Co-Director of the VA Suicide Risk Management Consultation Program at the VA Rocky Mountain Mental Illness Research, Education and Clinical Center (MIRECC) in Denver, Colorado, and assistant professor in the Departments of Psychiatry, and Physical Medicine and Rehabilitation at the University of Colorado, School of Medicine, Anschutz Medical Campus.

Lauren R. Khazem, is a graduate student in clinical psychology at the University of Southern Mississippi.

Bridget B. Matarazzo, PsyD, is the Co-Director of the Suicide Consultation Service and a clinical research psychologist at the VA Rocky Mountain Mental Illness Research, Education and Clinical Center (MIRECC) in Denver, Colorado, and assistant professor in the Department of Psychiatry at the University of Colorado, School of Medicine, Anschutz Medical Campus.

Laura L. Neely, PsyD, is the Associate Director of the Laboratory for the Treatment of Suicide-Related Ideation and Behavior at the Uniformed Services University of the Health Sciences.

M. David Rudd, PhD, ABPP, is the President of the University of Memphis and Scientific Director for the National Center for Veterans Studies.

Cemile Ceren Sonmez, is an assistant research scientist at the New York State Psychiatric Institute.

Barbara Stanley, PhD, is the Director of the Suicide Intervention Center at the New York State Psychiatric Institute and a professor of Medical Psychology in the Department of Psychiatry at Columbia University Medical Center.

Jennifer Tucker, PhD, is a postdoctoral fellow at the Laboratory for the Treatment of Suicide-Related Ideation and Behavior at the Uniformed Services University of the Health Sciences.

Series Editor's Foreword

The largest professional incongruity in the field of mental health is the fact that virtually all clinicians encounter suicidal patients in their practice, but most of those clinicians have had no or only minimal suicide-specific intervention training. As mental health professionals receive countless hours of education and training in areas such as psychodiagnostics, evidence-based psychotherapeutic techniques, and multiculturalism, it is mind boggling that most clinicians leave their graduate training ill prepared for managing the most serious of behaviors—suicide attempts. But things are changing.

A fortunate consequence of an incredibly unfortunate outcome of the wars in Iraq and Afghanistan is a renewed focus on the complexity of suicide. As a result of losing thousands of military personnel and veterans to this sad and preventable means of death, millions of dollars have been funneled to behavioral scientists to study the epidemiology and causes of and methods for preventing suicide. And the efforts are starting to bear fruit. Empirically supported interventions for suicide are proliferating throughout the Departments of Defense and Veterans Affairs, as well as among civilian clinicians who see active duty service members and veterans. Moreover, these same interventions are finding their ways into a variety of treatment settings and with a variety of patient populations.

Even though progress is being made in the area of suicide intervention, there is much more that needs to be done. Countless clinicians from the fields of psychology, counseling, social work, and psychiatry are in need of greater awareness of the theory behind why people die by suicide and evidence-based interventions for effectively managing those most at risk in a variety of settings. That's why this current volume is such a needed addition to the field of suicide prevention.

The fourth book in one of Routledge's newest series, *Clinical Topics in Psychology and Psychiatry*, *Cognitive Behavioral Therapy for Preventing Suicide Attempts: A Guide to Brief Treatments Across Clinical Settings* is a timely resource for clinicians who manage suicidal patients. Dr. Craig Bryan delivers a concise but comprehensive guide covering the most effective methods for treating suicidal patients in the most challenging settings. Consisting of the actual experts who have developed and researched these effective interventions, Dr. Bryan provides chapter after chapter of sound principles and techniques that will ready the average clinician for the most challenging patients.

Although there are numerous books available that deal with suicide, there are few that are as practical as the current volume. In addition to being a highly respected researcher, Dr. Bryan is also an accomplished clinician, educator, and trainer. Straddling the equally important sides of practice and science, Dr. Bryan is in the ideal position of delivering a depth and breadth of the topic that few can. And as a result of his experience, this volume will collect more wear from use than dust from sitting on the shelf.

Bret A. Moore, PsyD, ABPP
Series Editor
Clinical Topics in Psychology and Psychiatry

Introduction

Suicide research in the United States began in earnest during the 1950s with the work of Edwin Shneidman, Norman Farberow, and Robert Litman at the Los Angeles Suicide Prevention Center. Sixty years later, suicide continues to be a persistent and vexing public health issue and has remained among the top 10 causes of death in the United States for decades, with little indication that this trend will change in the near future. Over the past several years, public awareness of and attention to suicide has increased markedly in response to the tragic and steady rise in suicides among US military personnel and veterans, but shockingly few mental health clinicians have received formal training in the assessment, management, and treatment of actively suicidal patients. According to a recent report by the American Association of Suicidology (Schmitz et al., 2012), although approximately 90% of mental health professionals report having an actively suicidal patient on their caseloads, fewer than half received suicide-specific training while in graduate, medical, or professional training, and when training was received, it was typically less than a few hours in duration.

In the absence of sufficient training, myths and misconceptions about the effective care of suicidal patients abound, and inconsistencies in treatment and intervention approaches are the norm. Unfortunately, it is not possible to know with any certainty what type of care a suicidal individual will receive before he or she seeks out professional assistance, as there are no consistent or standardized training models or educational programs specific to this issue for mental health professionals. Of the many myths and misconceptions that exist about suicide among mental health professionals, perhaps the most persistent and pernicious assumption is that all therapies prevent suicide equally well. In my experience, few mental health clinicians actually agree with this statement, as most clinicians believe that their specific treatment approach works better than other treatment approaches (otherwise they wouldn't be using it). Nonetheless, most clinicians would agree with the suggestion that suicidal individuals should "get help" because "treatment works." Of course, the problem with this statement is that it does not tell the suicidal individual which treatments work and how to find a clinician who is able to provide it. In short, all treatments are not created equal; the brief cognitive behavioral therapies and interventions described in this book work better than other treatments.

Of course, stating that some treatments "work better" than others raises questions regarding what we mean by a treatment "working" with suicidal individuals. In this book, treatments are considered to be "better" than others if they have been tested in controlled scientific studies and have contributed to significant reductions in suicide attempts as compared to an alternative treatment. Because suicide attempts are considered to be the closest approximation to death by suicide (and because one must make a suicide attempt in order to die by suicide), incidence of suicide attempts during and following treatment is the most rigorous method for testing a treatment's efficacy. The brief cognitive behavioral therapies described in this book therefore "work better" than other treatments because they have been shown to reduce the likelihood of suicide attempts by over 50% for up to 2 years after treatment. The brief cognitive behavioral therapies described in this book also contribute to faster reductions in suicide ideation, depression, hopelessness, and other secondary outcomes.

Another common misconception about treating suicidal individuals is that being a warm and empathic clinician is the most important component of therapy and is the primary factor that reduces a patient's risk for suicide attempts. This is only partially true, however. Clinician warmth and empathy is certainly important, if not essential, when working with suicidal patients, but these variables are not sufficient to prevent suicide attempts in the absence of effective intervention. Rather, it is the combination of empirically supported interventions that are delivered by a caring, respectful, and collaborative clinician that prevents suicide attempts. To this end, all of the brief cognitive behavioral therapies and interventions described in this book begin with a narrative assessment in which the patient is allowed to "tell the story" of his or her suicidal crisis or suicide attempt without interruption or distraction. This assessment guides the clinician's case conceptualization and subsequent treatment plan, which entails selecting specific interventions from a predetermined set of options that have been empirically tested. In this way, the clinician customizes a standardized treatment approach to the unique needs of each individual patient.

Suicide is a problem that is not confined to mental health clinicians and the mental health care system. Suicidal individuals present to the emergency department, whether in crisis or following a suicide attempt, and they visit family practitioners in primary care medical settings. The therapies and interventions described in this book have therefore been adapted and adjusted to meet the unique needs and demands of different clinical settings and populations based upon a common foundation that has repeatedly proven to be effective for preventing suicide attempts. The strategies presented in this book are described by their primary developers and researchers, all of whom are friends and close collaborators. We have exchanged ideas, shared data, generated new hypotheses, critiqued each other's work, suggested new directions to pursue, and offered support and advice when faced with obstacles. We have worked together to identify and strengthen a signal for effective suicide prevention amidst the noise of myriad interventions and therapeutic approaches. My hope is that this book will provide a practical yet concise overview of the work completed to date. More work needs to be done, but we now have a clear direction forward.

References

Schmitz, W. M., Allen, M. H., Feldman, B. N., Gutin, N. J., Jahn, D. R., Kleespies, P. M., Quinnett, P., & Simpson, S. (2012). Preventing suicide through improved training in suicide risk assessment and care: An American Association of Suicidology Task Force report addressing serious gaps in U.S. mental health training. *Suicide and Life-Threatening Behavior, 42*, 292–304.

Part I
Understanding Suicide

one
The Problem of Suicide

Michael D. Anestis and Lauren R. Khazem

UNIVERSITY OF SOUTHERN MISSISSIPPI

Suicide attempt (also referred to as *suicidal self-directed violence* [SDV], see Chapter 2)—defined as deliberate and self-directed behavior resulting in injury or the potential for injury to oneself in the presence of at least some intent to die, whether implicit or explicit (Crosby, Ortega, & Melanson, 2011)—is a trans-diagnostic and tragic outcome that impacts individuals across demographic categories and geographic boundaries. Although certain populations are at particularly high risk—a point we will highlight later in this chapter—it is worth initially noting the overall impact that suicide has on both a global and national level and, in doing so, establishing with utmost clarity why suicide represents such a pressing problem.

First and foremost, by definition, suicide represents the premature end of a life, which serves as a substantial loss on its own. Additionally, loved ones who survive an individual's death by suicide are left to mourn and, due to natural responses and a variety of common misunderstandings regarding the nature and meaning of suicide attempts (e.g., Joiner, 2010), can experience outcomes ranging from normative grief to acute feelings of shame, stigma, and self-blame (e.g., Sveen & Walby, 2008). Indeed, Schneidman (1972) posited that the grief associated with the stigmatized death of a loved one (e.g., death by suicide) was distinctly different from that associated with deaths of loved ones through more socially accepted means (e.g., cancer). Similarly, individuals who have survived a nonlethal suicide attempt themselves are frequently met with stigma that could further interfere with recovery and future mental health–related outcomes (e.g., Batterham, Calear, & Christensen, 2013; Lester & Walker, 2006). In addition to the loss of life, death by suicide is associated with a substantial economic burden estimated to total approximately $34 billion per year in the United States, in addition to an estimated $8 billion per year in lost wages, lost productivity, and direct medical care for those who make suicide attempts (American Foundation for Suicide Prevention, 2013). As such, suicide attempts and, by extension, death by suicide, are problematic for reasons that extend beyond the act itself.

Although some interventions have been developed specifically to address suicide attempts (e.g., dialectical behavior therapy; Linehan & Heard, 1992), there remains a dearth of evidence-based approaches to prevent suicide attempts and limited implementation of those that exist (e.g., Jobes, 2012; Jobes & Berman, 1993; Jobes, Rudd, Overholser, & Joiner, 2008). As such, despite increased knowledge regarding risk factors for and correlates of suicide attempts (e.g., Bagge & Sher, 2008; Bostwick & Pankratz, 2000; Joiner, 2005; Nock, Joiner, Gordon, Lloyd-Richardson, & Prinstein, 2006), we remain somewhat ill equipped to stem the tide of death by suicide in a practical, cost-effective way. The purpose of summarizing the evidence underlying brief cognitive behavior therapy for suicidal individuals across a variety of settings is thus quite clear.

General Rates of Suicide and Suicide Attempts

Each year, approximately 1 million individuals die by suicide worldwide, translating to a rate of approximately 16 per 100,000 (World Health Organization, 2013). In 2010, the most recent year for which such data are currently available, 38,364 individuals died by suicide in the United States alone (50.5% by self-inflicted gunshot wounds), translating to an age-adjusted rate of approximately 12.08 per 100,000 (Centers for Disease Control and Prevention, 2013). This represents a stark increase relative to the early 2000s. In 2001, for instance, 30,622 individuals died by suicide (55.0% by self-inflicted gunshot wounds) in the United States, translating to an age-adjusted rate of 10.71 per 100,000 (CDC, 2013).

The overall increase in deaths by suicide within the United States has occurred among both males and females. In 2001, males represented 80.6% of US suicide deaths, with an age-adjusted rate of 18.17 per 100,000 (females died at a rate of 4.06 per 100,000). In 2010, males represented 78.9% of US suicide deaths, with an age-adjusted rate of 19.78 per 100,000 (females died at a rate of 4.99 per 100,000). Other demographic variables, however, reveal a substantial level of variability across groups over this time period.

Age is a particularly telling example of this phenomenon. In 2001, the rate for death by suicide was highest in older adults. Adults aged 75–79 died at a rate of 16.35 per 100,000, adults aged 80–84 died at a rate of 18.94 per 100,000, and adults aged 85 and older died at a rate of 17.83 per 100,000. These numbers declined by 2010, with adults aged 75–79 dying at a rate of 15.29 per 100,000, adults aged 80–84 dying at a rate of 16.24 per 100,000, and adults aged 85 and older dying at a rate of 17.62 per 100,000 (CDC, 2013). The trend for middle-aged adults, however, was quite different. In 2001, adults aged 45–49 died by suicide at a rate of 15.75 per 100,000, and adults aged 50–54 died by suicide at a rate of 14.35 per 100,000. In 2010, however, those numbers increased to 19.25 and 19.85 respectively (CDC, 2013). Given that middle-aged adults account for a substantially greater proportion of the population, this increase represents a potentially crucial explanation for the overall increase in deaths by suicide within the United States.

A substantial shift is also evident when examining the numbers by race. In 2001, the rates of death by suicide for Americans who self-identified as White, Black, American Indian/Alaskan Native, and Asian/Pacific Islander were 11.71, 5.45, 10.46, and 5.34 per 100,000, respectively (data were not reported for other racial groups; CDC, 2013). In 2010, however, whereas suicide rates remained relatively stable for those who identified as Black, American Indian/Alaskan Native, and Asian Pacific Islander (5.19, 10.87, and 6.19 per 100,000, respectively), the suicide rate for White Americans increased substantially (13.55 per 100,000). Given that White Americans represented 79.5% of the US population in 2010, the impact of this increase on the overall US suicide rate is clear.

Although obviously problematic, these numbers do not illustrate the entirety of the issue. Indeed, the impact of suicide attempts extends beyond death by suicide. In 2010, a total of 464,995 individuals (age-adjusted rate = 152.96 per 100,000) within the United States received treatment in an emergency room for all forms of self-directed violence, meaning that for every death by suicide (n = 38,364), there were 12.12 cases of suicidal and nonsuicidal SDV (CDC, 2013). Here again, a shift has emerged since 2001, when 323,370 Americans presented at emergency rooms for self-inflicted injuries, representing an age-adjusted rate of 112.82 per 100,000 and a ratio of nonlethal to lethal (n = 30,622) SDV of 10.56.

It is important to note that these numbers do not account for the presence of suicidal intent and, as such, it is entirely plausible that a number of these cases are better classified as *nonsuicidal self-injury* or *nonsuicidal self-directed violence* rather than suicide attempts; however, the use of emergency room data also undoubtedly severely underestimates the total number of suicide attempts that occur in the United States, as a substantial number of suicide attempts that result in no or minimal injury likely result in either no medical attention or limited care in alternative, nonemergency medical settings. As such, although nonlethal and lethal SDV can be accurately conceptualized as low base-rate behaviors, the scope of their impact on society is nonetheless considerable.

High-Risk Populations and Environments

The primary aim of this book is to describe the evidence supporting, methods for utilizing, and feasibility of implementing brief cognitive behavioral therapy for suicidal patients across diverse groups and clinical settings. Outpatient mental health settings, inpatient psychiatric settings, emergency departments, primary care, and military settings will be specifically considered in depth in later chapters. Before presenting such information, however, it seems worth noting why these settings were chosen and in what ways suicide represents a substantial problem for each.

Suicide Attempts Among Patients in Outpatient Mental Health Settings

Although outpatient mental health services can, in some ways, be seen as an indicator of less clinical severity than those treating patients with inpatient services, the veracity of such views can vary by setting, patient, and primary diagnostic presentations. Consequently, the presence of suicide attempts resulting in death remains a legitimate possibility. Indeed, efforts have been made to develop systematic methods for assessing suicide risk across outpatient settings (e.g., Joiner, Walker, Rudd, & Jobes, 1999), and evidence-based treatments specifically designed for highly suicidal patients have been created specifically for such populations (e.g., dialectical behavior therapy; Linehan & Heard, 1992).

Because outpatient populations represent such a diverse group, establishing a single rate of nonlethal versus lethal suicide attempts in such settings is challenging, and any such numbers should be interpreted within the context of the institutional environment (e.g., military versus civilian) and diagnostic composition (e.g., inpatient eating disorder treatment facilities versus inpatient units for acutely suicidal individuals) of the sample. Using two cohorts of veterans who utilized Veterans Affairs (VA) hospitals in 1997 and 2001, for instance, Desai, Rosenheck, and Desai (2008) reported a rate of death by suicide of 8.94 per 100,000 in outpatients as compared to 18.29 per 100,000 in inpatients; however, as we discuss in greater detail later in this chapter, these data were drawn from a period of time when the rate of death by suicide in military personnel was substantially lower than it is today. Steer, Brown, and Beck (2006) followed a group of 6,891 civilian outpatients over the course of 10 years and reported that the daily hazard rate for death by suicide decreased rapidly during the first 3 years after an initial psychiatric evaluation before reaching a level too low to predict, with 49 (0.7%) individuals dying by suicide during the course of the follow-up period. This group, however, encompassed a broad array of suicide risk and diagnostic statuses and does not necessarily speak to an overall trend in outpatient settings in general. Indeed, if a particular outpatient setting sees a higher proportion of clients diagnosed with conditions characterized by greater suicide risk (e.g., borderline personality disorder, bipolar disorder; Frances, Fyer, & Clarkin, 1986; Hawton, Sutton, Haw, Sinclair, & Harriss, 2005; Skodol et al., 2002), it would be reasonable to assume that rates of nonlethal and lethal suicide attempts would likely rise as well, highlighting the need for such settings to incorporate brief evidence-based treatments that directly impact suicide risk.

Suicide Attempts Among Patients in Inpatient Psychiatric Settings

Inpatient hospitalization for suicidal clients has undergone considerable change over the past several decades, with the length of stay and feasibility of insurance coverage for such stays diminishing (e.g., Olfson, Gameroff, Marcus, Greenberg, & Shaffer, 2005). This, along with debate regarding the effectiveness of repeated inpatient stays, has led many to advocate for caution in the use of inpatient hospitalization (e.g., Jobes, 2006; Jobes, Rudd, Overholser, & Joiner, 2008). In some areas, the number of available inpatient beds has decreased dramatically, further contributing to changes in how decisions about this treatment modality occur. For example, between 1995 and 2001, the Department of Veterans Affairs (VA) closed two-thirds of their previously available inpatient beds (Desai et al., 2008). The need for inpatient hospitalization in moments of severe and imminent risk remains largely uncontested; however, it is important to consider the risk of suicide attempts in such settings and the best practices for preventing such outcomes.

A number of studies have indicated that the majority of inpatient psychiatric units utilize "no-suicide contracts" with patients, in which the patient signs his or her name on a binding contract (although such contracts are not truly legally binding) to indicate that they agree not to make a suicide attempt during the course of treatment (e.g., Drew, 2001). Importantly, evidence indicates that these contracts are at best ineffective (e.g., Jobes et al., 2008; Rudd, Mandrusiak, & Joiner, 2006) and at worst iatrogenic (e.g., Drew, 2001). As such, the form of treatment reserved for acute crises (inpatient psychiatric units) is characterized by the frequent use of a problematic procedure.

Compounding this situation is the frequency with which suicide attempts occur in inpatient units. Although, like suicide in general, this phenomenon is a low base-rate outcome, the raw numbers are nonetheless problematic. In 2003, the American Psychiatric Association reported a total of roughly 1,500 deaths by suicide in inpatient units in the United States. Furthermore, it noted that one in three of those deaths occurred while individuals were on 15-minute checks in which hospital staff regularly checked on the safety of the patient. Approximately 75% of those deaths resulted from hanging, with jumping from a high place serving as the second leading cause (Joint Commission Sentinel Event Report, 1998). More recently, Mills, King, Watts, and Hemphill (in press) examined rates of suicide attempts within inpatient mental health units in Veterans Affairs (VA) hospitals between the years of 1999 and 2011 and found that a total of 243 suicide deaths occurred in such settings over that time period, with the most frequent methods being hanging (43.6%), cutting (22.6%), and strangulation (15.6%).

These numbers highlight the point that simple hospitalization in and of itself may not be sufficient as a treatment option and that even when staff diligently check on the safety of patients on a regular and fairly high-frequency schedule, prevention of death by suicide cannot always be assured. This highlights the discomforting fact that even in settings where means for suicide can be highly restricted, a patient with a strong desire to die can often find a method by which to arrive at that outcome. Therefore, the importance of developing brief and effective evidence-based treatment approaches for suicidal patients in such settings is critical.

Suicide Attempts Among Patients Presenting to Emergency Departments

Between the years of 1993 and 2008, an average of 420,000 individuals within the United States presented to emergency departments (EDs) each year due to an episode of SDV, whether with or without suicidal intent (Ting, Sullivan, Boudreaux, Miller, & Camargo, 2012). Individuals who present to emergency departments (EDs) in the midst of a suicidal crisis represent an important clinical concern. Indeed, although releasing acutely suicidal individuals from such settings without treatment is clearly suboptimal, data indicate that the decision to hospitalize acutely suicidal individuals often produces similarly disappointing results. For example, between the years of 2004 and 2006, 16.09% of individuals who died by suicide in Florida had experienced an emergency commitment during the 4 years preceding their deaths, with 14.7% of those individuals dying within a month of their commitment and 7.1% within 2 weeks (Roggenbaum et al., 2008). Gairin, House, and Owns (2003) similarly reported in an independent study that 39% of a sample of 85 suicide decedents had visited an ED in the year prior to their death.

The fact that many suicide decedents presented to EDs not long before their deaths highlights the point that EDs serve as a vital point of intervention. Proper training in brief, evidence-based treatments geared specifically toward the mitigation of suicide risk is therefore critical for clinicians working in this setting. Indeed, evidence has shown that educating ED personnel on their role as gatekeepers in identifying suicide risk is associated with reductions in suicide rates (Mann et al., 2005), and training staff to educate patients on means restriction results in greater efforts on the parts of families to reduce access to highly lethal means within their homes (e.g., Kruesi et al., 1999). These results indicate that EDs have the potential to provide high-yield results during short interactions with high-risk individuals.

Suicide Attempts Among Patients Treated in Primary Care Medical Settings

Although studies show that only a small percentage of primary care providers have specific and adequate training in suicide risk assessment (e.g., Stuber & Quinnett, 2013), up to 75% of suicide decedents come into contact with such providers within 30 days of their death (e.g., Appleby et al., 1999; Arean, Alvidrez, Barera, Robinson, & Hicks, 2002). This indicates that a large proportion of individuals at the greatest risk for imminent death by suicide are seeking services in settings that are not optimally prepared to address their needs. Along these lines, rates of visits to primary care providers substantially exceed the rates of visits to mental health specialists amongst individuals who die by suicide in the time leading up to their deaths, further highlighting the vital role that primary care providers could play in the detection and mitigation of risk if given proper training in brief and effective intervention techniques (e.g., Luoma, Martin, & Pearson, 2002; Schulberg et al., 2004).

Unfortunately, recent data indicate that thorough risk assessments in primary care settings are fairly uncommon, with physicians reporting they ask their patients about suicide risk only 36% of the time (Hooper et al., 2012). The decision to assess for risk is often driven by the presence of overt risk factors (e.g., severe depression); however, data indicate that only 19–54% of individuals who die by suicide after visiting a primary care physician report to their physician that they are experiencing suicidal ideation during their appointment (Schulberg et al., 2004). Consequently, a large proportion of high-risk individuals presenting in primary care settings end up not being assessed for suicide risk because they do not volunteer information or demonstrate any objective indicators of suicide risk factors. The need for the systematic implementation of proper risk assessment procedures and the provision of brief evidence-based interventions for suicidal patients in primary care settings is thus essential.

Suicide Attempts Among Military Personnel

Historically, the rate of death by suicide in the military has been lower than that of the general population (e.g., Rothberg et al., 1990); however, in recent years this trend has reversed, with the military suicide rate now exceeding that of the civilians (e.g., Department of Defense Task Force on the Prevention of Suicide by Members of the Armed Forces [DOD TFPS], 2010; Lorge, 2008). Data indicate that deployment factors alone do not exhibit a robust association with death by suicide (e.g., LeardMann et al., 2013) and instead point toward risk factors similar to those in the general population as well as the cumulative stress of military life during an extended period of war.

In another troubling development, recent data have indicated that the ratio of nonlethal to lethal suicide attempts among military personnel (3.07 to 1) is significantly lower than that of the general population (12.12 to 1)—a finding that remains unchanged regardless of sex and age and whether or not self-inflicted gunshot wounds are included in the analysis (Anestis & Bryan, 2013). These numbers indicate that when service members engage in suicide attempts, they are substantially more likely to die as a result than the members of the general population. Indeed, studies have found that US Air Force personnel who recently completed basic training exhibit higher mean levels of the capacity for suicide (Joiner, 2005) than civilians in outpatient mental health treatment, which included civilians with a history of multiple suicide attempts (Bryan, Morrow,

Anestis, & Joiner, 2010). This greater capacity for suicide attempts, in combination with the greater likelihood that service members will select a high-lethality method for suicide attempts such as self-inflicted gunshot wound (e.g., Anestis & Bryan, 2013; Kaplan, Huguet, McFarland, & Newson, 2007), creates a truly problematic situation in which suicidal desire among service members is more likely to be associated with a willingness and capability of enacting a plan with a high probability of resulting in death.

Given that suicidal desire is more likely to be accompanied by the capability for enacting lethal suicide attempts in military populations, detecting risk early and implementing brief evidence-based approaches to reduce suicide attempts among military personnel is paramount. That being said, organizational (e.g., fear of risking future promotions) and cultural (e.g., fear of stigma) obstacles can deter service members from voicing distress and seeking mental health care. As such, culturally sensitive methods for disseminating evidence-based treatments in this population, along with continued efforts to encourage fellow service members to seek help without fear of repercussion represent vital goals in coming years.

Summary

Suicide attempts are a relatively low base-rate phenomenon, but the scope of their impact is remarkably large and extends to a broad array of populations across the full spectrum of health care settings. No demographic group is immune to this outcome (or the effects of losing someone to suicide); however, some groups are at particularly high risk and some environments represent robust opportunities for reducing risk and saving lives. In this chapter, we discussed the overall impact of suicide attempts globally and within the United States and then focused on five subgroups that will be of primary interest in this book: outpatient mental health settings, inpatient psychiatric settings, emergency departments, primary care, and the military. By more successfully implementing evidence-based treatments in a manner that is plausible given the demands of each environment, clinicians have an opportunity to reverse many of the troubling trends discussed in this chapter and, in doing so, reduce the burden of grief and pain associated with suicide.

References

American Foundation for Suicide Prevention (2013). *Facts and figures*. Retrieved from www.afsp.org/understanding-suicide/facts-and-figures

Anestis, M. D., & Bryan, C. J. (2013). Means and capacity for suicidal behavior: A comparison of the ratio of suicide attempts and deaths by suicide in the US military and general population. *Journal of Affective Disorders, 148*, 42–47.

Appleby, L., Shaw, J., Amos, T., McDonnel, R., Harris, C., McCann, K. et al. (1999). Suicide within 12 months of contact with mental health services: National clinical survey. *British Medical Journal, 318*, 1235–1239.

Arean, P. A., Alvidrez, J., Barrera, A., Robinson, G. S., & Hicks, S. (2002). Would older medical patients use psychological services? *Gerontologist, 42*, 392–398.

Bagge, C. L., & Sher, K. J. (2008). Adolescent alcohol involvement and suicide attempts: Toward the development of a conceptual framework. *Clinical Psychology Review, 28*, 1283–1296.

Batterham, P. J., Calear, A. L., & Christensen, H. (2013). The Stigma of Suicide Scale: Psychometric properties and correlates of the stigma of suicide. *Crisis: The Journal of Crisis Intervention and Suicide Prevention, 34*, 13–21.

Bostwick, J. M., & Pankratz, V. S. (2000). Affective disorders and suicide risk: A reexamination. *American Journal of Psychiatry, 157*, 1925–1932.

Bryan, C. J., Morrow, C. E., Anestis, M. D., & Joiner, T. E. (2010). A preliminary test of the interpersonal-psychological theory of suicidal behavior in a military sample. *Personality and Individual Differences, 48*, 47–50.

Centers for Disease Control and Prevention (2013). *Web-Based Injury Statistics Query and Reporting System* (WISQARS). Retrieved from www.cdc.gov/injury/wisqars/index.html

Crosby, A. E., Ortega, L., & Melanson, C. (2011). *Self-directed violence surveillance: Uniform definitions and recommended data elements, Version 1.0.* Atlanta, GA: Centers for Disease Control and Prevention, National Center for Injury Prevention and Control. Retrieved from www.cdc.gov/violenceprevention/pdf/Self-Directed-Violence-a.pdf

Department of Defense Task Force on the Prevention of Suicide by Members of the Armed Forces [DOD TFPS]. (2010). The challenge and the promise: Strengthening the force, preventing suicide, and saving lives. Washington, DC: Department of Defense.

Desai, M. M., Rosenheck, R. A., & Desai, R. A. (2008). Time trends and predictors of suicide among mental health outpatients in the Department of Veterans Affairs. *Journal of Behavioral Health Services & Research, 35*, 115–124.

Drew, B. L. (2001). Self-harm behavior and no-suicide contracting in psychiatric inpatient settings. *Archives of Psychiatric Nursing, 15*, 99–106.

Frances, A., Fyer, M., & Clarkin, J. (1986). Personality and suicide. *Annals of the New York Academy of Sciences: Psychobiology of Suicidal Behavior, 487*, 281–293.

Gairin, I., House, A., & Owns, D. (2003). Attendance at the accident and emergency department in the year before suicide: Retrospective study. *The British Journal of Psychiatry, 183*, 28–33.

Hawton, K., Sutton, L., Haw, C., Sinclair, J., & Harriss, L. (2005). Suicide and attempted suicide in bipolar disorder: A systematic review of risk factors. *Journal of Clinical Psychiatry, 66*, 693–704.

Hooper, L. M., Epstein, S. A., Weinfurt, K. P., DeCoster, J., Qu, L., & Hannah, N. J. (2012). Predictors of primary care physicians' self-reported intention to conduct suicide risk assessments. *Journal of Behavioral Health Services & Research, 39*, 103–115.

Jobes, D. A. (2006). *Managing suicidal risk: A collaborative approach.* New York: Guilford Press.

Jobes, D. A. (2012). The Collaborative Assessment and Management of Suicidality (CAMS): An evolving evidence-based clinical approach to suicidal risk. *Suicide and Life-Threatening Behavior, 42*, 640–653.

Jobes, D. A., & Berman, A. L. (1993). Suicide and malpractice liability: Assessing and revisiting policies, procedures, and practice in outpatient settings. *Professional Psychology: Research and Practice, 24*, 91–99.

Jobes, D. A., Rudd, M. D., Overholser, J. C., & Joiner, T. E. (2008). Ethical and competent care of suicidal patients: Contemporary challenges, new developments, and considerations for clinical practice. *Professional Psychology: Research and Practice, 39*, 405–413.

Joiner, T. E. (2005). *Why people die by suicide.* Cambridge, MA: Harvard University Press.

Joiner, T. E. (2010). *Myths about suicide.* Cambridge, MA: Harvard University Press.

Joiner, T. E., Walker, R. L., Rudd, M. D., & Jobes, D. A. (1999). Scientizing and routinizing the assessment of suicidality in outpatient practice. *Professional Psychology: Research and Practice, 30,* 447–453.

Joint Commission Sentinel Event Alert (1998, November 6). Issue 7: Inpatient suicides: Recommendations for prevention. Retrieved from www.jointcommission.org/assets/1/18/SEA_7.pdf

Kaplan, M. S., Huguet, N., McFarland, B. H., & Newsom, J. T. (2007). Suicide among male veterans: A prospective population-based study. *Journal of Epidemiology and Community Health, 61,* 619–624.

Kruesi, M. J., Grossman, J., Pennington, J. M., Woodward, P. J., Duda, D., & Hirsh, J. G. (1999). Suicide and violence prevention: Parent education in the emergency department. *Journal of the American Academy of Child and Adolescent Psychiatry, 38,* 250–255.

LeardMann, C. A., Powell, T. M., Smith, T. C., Bell, M. R., Smith, B., Boyko, E. J. et al. (2013). Risk factors associated with suicide in current and former US military personnel. *Journal of the American Medical Association, 310,* 496–506.

Lester, D., & Walker, R. L. (2006). The stigma for attempting suicide and the loss to suicide prevention efforts. *Crisis: The Journal of Crisis Intervention and Suicide Prevention, 27,* 147–148.

Linehan, M. M., & Heard, H. L. (1992). Dialectical behavior therapy for borderline personality disorder. In J. F. Clarkin, E. Marziali, & H. Munroe-Blum (Eds.), *Borderline personality disorder: Clinical and empirical perspectives* (pp. 248–267). New York: Guilford Press.

Lorge, E. (2008). Army responds to rising suicide rates. Retrieved from www.army.mil/article/7222/Army_Responds_to_Rising_Suicide_Rates/

Luoma, J. B., Martin, C., & Pearson, J. L. (2002). Contact with mental health and primary care providers before suicide: A review of the evidence. *American Journal of Psychiatry, 159,* 909–916.

Mann, J. J., Apter, A., Bertolote, J., Beautrais, A., Currier, D., Haas, A. et al. (2005). Suicide prevention strategies: A systematic review. *Journal of the American Medical Association, 294,* 2064–2074.

Mills, P. D., King, L. A., Watts, B. V., & Hemphill, R. R. (in press). Inpatient suicide on mental health units in Veterans Affairs (VA) hospitals: Avoiding environmental hazards. *General Hospital Psychiatry.*

Nock, M. K., Joiner, T. E., Gordon, K. H., Lloyd-Richardson, E., & Prinstein, M. J. (2006). Non-suicidal self-injury among adolescents: Diagnostic correlates and relation to suicide attempts. *Psychiatry Research, 144,* 65–72.

Olfson, M., Gameroff, M. J., Marcus, S. C., Greenberg, T., & Shaffer, D. (2005). National trends in hospitalization of youth with intentional self-inflicted injuries. *American Journal of Psychiatry, 162,* 1328–1335.

Roggenbaum, S., Christy, A., LeBlanc, A., McCranie, M., Murrin, M. R., & Li, Y. (2008). *The relationship of suicide death to Baker Act examination, client characteristics and severe use patterns.* Tampa, FL: University of South Florida, Louis de la Parte Florida Mental Health Institute.

Rothberg, J. M., Bartone, P. T., Holloway, H. C., & Marlowe, D. H. (1990). Life and death in the U.S. Army. *Journal of the American Medical Association, 264,* 2241–2244.

Rudd, M. D., Mandrusiak, M., & Joiner, T. E. (2006). The case against no-suicide contracts: The commitment to treatment statement as a practice alternative. *Journal of Clinical Psychology: In Session, 62,* 243–251.

Schneidman, E. S. (1972). Forward to A. C. Cain (Ed.), *Survivors of suicide*. Springfield, Ill: Charles C. Thomas.

Schulberg, H. C., Bruce, M. L., Lee, P. W. et al. (2004). Preventing suicide in primary care patients: The primary care physician's role. *General Hospital Psychiatry, 26*, 337–345.

Skodol, A. E., Gunderson, J. G., Pfohl, B., Widiger, T. A., Livesley, W. J. et al. (2002). The borderline diagnosis I: Psychopathology, comorbidity, and personality structure. *Biological Psychiatry, 51*, 936–950.

Steer, R. A., Brown, G. K., & Beck, A. T. (2006). When does the daily hazard rate for committing suicide stabilize in psychiatric outpatients? *Psychological Reports, 99*, 462–464.

Stuber, J., & Quinnett, P. (2013). Making the case for primary care and mandated suicide prevention education. *Suicide and Life-Threatening Behavior, 43*, 117–124.

Sveen, C-A., & Walby, F. A. (2008). Suicide survivors' mental health and grief reactions: A systematic review of controlled studies. *Suicide and Life-Threatening Behavior, 38*, 13–29.

Ting, S. A., Sullivan, A. F., Boudreaux, E. D., Miller, I., & Camargo, C. A. (2012). Trends in US emergency department visits for attempted suicide and self-inflicted injury, 1993–2008. *General Hospital Psychiatry, 34*, 557–565.

World Health Organization (2013). Suicide prevention (SUPRE). Retrieved from www.who.int/mental_health/prevention/suicide/suicideprevent/en/

two
The Language of Suicide

Bridget B. Matarazzo, Beeta Y. Homaifar,
Samantha A. Farro, and Lisa A. Brenner

VISN 19 MIRECC, DENVER VETERANS AFFAIRS
MEDICAL CENTER

The field of suicidology has been challenged by a lack of conceptual clarity about suicidal thoughts and behaviors, as well as associated terms (e.g., suicidal intent; Institute of Medicine, 2002). As a result, the theoretical and scientific literature on suicide is replete with confusing terms, definitions, and classifications, making it difficult to compare and contrast one clinical case, research study, or epidemiological survey with another (Fischer, Comstock, Monk, & Sencer, 1993). Further, terms that are used within the literature are at times pejorative and based on incorrect notions about the seriousness of behaviors (e.g., suicide attempts described as manipulative).

This chapter describes clinical, research, and public policy–related challenges that result from not having a consistent language related to self-directed violence (SDV). SDV encompasses a range of related yet distinct thoughts and behaviors. Examples of terms used to describe SDV include suicidal ideation, preparatory behavior, suicide attempts, and suicide. The Self-Directed Violence Classification System (SDVCS) is introduced as a solution to these challenges, and its structure is briefly discussed, with a table and figure to facilitate ease of use. Relevant examples of how the SDVCS can be used to facilitate communication in clinical, research, and policy settings are offered. Dissemination and implementation efforts are then discussed. Lastly, future directions and conclusions are suggested.

Challenges of Inconsistent Language

The need for a common language related to SDV has been thoroughly documented in the literature (De Leo, Burgis, Bertolote, Kerkhof, & Bille-Brahe, 2006; Silverman, 2006). A *nomenclature* refers to "a set of commonly understood, widely acceptable, comprehensive terms that define the base clinical phenomena of suicide and suicide-related behaviors" (Silverman, 2006, p. 520). Silverman (2006) points out that an ideal nomenclature is theory neutral, culturally normative, and contains mutually exclusive terms. Whereas a nomenclature helps professionals to specify and define SDV, a *classification system* allows for the categorization of thoughts and behaviors into distinct groups (Silverman, 2006). Classification systems are dependent upon the nomenclature on which they are based. The lack of a useful nomenclature precludes the development of a classification system, which in turn can impact clinical practice, research, surveillance, and public policy efforts.

With respect to clinical practice, inconsistent language can impede communication between providers, thereby negatively impacting case conceptualization and treatment planning. For example, one provider may document a patient's behavior as a "suicide attempt," whereas another provider may describe the same behavior as a "suicide gesture." Current or future providers reading the medical record may find it challenging to determine whether or not suicidal intent was present at the time of the behavior. In turn, the presence or absence of intent would be expected to impact treatment planning and decision making regarding indicated evidence-based interventions. Use of the two terms to describe the same behavior may also lead to additional confusion regarding whether they are being used to describe the same or different episodes of SDV.

In addition to the above noted impact on clinical practice, lack of a consistent nomenclature impedes progress and clarity of research regarding populations with a history of and/or increased risk for SDV. Specifically, inconsistent use of language to describe cohorts being studied or outcomes of interest negatively impacts the ability to compare or combine results or to generalize results. Consequently, it may be difficult for clinicians to know when and with whom to implement findings.

Similar to the impacts seen in clinical practice and research, a major barrier to implementing effective public policy for preventing and addressing the problem of SDV is that even basic surveillance efforts regarding SDV incidence rates are hindered by the inconsistent use of terms and definitions across agencies and studies. Silverman et al. (2007a) note that national surveys estimating rates of occurrence use different definitions for "suicidal behavior" and that, in order to conduct meaningful surveillance, behaviors of interest need to be defined and distinguishable from one another. Additionally, the accuracy of data collected on cultural and sociodemographic trends/differences in suicidal thoughts/behaviors is likely compromised by the lack of a common nomenclature. This in turn could result in inadequate attention being paid to under-recognized at-risk populations (Crosby, Ortega, & Melanson, 2011). Consequently, the development of *effective* public policy is hindered because policies are informed and guided by imprecise data.

The Self-Directed Violence Classification System (SDVCS)

With the goal of increasing suicide prevention efforts, the former Secretary of the Department of Veterans Affairs (VA), Dr. James B. Peake, formed the "Blue Ribbon Work Group on Suicide Prevention in the Veterans Population" (Department of Veterans Affairs, 2008a). Members of the Blue Ribbon panel noted the absence of clearly operationalized definitions of terms related to SDV as a long-standing problem (Department of Veterans Affairs, 2008b). Given the implications of this conclusion, adoption of a "standard definition" for terms, particularly for "suicide" and "suicide attempts," was recommended by the work group (Department of Veterans Affairs, 2008b). In response to this recommendation, in 2008, clinical researchers at the Veterans Integrated Service Network 19 Mental Illness, Research, Education and Clinical Center (VISN 19 MIRECC) began creating a nomenclature and associated classification system to be used for clinical purposes.

Similarly, the Centers for Disease Control and Prevention (CDC) highlighted that communication among professionals such as researchers and clinicians will be improved with the use of consistent terminology with standardized definitions (Crosby et al., 2011). In response to the need for uniform definitions of terms related to SDV, the CDC proposed a set of definitions for SDV surveillance. The authors of this system noted that the uniform definitions were defined in a general sense and that users other than those working in public health surveillance, such as in clinical practice, may need to further refine the terms.

In response to and in collaboration with the CDC, the VISN 19 MIRECC further refined the CDC-proposed SDV terms and developed the SDVCS. The SDVCS is a taxonomy of terms and corresponding definitions for thoughts and behaviors related to suicidal and non-suicidal SDV. The classification system was developed on the basis of prior nomenclatures and classification systems for SDV (O'Carroll, Berman, Maris, Moscicki, Tanney, & Silverman, 1996; Silverman, Berman, Sanddal, O'Carroll, & Joiner, 2007b; Beck et al., 1972) and was informed by researchers, clinicians, and policy experts in the field of suicide (Silverman et al., 2007a; Silverman et al., 2007b; Posner, Oquendo, Gould, Stanley, & Davies, 2007; Brenner et al., 2011; Rosenberg et al., 1988).

Structure of the SDVCS

The SDVCS is comprised of 22 terms related to suicidal and non-suicidal SDV (see Table 2.1) that are categorized into two groups, *thoughts* and *behaviors*, which are further divided into subtypes. Thoughts are categorized as either "non-suicidal

TABLE 2.1. Self-Directed Violence Classification System

Type	Subtype	Definition	Modifiers	Terms
Thoughts	Non-Suicidal Self-Directed Violence Ideation	Self-reported thoughts regarding a person's desire to engage in self-inflicted potentially injurious behavior. There is no evidence of suicidal intent. For example, persons engage in Non-Suicidal Self-Directed Violence Ideation in order to attain some other end (e.g., to seek help, regulate negative mood, punish others, receive attention).	N/A	• Non-Suicidal Self-Directed Violence Ideation
	Suicidal Ideation	Thoughts of engaging in suicide-related behavior. For example, intrusive thoughts of suicide without the wish to die would be classified as Suicidal Ideation, Without Intent.	• Suicidal Intent: —Without —Undetermined —With	• Suicidal Ideation, Without Suicidal Intent • Suicidal Ideation, With Undetermined Suicidal Intent • Suicidal Ideation, With Suicidal Intent
Behaviors	Preparatory	Acts or preparation toward engaging in Self-Directed Violence but before potential for injury has begun. This can include anything beyond a verbalization or thought, such as assembling a method (e.g., buying a gun, collecting pills) or preparing for one's death by suicide (e.g., writing a suicide note, giving things away). For example, hoarding medication for the purpose of overdosing would be classified as Suicidal Self-Directed Violence, Preparatory.	• Suicidal Intent: —Without —Undetermined —With	• Non-Suicidal Self-Directed Violence, Preparatory • Undetermined Self-Directed Violence, Preparatory • Suicidal Self-Directed Violence, Preparatory

Continued overleaf

TABLE 2.1. *(continued).* Self-Directed Violence Classification System

Type	Subtype	Definition	Modifiers	Terms
	Non-Suicidal Self-Directed Violence	Behavior that is self-directed and deliberately results in injury or the potential for injury to oneself. There is no evidence, whether implicit or explicit, of suicidal intent. For example, persons engage in Non-Suicidal Self-Directed Violence in order to attain some other end (e.g., to seek help, regulate negative mood, punish others, receive attention).	• Injury: —Without —With —Fatal • Interrupted by Self or Other	• Non-Suicidal Self-Directed Violence, Without Injury • Non-Suicidal Self-Directed Violence, Without Injury, Interrupted by Self or Other • Non-Suicidal Self-Directed Violence, With Injury • Non-Suicidal Self-Directed Violence, With Injury, Interrupted by Self or Other • Non-Suicidal Self-Directed Violence, Fatal
	Undetermined Self-Directed Violence	Behavior that is self-directed and deliberately results in injury or the potential for injury to oneself. Suicidal intent is unclear based upon the available evidence. For example, the person is unable to admit positively to the intent to die (e.g., unconsciousness, incapacitation, intoxication, acute psychosis, disorientation, or death); **OR** the person is reluctant to admit positively to the intent to die for other or unknown reasons.	• Injury: —Without —With —Fatal • Interrupted by Self or Other	• Undetermined Self-Directed Violence, Without Injury • Undetermined Self-Directed Violence, Without Injury, Interrupted by Self or Other • Undetermined Self-Directed Violence, With Injury • Undetermined Self-Directed Violence, With Injury, Interrupted by Self or Other • Undetermined Self-Directed Violence, Fatal
	Suicidal Self-Directed Violence	Behavior that is self-directed and deliberately results in injury or the potential for injury to oneself. There is evidence, whether implicit or explicit, of suicidal intent. For example, a person with the wish to die cutting her wrists with a knife would be classified as Suicide Attempt, With Injury.	• Injury: —Without —With —Fatal • Interrupted by Self or Other	• Suicide Attempt, Without Injury • Suicide Attempt, Without Injury, Interrupted by Self or Other • Suicide Attempt, With Injury • Suicide Attempt, With Injury, Interrupted by Self or Other • Suicide

self-directed violence ideation" or "suicidal ideation," and behaviors are categorized as either "preparatory," "non-suicidal self-directed violence," "undetermined self-directed violence," or "suicidal self-directed violence." Subtypes of behaviors are then modified by intent, interruption by self or other, and injury. The resulting 22 terms are theory and culture neutral and mutually exclusive, such that any example of ideation or behavior can only be classified by one term (Brenner et al., 2011).

Key Terms

Self-Directed Violence: Behavior that is self-directed and deliberately results in injury or the potential for injury to oneself.

Suicidal Intent: There is past or present evidence (implicit or explicit) that an individual wishes to die, means to kill him/herself, and understands the probable consequences of his/her actions or potential actions. Suicidal intent can be determined retrospectively and in the absence of suicidal behavior.

Physical Injury: A (suspected) bodily lesion resulting from acute overexposure to energy (this can be mechanical, thermal, electrical, chemical, or radiant) interacting with the body in amounts or rates that exceed the threshold of physiological tolerance. In some cases an injury results from an insufficiency of vital elements, such as oxygen. Acute poisonings and toxic effects, including overdoses of substances and wrong substances given or taken in error are included, as are adverse effects and complications of therapeutic, surgical, and medical care. Psychological injury is excluded in this context.

Interrupted by Self or Others: A person takes steps to injure self but is stopped by self/another person prior to fatal injury. The interruption may occur at any point.

Suicide Attempt: A nonfatal self-inflicted potentially injurious behavior with any intent to die as a result of the behavior.

Suicide: Death caused by self-inflicted injurious behavior with any intent to die as a result of the behavior.

To facilitate use of the SDVCS in clinical practice, the VISN 19 MIRECC staff created a SDVCS Table and SDVCS Clinical Tool (see Figure 2.1). The development of this tool was informed by clinician stakeholder feedback, which suggested that a decision tree format would be user-friendly and would improve the accuracy of term identification (Brenner et al., 2011). In order to identify the correct SDVCS

Self-Directed Violence (SDV) Classification System
Clinical Tool

BEGIN WITH THESE 3 QUESTIONS:

1. Is there any indication that the person engaged in self-directed violent behavior that was lethal, preparatory, or potentially harmful? (Refer to Key Terms on reverse side)
   If NO, proceed to Question 2
   If YES, proceed to Question 3

2. Is there any indication that the person had self-directed violence related thoughts?
   If NO to Question 1 and 2, there is insufficient evidence to suggest self-directed violence? → NO SDV TERM
   If YES, proceed to Decision Tree A

3. Did the behavior involve any injury or did it result in death?
   If NO, proceed to Decision Tree B
   If YES, proceed to Decision Tree C

DECISION TREE A: THOUGHTS

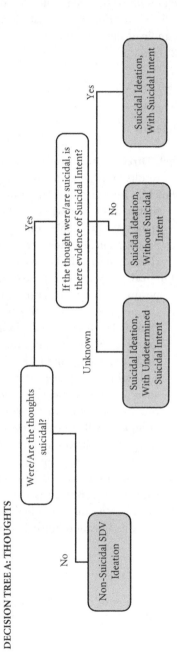

FIGURE 2.1. Implementation of a suicide nomenclature within two VA healthcare settings. *Journal of Clinical Psychology in Medical Settings, 18*(2), 116–128.

Brenner, L. A., Breshears, R. E., Betthauser, L.M., Bellon, K.K., Holman, E., Harwood, J.E., . . . Nagamoto, H. T. (2011).

DECISION TREE B: BEHAVIORS, WITHOUT INJURY

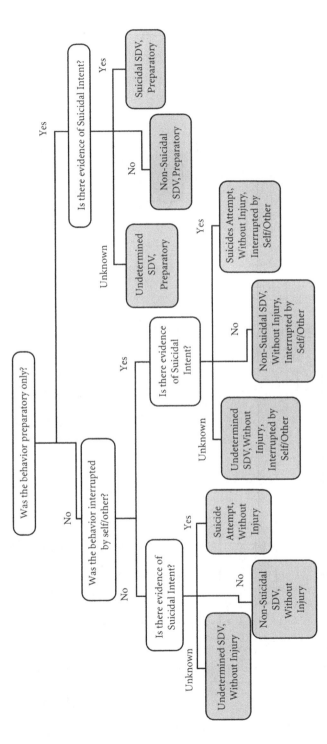

FIGURE 2.1. (continued). Implementation of a suicide nomenclature within two VA healthcare settings. *Journal of Clinical Psychology in Medical Settings, 18*(2), 116–128.

DECISION TREE C: BEHAVIORS, WITH INJURY

FIGURE 2.1. *(continued).* Implementation of a suicide nomenclature within two VA healthcare settings. *Journal of Clinical Psychology in Medical Settings, 18*(2), 116–128.

Self-Directed Violence (SDV) Classification System
Clinical Tool

Key Terms (center for Disease Control and Prevention)

Self-Directed Violence:	Behavior that is self-directed and deliberately results in injury or potential for injury to oneself.
Suicidal Intent:	There is past or present evidence (implicit or explicit) that an individual wishes to die, means to kill him/herself, and understands the probable consequences of his/her actions or potential actions. Suicidal intent can be determined retrospectively and in the absence of suicidal behavior.
Preparatory Behavior:	Acts of preparation towards engaging in Self-Directed Violence, but before potential for injury has begun. This can include anything beyond a verbalization or thought, such as assembling a method (e.g. buying a gun, collecting pills), or preparing for ones's death by suicide (e.g., writing a suicide note, giving things away).
Physical Injury (paraphrased):	A body lesion resulting from acute overexposure to energy (this can be mechanical, thermal, electrical, chemical, or radiant) interacting with the body in amounts or rates that exceed the threshold of physiological tolerance (e.g. bodily harm due to suffocation, poisoning or overdose, lacerations, gunshot wounds, etc.). Refer to the Classification System for the Centers for Disease Control and Prevention definitions.
Interrupted by Self or Others:	A person takes steps to injure self but is stopped by self/another person prior to fatal injury. The interruption may occur at any point.
Suicide Attempt:	A nonfatal self-inflicted potentially injurious behavior with any intent to die as a result of the behavior.
Suicide:	Death caused by self-inflicted injurious behavior with any intent to die as a result of the behavior.

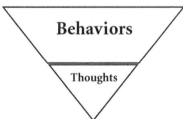

Reminder: Behaviors Trump Thoughts

FIGURE 2.1. *(continued)*. Implementation of a suicide nomenclature within two VA healthcare settings. *Journal of Clinical Psychology in Medical Settings, 18*(2), 116–128.

term, the user first answers the three questions at the top of the SDVCS Clinical Tool:

1. Is there any indication that the person engaged in self-directed violent *behavior* that was lethal, preparatory, or potentially harmful?
2. Is there any indication that the person had self-directed violence related *thoughts*?
3. Did the behavior involve any *injury* or did it result in death?

These questions help the clinician to differentiate between thoughts and behaviors (i.e., the two types of SDV included in SDVCS) and injury (i.e., one of the modifiers within SDVCS). The clinician then follows the prompts after each question, which lead to the appropriate decision tree.

Clinicians who use the SDVCS Clinical Tool will find that they are able to most effectively answer all questions if they have gained certain information about the SDV related to intent, injury, and interruption. Specifically, the clinician will need to know if the patient intended to kill him- or herself by engaging in the potentially self-injurious behavior. This will help the clinician to determine if a non-suicidal SDV or suicidal SDV term is accurate. If the patient did engage in an SDV behavior, it must be known whether the behavior resulted in any level of injury and whether it was interrupted by the patient or someone else. Thus, clinicians and researchers are encouraged to assess for suicidal intent, injury resulting from the behavior, and whether or not the behavior was interrupted or "cut short" by the patient or by someone else as a part of their clinical interviews. The SDVCS Clinical Tool is also available in a clipboard format, which allows the clinician to easily access it throughout an interview to ensure that he or she is gaining enough information to correctly identify the SDVCS term that best classifies the patient's type of ideation or behavior. The SDVCS Clinical Tool can be accessed and clipboards can be ordered via the VISN 19 MIRECC website at www.mirecc.va.gov/visn19/education/nomenclature.asp.

How Does the SDVCS Address the Challenges of Inconsistent Language?

The SDVCS is currently in use by three large federal organizations (i.e., CDC, VA, and the Department of Defense [DOD]), including the largest health care system in the United States (i.e., VA; Department of Veterans Affairs, 2013), and offers a solution to the multitude of problems associated with not having a consistent language to describe SDV. In the next section, examples of how the SDVCS addresses challenges in the realms of clinical practice, research, and surveillance/public policy efforts will be addressed.

The SDVCS and Clinical Practice

To demonstrate the utility of the SDVCS in clinical practice, consider the following case example. A clinician is preparing for his next Mental Health Clinic intake appointment. In the medical record, he reads a note documenting the patient's recent visit to the Emergency Department (ED). The note states that the patient, a physically healthy 21-year-old female, was brought by her boyfriend to the ED after telling him she ingested six to eight regular strength acetaminophen (Tylenol) capsules. She reported no ill effects. Lab tests done at the time of admission to the ED indicated her acetaminophen level was within the therapeutic range. During triage, she stated that before she took the capsules she was upset, but she feels better now and would like to go home.

This example illustrates a case in which a clinician can utilize the SDVCS Clinical Tool to inform assessment. Upon reading the information in the medical record, the clinician realizes that he does not have enough information to determine whether this SDV behavior was a suicide attempt. He is interested in clarifying the patient's history of past SDV, as it will inform his estimation of the patient's level of current risk. Gaining a better understanding of the intention behind the patient's behavior (i.e., ingesting six to eight regular strength acetaminophen capsules) is a critical component of this process because understanding her past behavior and current risk will influence his decisions regarding recommended interventions. To facilitate this process, the clinician reviews the SDVCS Clinical Tool prior to his session with this patient and answers as many questions as he can regarding the behavior, noting what additional information is needed. He is able to answer Question 1 that yes, the person engaged in SDV behavior. Moving to Question 3, he answers no, the documentation does not identify any injury (the patient's acetaminophen level was in the therapeutic range). This directs the clinician to move to Decision Tree B. The behavior was not preparatory only since the patient did engage in SDV, and it was not interrupted because she told her boyfriend about it only after she took the pills, but the clinician is unsure if there is evidence of suicidal intent because the note only documents the patient as stating that she "was upset." Because the patient's suicidal intent is unknown at this time, the patient's SDV is best classified as "undetermined SDV, without injury." The clinician now knows that during the course of the intake, he will need to ask questions regarding the patient's intent in order to determine if the behavior was a "suicide attempt, without injury" or "non-suicidal SDV, without injury." The clinician can then accurately document this in the medical record.

This example highlights how the SDVCS and the associated Clinical Tool can improve clinical practice. First, it helps clinicians to know what questions are important to ask during a clinical assessment, a need noted in the literature (Silverman et al., 2007a). In this example, the clinician identified the need to ask questions related to intent. In other instances, clinicians may need more information about injury and/or interruption of the behavior by self or others. Second, use of the SDVCS improves communication between clinicians, as this clinician can now document the SDV in the medical record in a specific and descriptive manner. Finally, the clarification gained from using the Clinical Tool will likely guide this clinician's assessment of the patient's current level of suicide risk and associated indicated interventions. For example, the clinician is likely to intervene differently if the patient made a suicide attempt versus non-suicidal

SDV, perhaps by scheduling therapy appointments more frequently if intent to die was present.

The SDVCS and Research

The SDVCS can also facilitate research in a number of ways, as illustrated in the following research case example. A researcher is selecting eligibility criteria for a study aimed at increasing understanding of the relationship between executive dysfunction (higher-order mental activities [initiation, planning, and self-regulation of goal-directed behavior] primarily governed by the frontal lobes of the brain; cf. Lezak, Howieson, & Loring, 2004; McDonald, Flashman, & Saykin, 2002) and suicide attempt history. She is interested in including participants with a history of suicide attempt and excluding those with a history of non-suicidal SDV and is trying to determine the best way to ensure that she accurately classifies SDV during screening procedures.

In this example, the researcher may come across a wide variety of definitions for suicide attempt and non-suicidal SDV, and may feel frustrated by the lack of clarity among and between these definitions. Utilizing the SDVCS, however, offers a solution to this problem, as each behavior can only be categorized by one term and each term is accompanied by a specific definition. Similar to the clinical example discussed above, the researcher and her team can use the SDVCS Clinical Tool during the screening process to assure that they collect all necessary information to classify research participants' behaviors correctly, thereby only including members of the population of interest.

In addition, articulating use of the SDVCS in study methods provides the reader with clear information regarding who is included in study samples. Such clarity also allows researchers to aggregate and compare data across studies (Institute of Medicine, 2002). Moreover, consumers of the literature can more appropriately apply research findings to populations with whom they work. For example, a clinician reading the results from the above described study would be more confident that the study's findings apply to his or her patients with a history of attempt but not to patients with non-suicidal SDV.

The SDVCS can also facilitate research that utilizes SDV-related assessment measures, such as the Columbia Suicide Severity Rating Scale (C-SSRS; Posner et al., 2006). The SDVCS/C-CASA (Columbia Classification Algorithm for Suicide Assessment; Posner et al., 2007) Crosswalk Table (Matarazzo, Clemans, Silverman, & Brenner, 2013) can be used by professionals who utilize the C-SSRS in their work. The C-SSRS maps onto the C-CASA, but the terms employed in this measure can be "crosswalked" to the SDVCS via the SDVCS/C-CASA Crosswalk Table. If the researcher in the example above is interested in using a measure to obtain SDV history during screening, she can use the C-SSRS to assess history of SDV and then utilize the Crosswalk to identify the appropriate SDVCS terms to define the behavior. Users should be aware, however, that in order to successfully identify the correct SDVCS term, they may need to gain additional information with respect to intent, injury, or interruption of the behavior (see Table 2.2; Matarazzo et al., 2013). The Crosswalk may be of particular interest to researchers in the VA and DOD who are required to utilize the SDVCS in their work.

TABLE 2.2. Self-Directed Violence Classification System (SDVCS)[a] and Columbia Classification Algorithm of Suicide Assessment (C-CASA)[b] Crosswalk

SDVCS Subtype	SDVCS Term	Closest-Matched C-CASA Classification/ Category
Suicidal Ideation	Suicidal Ideation, Without Suicidal Intent Suicidal Ideation, With Undetermined Suicidal Intent Suicidal Ideation, With Suicidal Intent	Suicidal Ideation[c]
Preparatory	Suicidal Self-Directed Violence, Preparatory	Preparatory Acts Toward Imminent Suicidal Behavior[c,d]
Non-Suicidal Self-Directed Violence	Non-Suicidal Self-Directed Violence, Without Injury Non-Suicidal Self-Directed Violence, Without Injury, Interrupted by Self or Other Non-Suicidal Self-Directed Violence, With Injury Non-Suicidal Self-Directed Violence, With Injury, Interrupted by Self or Other Non-Suicidal Self-Directed Violence, Fatal	Self-Injurious Behavior Without Suicidal Intent
Undetermined Self-Directed Violence	Undetermined Self-Directed Violence, Without Injury Undetermined Self-Directed Violence, Without Injury, Interrupted by Self or Other Undetermined Self-Directed Violence, With Injury Undetermined Self-Directed Violence, With Injury, Interrupted by Self or Other Undetermined Self-Directed Violence, Fatal	Self-Injurious Behavior, Suicidal Intent Unknown[e]

Continued overleaf

TABLE 2.2. *(continued).* Self-Directed Violence Classification System (SDVCS)[a] and Columbia Classification Algorithm of Suicide Assessment (C-CASA)[b] Crosswalk

SDVCS Subtype	SDVCS Term	Closest-Matched C-CASA Classification/ Category
Suicidal Self-Directed Violence	Suicide	Completed Suicide
	Suicide Attempt Without Injury	
	Suicide Attempt Without Injury, Interrupted by Self or Other	Suicide Attempt[e]
	Suicide Attempt With Injury	
	Suicide Attempt With Injury, Interrupted by Self or Other	

[a]SDVCS terms not included in table: Non-Suicidal Self-Directed Violence Ideation; Undetermined Self-Directed Violence, Preparatory; Non-Suicidal Self-Directed Violence, Preparatory
[b]C-CASA terms not included in table: Other, No Deliberate Self-Harm; Not Enough Information
[c]To match this C-CASA term to one of the SDVCS terms, additional information is needed regarding intent.
[d]The Columbia-Suicide Severity Rating Scale yields two classifications/categories not included in C-CASA: Interrupted Attempt and Aborted Attempt, which most closely correspond with the SDVCS term Suicidal Self-Directed Violence, Preparatory.
[e]To match this C-CASA term to one of the SDVCS terms, additional information is needed regarding injury and interruption by self or other.

The SDVCS and Surveillance Efforts/Public Policy

As noted above, the SDVCS can also address issues related to inconsistent use of nomenclature in the realm of surveillance and public policy. Consider, as an example, that the Centers for Disease Control and Prevention (CDC) conducts a Youth Risk Behavior Survey every year. In 2003, the CDC found that 16.9% of adolescents (grades 9–12) seriously considered attempting suicide, 16.5% made a plan, and 8.5% attempted suicide (CDC, 2005). During a similar timeframe, from 2001–2003, an epidemiologic study surveyed US citizens aged 18–54 years to determine the presence of suicidal thoughts/behaviors in the last year. Results indicated that 3.3% reported suicidal ideation, 1.0% reported a plan, and 0.6% reported a suicide attempt (Kessler, Berglund, Borges, Nock, & Wang, 2005).

In allocating resources to suicide prevention efforts, a consumer of the literature would likely embark on a process of comparing existing findings (e.g., CDC data and data from Kessler et al., 2005). Without clear definitions of terms, however, it becomes difficult to compare and combine data across multiple studies. Use of SDVCS terms, however, could inform the development of surveys in which thoughts and behaviors are defined consistently. In turn, more precise data collection allow for data to be aggregated and compared across organizations, systems of care, and geographic regions. Estimates regarding SDV incidence and prevalence would be improved (Crosby et al., 2011). Not only would this facilitate enhanced communication and improved transfer of information regarding mental health, but improved reliability related to facility reporting would more accurately inform public policy and funding efforts aimed at addressing existing needs.

SDVCS Dissemination and Implementation Efforts

VA, CDC, and DOD adoption of the SDVCS common terms marks a fundamental step toward improving care, research, and surveillance regarding SDV. Nevertheless, existing literature suggests that the process of implementing new practices in health care systems are nonlinear and challenging (Kitson, Harvey, & McCormack, 1998; Rycroft-Malone, 2004). Historically, barriers to adoption of a standard system include factors such as clinicians' unfamiliarity with the new terminology; complexity of the system being implemented; and/or implementation of systems that do not fully meet the needs of clinicians, researchers, and those involved in surveillance and public policy efforts (Rosenberg et al., 1988). Improving health care quality via the successful system-wide adoption of the SDVCS will therefore require a strategic implementation plan (Stetler, Mittman, & Franics, 2008).

Utilizing guidance offered by the implementation science literature (e.g., Green, Kreuter, Deeds, & Partridge, 1980; Rubenstein et al., 2002, 2006), Brenner and colleagues (2011) conducted a pilot project aimed at facilitating implementation of the SDVCS at two VA Medical Centers. Research staff trained mental health providers on the SDVCS and collected data regarding professionals' impressions of the SDVCS, with results suggesting that use of the SDVCS may enhance clarity of communication across clinical, policy, and research settings (Brenner et al., 2011). Implementation data also suggest the SDVCS and its associated SDVCS Clinical Tool are acceptable and useful to mental health clinicians in the VA system (Brenner et al., 2011). Additionally, results spoke to the need for widespread implementation efforts to address both clinician- and organization-level barriers, such as initial unfamiliarity with terms. As such, it is recommended that professionals starting to utilize the SDVCS identify training methods applicable to their setting. For example, clinicians could practice using case vignettes and the SDVCS Clinical Tool in order to increase their familiarity with the system prior to using it in clinical practice.

Next Steps

Data from Brenner et al. (2011) suggest that enhanced training alone will be insufficient to facilitate adoption of the SDVCS. In order to facilitate adoption and sustain changes over time, efforts must be made to understand clinician behavior regarding the use of terminology. This could be accomplished by direct observation, indirect observation (e.g., via examination of clinician documentation in electronic medical records), and/or self-report. Direct observation of clinician behavior is challenging, however. Additionally, research suggests that clinicians are not aware of their own rate of adherence to health care guidelines (Steinman et al., 2004), thus making self-report an unreliable research method. Therefore, research involving indirect observation is indicated as a critical component of implementation of the SDVCS.

Additionally, future research is needed to explore the impact of using this particular standardized nomenclature across clinical, research, and surveillance/public policy settings. For example, the field would benefit from evidence identifying if different terms, such as *suicide attempt with injury* versus *without injury*, led to different SDV- and health-related outcomes. Similarly, clinical assessment and intervention would benefit from empirical evidence regarding any associations between the unique SDVCS terms and suicide risk stratification. Finally, no assessment measure utilizing the SDVCS currently exists (Matarazzo et al., 2013). Because most instruments assume that respondents have the same definition for suicidal ideation or attempts, researchers often assume that responses to self-report instruments are based on the same conceptualization and definitions of suicide-related terms (Silverman et al., 2007a). Therefore, the field would greatly benefit from the development of an SDVCS risk assessment tool.

Summary

This chapter considered how the use of inconsistent language specific to SDV creates barriers for effective clinical practice, rigorous research, and meaningful surveillance efforts/public policy. Use of a newly developed classification system called the SDVCS was therefore recommended for addressing these challenges. Real-world examples were provided from three different settings (i.e., clinical, research, and surveillance efforts/public policy) to illustrate the practical benefits of using the SDVCS. The SDVCS Clinical Tool was introduced and discussed as a practical tool for clinicians and researchers to reliably classify SDV, and suggestions were offered for facilitating the SDVCS's adoption, dissemination, and widespread implementation, particularly within health care settings. Finally, future steps for advancing the use of nomenclature in the health care field using the SDVCS were discussed, including a brief overview of research focused on understanding clinician behavior related to use of nomenclature and research exploring the impact of SDVCS use across clinical, research, and surveillance/public policy settings.

References

Beck, A. T., Davis, J. H., Frederick, C. J., Perlin, S., Pokorny, A. D., Schulman, R. E., Seiden, R. H., …Wittlin, B.J. (1972). Classification and nomenclature. In H. L. P. Resnik & B. C. Hathorne (Eds.), *Suicide prevention in the seventies* (pp. 7–12). Washington, DC: U.S. Government Printing Office.

Brenner, L. A., Breshears, R. E., Betthauser, L. M., Bellon, K. K., Holman, E., Harwood, J. E., ... Nagamoto, H. T. (2011). Implementation of a suicide nomenclature within two VA healthcare settings. *Journal of Clinical Psychology in Medical Settings, 18*(2), 116–128.

Centers for Disease Control and Prevention. (2005). *Youth risk behavior surveillance system.* Retrieved from www.cdc.gov/HealthyYouth/yrbs/index.htm

Crosby, A. E., Ortega, L., & Melanson, C. (2011). *Self-directed violence surveillance: Uniform definitions and recommended data elements, version 1.0.* Atlanta, GA: Centers for Disease Control and Prevention, National Center for Injury Prevention and Control.

De Leo, D., Burgis, S., Bertolote, J. M., Kerkhof, A. J., & Bille-Brahe, U. (2006). Definitions of suicidal behavior: Lessons learned from the WHO/EURO Multicentre Study. *Crisis, 27*(1), 4–15.

Department of Veterans Affairs (2008a). *VA secretary appoints panel of national suicide experts.* Retrieved from www1.va.gov/opa/pressrel/pressrelease.cfm?id=1506

Department of Veterans Affairs (2008b). *Report of the Blue Ribbons Work Group on suicide prevention in the Veteran population.* Retrieved from www.mentalhealth.va.gov/suicide_prevention/Blue_Ribbon_Report-FINAL_June-30-08.pdf

Department of Veterans Affairs (2013). *Veterans Health Administration.* Retrieved from www.va.gov/health/aboutVHA.asp

Fischer, E. P., Comstock, G. W., Monk, M. A., & Sencer, D. J. (1993). Characteristics of completed suicides: Implications of differences among methods. *Suicide and Life Threatening Behavior, 23*(2), 91–100.

Green, L. W., Kreuter, M. W., Deeds, S. G., & Partridge, K. B. (1980). Health education planning model (PRECEDE). In L. W. Green (Ed.), *Health education planning: A diagnostic approach* (pp. 86–115). Palo Alto, CA: Mayfield Publishing Company.

Institute of Medicine (2002). Barriers to research and promising approaches. In S. K. Goldsmith, T. C. Pellmar, A. M. Kleinman, & W. E. Bunney (Eds.), *Reducing suicide: A national imperative* (p. 375). Washington, DC: The National Academies Press.

Kessler, R., Berglund, P., Borges, G., Nock, M., & Wang, P. S. (2005). Trends in suicide ideation, plans, gestures, and attempts in the United States, 1990–1992 to 2001–2003. *Journal of the American Medical Association, 293,* 2487–2495.

Kitson, A., Harvey, G., & McCormack, B. (1998). Enabling the implementation of evidence based practice: A conceptual framework. *Quality in Health Care, 7*(3), 149–158.

Lezak, M. D., Howieson, D. B., & Loring, D. W. (2004). *Neuropsychological assessment* (4th ed.). New York, NY: Oxford University Press.

Matarazzo, B. B., Clemans, T. A., Silverman, M. M., & Brenner, L. A. (2013). The Self-Directed Violence Classification System and the Columbia Classification Algorithm for Suicide Assessment: A crosswalk. *Suicide and Life-Threatening Behavior, 43*(3), 235–249.

McDonald, B. C., Flashman, L. A., & Saykin, A. J. (2002). Executive dysfunction following traumatic brain injury: Neural substrates and treatment strategies. *NeuroRehabilitation, 17,* 333–344.

O'Carroll, P. W., Berman, A. L., Maris, R. W., Moscicki, E. K., Tanney, B. L., & Silverman, M. M. (1996). Beyond the Tower of Babel: A nomenclature for suicidology. *Suicide and Life-Threatening Behavior, 26*(3), 237–252.

Posner, K., Brent, D., Lucas, C., Gould, M., Stanley, B., Brown, G., ... Mann, J. (2006). *Columbia-Suicide Severity Rating Scale (C-SSRS).* New York, NY: New York State Psychiatric Institute.

Posner, K., Oquendo, M. A., Gould, M., Stanley, B., & Davies, M. (2007). Columbia Classification Algorithm of Suicide Assessment (C-CASA): Classification of suicidal events in the FDA's pediatric suicidal risk analysis of antidepressants. *American Journal of Psychiatry, 164*(7), 1035–1043.

Rosenberg, M. L., Davidson, L. E., Smith, J. C., Berman, A. L., Buzbee, H., Ganter, G., . . . Murray, D. (1988). Operational criteria for the determination of suicide. *Journal of Forensic Sciences, 33*(6), 1445–1456.

Rubenstein, L. V., Meredith, L. S., Parker, L. E., Gordon, N. P., Hickey, S. C., Oken, C., & Lee, M. L. (2006). Impacts of evidence-based quality improvement on depression in primary care: a randomized experiment. *Journal of General Internal Medicine, 21*(10), 1027–1035.

Rubenstein, L. V., Parker, L. E., Meredith, L. S., Altschuler, A., dePillis, E., Hernandez, J., & Gordon, N. P. (2002). Understanding team-based quality improvement for depression in primary care. *Health Services Research, 37*(4), 1009–1029.

Rycroft-Malone, J. (2004). The PARIHS framework—a framework for guiding the implementation of evidence-based practice. *Journal of Nursing Care Quality, 19*(4), 297–304.

Silverman, M. M. (2006). The language of suicidology. *Suicide and Life Threatening Behavior, 36*(5), 519–532.

Silverman, M. M., Berman, A. L., Sanddal, N. D., O'Carroll, P. W., & Joiner, T. E. (2007a). Rebuilding the tower of Babel: A revised nomenclature for the study of suicide and suicidal behaviors. Part 1: Background, rationale, and methodology. *Suicide and Life Threatening Behavior, 37*(3), 248–263.

Silverman, M. M., Berman, A. L., Sanddal, N. D., O'Carroll, P. W, & Joiner, T. E. (2007b). Rebuilding the tower of Babel: A revised nomenclature for the study of suicide and suicidal behaviors. Part 2: Suicide-related ideations, communications, and behaviors. *Suicide and Life Threatening Behavior, 37*(3), 264–277.

Steinman, M. A., Fischer, M. A., Shlipak, M. G., Bosworth, H. B., Hoffman, B. B., & Goldstein, M. K. (2004). Clinician awareness of adherence to hypertension guidelines. *American Journal of Medicine, 117*(10), 747–754.

Stetler, C. B., Mittman, B. S., & Francis, J. (2008). Overview of the VA Quality Enhancement Research Initiative (QUERI) and QUERI theme articles: QUERI Series. *Implementation Science, 3*, 8.

three

What We Know and Don't Know About Treating Suicide Risk

Ann Marie Hernandez

UNIVERSITY OF TEXAS HEALTH SCIENCE CENTER
AT SAN ANTONIO

Approximately 1 million people take their own lives each year worldwide (World Health Organization [WHO], 2012). In fact, suicide will account for greater than 2% of the total global burden of disease by 2020 (WHO, 2012). Within the United States alone, nearly 40,000 individuals took their own lives in 2010, making suicide the 10th-leading cause of death in the United States for all ages in 2010, with approximately 105 suicides per day (Centers for Disease Control [CDC], 2012). However, these rates only highlight the fatal endpoint of a continuum of suicide risk, broadly defined as any form of self-directed violence, to include thoughts and behaviors. For every death by suicide, there are approximately 30 suicide attempts (Gelder, Mayou, & Cowen, 2001). Moreover, the lifetime prevalence rate of suicidal ideation is approximately 13–15% (Kerkof & Arensman, 2001). Research suggests that individuals move along this continuum of risk from suicidal ideation to plan (34%), and from ideation to attempt (29%; Nock et al., 2008), with most suicide attempts occurring during the first year after the onset of suicidal ideation.

Despite the obvious need for an efficacious treatment for suicidal self-directed violence, the vast majority of the literature over the past 50 years has focused on the identification of risk factors and theory development. Intervention studies have only recently revealed a number of methods for adequately reducing the risk of suicide attempts. The aim of this chapter is to highlight recent advances in the intervention arena, with an emphasis on cognitive behavioral approaches that target risk for suicide attempts exclusively. Few psychological approaches have garnered as much empirical support as cognitive behavioral interventions, which propose to decrease emotional distress and improve adaptive coping by altering maladaptive thoughts and assumptions. The current chapter provides a review of randomized controlled trials on psychological and pharmacological treatments specifically aimed at preventing suicide attempts. While many uncontrolled studies of various treatments are available for review, they are not included here because little causal information about the efficacy of such treatments can be determined without experimental control and randomization. This review included studies that met the following criteria: (1) selected participants based on their high risk for suicide or history of attempts; (2) reported outcomes on suicide ideation and suicide attempts; (3) evaluated a psychosocial or pharmacological intervention; and (4) utilized randomization and a control condition. A brief discussion of medication trials and outcomes is discussed. In addition, the therapeutic ingredients shared by each of the interventions with demonstrated effectiveness will be outlined.

Psychotherapy Studies for Reducing Suicide Attempts

A number of reviews focused on interventions for reducing suicide risk exist in the literature (Comtois & Linehan, 2006; Hawton et al., 1999; Mann et al., 2005). The most recent exhaustive review was conducted by Hawton and colleagues (1999), which uncovered the largely mediocre effect of suicide prevention efforts. Their review included 23 randomized controlled trials, all published between 1997 and 1999, which compared psychosocial or psychopharmacological treatments to standard care in the treatment of self-directed violence. All studies met the following criteria: 1) a direct comparison of psychological or psychopharmacological treatment versus treatment as usual; 2) inclusion of participants who had engaged in self-directed violence of some kind (defined by the authors as "self-injury or poisoning") shortly before the initiation of the trial; and 3) random assignment of participants to treatment and control groups. Active interventions varied greatly and included problem-solving therapy, intensive intervention, emergency contact cards, dialectical behavior therapy (DBT), inpatient treatment, family therapy, antidepressants, and flupenthixol (an antipsychotic medication). Most of the trials used standard care as the comparison condition, which was generally limited to referral for outpatient services and increased clinical contact. Findings indicated significantly reduced rates of suicide attempts in both the flupenthixol (Montgomery et al., 1979) and DBT (Linehan et al., 1991) trials. However, the sample sizes of these trials were so small that the reviewers were unable to make any conclusive statements regarding effectiveness. A trend toward reduced suicide attempts among patients receiving problem-solving therapy (Salkovskis, Atha, & Storer, 1990; Evans et al., 1999) and contact cards (Cotgrove, Zirinsky, Black, & Weston, 1995) was also found; however, conclusions were limited by low statistical power. Overall, Hawton and colleagues were unable to make any recommendations regarding the superiority of any particular treatment due to significant methodological concerns. As such, calls for additional randomized controlled trials with greater statistical power were made to address the significant gap in the intervention literature. Fortunately, experimental investigations focused on the treatment of suicidal ideation and suicide attempts have grown exponentially since this early review, with recent trials suggesting superior efficacy of cognitive behavioral methods.

Brown and colleagues (2005) aimed to test the effectiveness of a brief cognitive intervention in reducing repeat suicide attempts relative to treatment as usual in adults recently treated in the emergency room for a suicide attempt. All patients (n = 350) who presented to the emergency room between October 1999 and September 2002 for medical treatment subsequent to a suicide attempt were consecutively approached within 48 hours of hospital admission. Of the 350 patients screened, 66 refused participation, 164 were ineligible, and 120 were randomly assigned to either brief cognitive therapy or treatment as usual. The cognitive therapy intervention was delivered over 10 sessions and utilized techniques such as identification and modification of cognitions and core beliefs that were activated during the suicidal episode, problem-solving strategies, behavioral activation, impulse control, and relapse prevention training. The relapse prevention training required that the patient identify an alternative adaptive response during a future hypothetical suicidal crisis. Of note, compliance of both the patient to treatment and therapist to the protocol was emphasized throughout the study. Each therapy session was audiotaped and rated for fidelity using the Cognitive Therapy Rating Scale (CTRS; Young & Beck, 1980). Both groups received treatment as usual, which included referral to case managers and mental health services in the community. The primary outcome variable was repeat suicide attempt during the 18 months follow-up period. By the end of the follow-up period, 13 participants (24.1%) in the brief cognitive intervention group and 23 participants (41.6%) in the usual care group made at least one repeat suicide attempt. Participants in the intervention group were therefore 50% less likely to reattempt suicide than the usual care group. Interestingly, both groups endorsed comparable declines in suicidal ideation. In addition, participants who underwent cognitive therapy reported significantly lower depression and hopelessness at follow up. These findings underline the important roles that depression and hopelessness may have during a suicidal crisis. Furthermore, the study underlines the feasibility and utility of targeting risk for suicide attempts specifically, even among high-risk populations.

Turner (2000) investigated the effects of DBT (Linehan et al., 1993) on repeat suicide attempts in comparison to client-centered treatment (CCT) among patients with BPD undergoing treatment for a recent suicide attempt. DBT is a cognitive behavioral treatment program developed to treat individuals with BPD who are suicidal or engage in self-harm or treatment interfering behaviors by addressing emotional regulation issues, behavioral capabilities, and reality testing. DBT combines cognitive behavioral techniques with meditation, acceptance, and mindfulness in a multifaceted approach to include individual therapy, group therapy, therapist contact between sessions, and ongoing support for the treating therapists. CCT differed from DBT in that it primarily provided a supportive environment and empathic reflection without interpretation, cognitive restructuring, or other cognitive behavioral techniques (Carkuff, 1969). Individuals were only excluded if they also had a diagnosis of schizophrenia, schizoaffective disorder, bipolar disorder, organic mental disorder, or mental retardation. Twenty-four study participants were randomly assigned to 12 months of weekly DBT or CCT. The study experienced significant attrition, such that only nine participants remained in DBT and three in CCT. However, all 24 participants completed both 6-month and 12-month follow-up assessments. Intent-to-treat analyses indicated that DBT was more effective in reducing suicide attempts, non-suicidal self-injury, suicidal ideation, depression, impulsivity, and psychological functioning than CCT. While the generalizability of this study is limited given the small sample size, the results suggest that cognitive-based treatment has a unique and superior treatment effect for suicide attempts compared to supportive therapy. Therefore, it is unlikely that the improvement in suicide attempts can be attributed solely to general therapeutic factors.

More evidence supporting the use of DBT was provided by Linehan and colleagues (2006), who conducted a 2-year randomized controlled trial comparing DBT to a nonbehavioral psychotherapy treatment by experts in the prevention of suicide attempts. As in the study described above, the objective was to determine if successful treatment of suicidal ideation and behaviors was the function of general psychotherapeutic effects or due to unique contributions made by DBT. Participants were recruited from university outpatient clinics and community treatment centers and consisted of females with a BPD diagnosis, aged 18 to 45, with a minimum of two suicide attempts or non-suicidal self-injury within the past 5 years, with at least one occurring within the 8 weeks before enrollment. Individuals were excluded on the basis of a diagnosis of schizophrenia, schizoaffective disorder, bipolar disorder, psychotic disorder, mental retardation, seizure disorder, treatment mandate, and/or need for concurrent treatment for another psychiatric condition. Of the 186 individuals screened, 22 refused participation, 53 did not meet inclusion criteria, and 111 were randomly assigned to 1 year of DBT or community treatment by experts. Community treatment was delivered by experts in the field nominated by community mental health leaders who self-described their clinical approach as either "eclectic but nonbehavioral" or "mostly psychodynamic." Consistent with previous findings, intent-to-treat analyses indicated that DBT outperformed community treatment by experts during the treatment and follow-up periods across a number of domains. Participants who received DBT were half as likely to make a suicide attempt, required fewer hospitalizations, and were less likely to drop out of treatment. These two studies suggest that the effectiveness of DBT in reducing risk for suicide attempts is not solely based on general psychotherapeutic factors and instead is the result of the unique cognitive behavioral tenets upon which the treatment is based.

Additional research suggests that cognitive behavioral treatments can be successfully applied to other groups of great interest, namely adolescents and active duty service members, with encouraging results. This is particularly pertinent given the alarming rate of suicide among both populations. Esposito-Smythers and Spirito (2004) compared a manualized cognitive behavioral treatment to treatment as usual in a psychiatric inpatient group of adolescents with substance use disorder and a suicide attempt within the past 3 months. Forty adolescents were randomly assigned to the cognitive behavioral intervention for co-occurring suicide risk and substance abuse (I-CBT) or enhanced treatment as usual (E-TAU). I-CBT is based on social cognitive theory, which views current difficulties as learned behaviors. The primary techniques used in I-CBT involved cognitive restructuring of maladaptive thoughts and behaviors thought to underlie both suicide attempts and substance abuse, problem solving, substance refusal skills, motivational interviewing, emotional regulation, and family/parent skills training. I-CBT was designed to be delivered in three phases: 1) phase one consists of the first 6 months of treatment where individual, family, and parenting sessions were held bi-weekly; 2) phase two marks the continuation phase where teens attended bi-weekly sessions and parents attended bi-weekly to monthly sessions; and 3) phase three is the maintenance phase where all sessions are held on a monthly basis. Consistent with studies described above, I-CBT therapists underwent rigorous training, received ongoing feedback from audiotaped sessions, and were rated for fidelity using the CTRS (Young & Beck, 1980). E-TAU treatment was largely at the discretion of community providers, of which none described themselves as utilizing a cognitive behavioral intervention. Treatment as usual was enhanced with respect to the provision of psychiatric medication prescribed by the study psychiatrist. Participants were assessed at pretreatment and at 3, 6, 12, and 18 months post-enrollment for affective disorders, suicidal ideation, suicide attempts, and substance use. Intent-to-treat analyses indicated that I-CBT was associated with significant improvement in substance use, suicide attempts (six attempts in E-TAU and one in I-CBT), emergency department visits, and arrests. Similar to the study by Brown and colleagues (2005), both groups endorsed an equivalent reduction in suicidal ideation. Of note is the superior treatment adherence exhibited by the I-CBT group, in which 74% of adolescent completed all 24 sessions in comparison to only 44% of the E-TAU group. A similar pattern of treatment adherence was displayed in parents and families. This study not only supports the use of I-CBT in the treatment of adolescents with substance use disorders who have also made a suicide attempt, but it also revealed a tendency toward greater treatment adherence. Additionally, the study underlines the ability to successfully reduce suicide attempts without exclusively addressing the accompanying psychiatric disorder. In fact, while this treatment focused on improving suicide risk, there was significant improvement in other salient areas including substance use, arrest, and emergency room visits, suggesting that treatment effects may generalize to other important domains.

Until recently, the feasibility and generalizability of a cognitive behavioral treatment for the reduction of suicide attempts in a military population had not been tested. Rudd and colleagues (2014) aimed to test the effectiveness of a Brief Cognitive Behavioral Treatment (BCBT) in the treatment of active duty service members with either current suicidal ideation with intent to die and/or a recent suicide attempt as compared to treatment as usual (TAU). BCBT integrated the effective components of cognitive behavioral interventions and delivered them in a brief, manualized approach across three phases. The initial phase (five sessions) was primarily directed at crisis management, emotional regulation, and the development of a cognitive behavioral conceptualization of the suicidal crisis. The second phase (five sessions) involved cognitive restructuring of the suicidal belief system, problem-solving skills, and methods to increase cognitive flexibility. The third and final phase (two sessions) focused on relapse prevention, where the patient is asked to imagine the circumstances of the suicidal crisis while implementing previously mastered skills to disrupt the suicidal crisis. Treatment as usual (TAU) was at the discretion of both military- and community-based mental health providers. Participants were eligible based on the following criteria: 1) endorsement of suicidal ideation with intent to die within the past week and/or a suicide attempt within the past month; 2) active duty military status; 3) age 18 or older; 4) English-speaking ability; and 5) ability to provide informed consent. Participants were excluded if a medical or psychiatric diagnosis (i.e., psychosis or mania) prohibited their ability to provide informed consent or engage in outpatient treatment. A total of 152 Army soldiers were randomly assigned to BCBT or TAU. Participants in BCBT received 12 outpatient individual psychotherapy sessions on a weekly or bi-weekly basis. Follow-up assessments were completed at 3, 6, 12, 18, and 24 months post-enrollment. Results indicate that participants in BCBT were significantly less likely to make a suicide attempt. Eight participants in B-CBT (13.8%) and 16 participants in TAU (35.6%) made at least one suicide attempt, which suggests participants in active treatment were 60% less likely to attempt suicide during follow-up than participants in TAU. This was the first treatment study specifically designed to meet the unique needs and environmental demands of the military that demonstrated efficacy for preventing suicide attempts among high-risk active duty military service members. Of note, military personnel in BCBT were also less likely to be medically separated from the military, indicating the treatment may also improve career outcomes in this population.

Pharmacological Treatments to Reduce Suicide Attempts

The treatment of mood and other psychiatric disorders using pharmacotherapy is central to suicide prevention efforts given the rate of psychiatric disorders present and largely untreated at the time of death by suicide (Henriksson, Boëthius, & Isacsson, 2001). In fact, one of the primary ways in which suicide risk is managed is through a combination of pharmacotherapy and psychotherapy (Brown et al., 2005). However, the evidence supporting the use of medication as a stand-alone treatment or in combination with psychotherapy is lacking. Meta-analyses of randomized controlled trials have yet to detect any positive effect on suicide attempts in studies of antidepressants used to treat mood disorders or other psychiatric disorders (Fergusson et al., 2005; Gunnel, Saperia, & Ashby, 2005). Currently, clozapine is approved by the Food and Drug Administration for suicide prevention in patients diagnosed with psychotic disorders. This is based on research suggesting that among individuals with schizophrenia, clozapine accounted for a 50% reduction in suicide attempts in comparison to a newer antipsychotic, olanzapine (7.7% vs. 13.8%, respectively; Meltzer et al., 2003). While lithium has also received considerable attention as a form of treatment to reduce suicide attempts among patients with bipolar disorder (Cipriani, Pretty, Hawton, & Geddes, 2005), the evidence base supporting this perspective is largely based on naturalistic research, secondary analyses of randomized controlled trials, and open-label medication trials (Oquendo et al., 2011). A recent randomized controlled trial compared the effectiveness of lithium relative to valproate for the prevention of suicide attempts in patients with bipolar disorder, with results finding no difference between groups (Oquendo et al., 2011). These findings suggest that lithium may be no more effective for reducing suicide attempts than other medications commonly used for bipolar disorders. As such, the current state of the evidence suggests that medications may have an indirect effect on suicide attempts by aiding in the management of acute psychiatric symptoms of related conditions that may contribute to suicide attempts (Clinical Care and Intervention Task Force to the National Action Alliance for Suicide Prevention [NAASP], 2011). Randomized controlled trials investigating the ability for medications to reduce suicidal ideation and suicide attempts alone or in combination with psychotherapy are needed.

Common "Ingredients" to Effective Treatments

Across clinical trials focused on the reduction of risk for suicide attempts, several common features have been observed (cf. Rudd, 2012): 1) a primary emphasis on reducing suicidal ideation and risk for suicide attempts; 2) use of a clear theoretical framework; 3) a skills-building focus; 4) access to crisis management services; 5) means restriction; 6) emphasis on personal responsibility by the patient; 7) patient compliance; and 8) treatment adherence and competence on the part of the therapist.

Emphasis on Suicide Ideation and Risk for Suicide Attempts

First and foremost, effective treatments directly target suicidal thoughts and the problems that are believed to be proximally related to risk for suicide attempts and view suicide risk as distinct from psychiatric diagnoses. This is in direct contrast to traditional psychotherapeutic approaches, which assume that treatment of the accompanying psychiatric disorders will result in an equivalent decrease in suicidal risk (Linehan, 2008). Instead, more recent suicide-specific cognitive behavioral approaches aim to identify and modify thoughts and behaviors that contribute to suicidal crises specifically, with a secondary emphasis on addressing any co-occurring psychiatric condition such as depression and anxiety. This allows both the patient and clinician to target the most life-threatening symptoms by way of cognitive restructuring, emotional regulation, and problem solving. In doing so, the patient can be expected to be better suited to engage in treatment for any associated psychiatric condition after his or her suicidal thoughts are appropriately managed. As indicated above, this method has proved useful across a number of settings and populations.

Use of a Clear Theoretical Framework

Inherent to a cognitive behavioral approach to treatment is the use of a well-defined, empirically supported model of behavior, which serves to clearly delineate the underlying cognitions, emotions, and behaviors proximal to maladaptive coping responses such as suicide attempts. In this case, suicide attempts are conceptualized as the outcome of automatic thoughts and core beliefs that are activated at the time of the suicidal crisis (Beck, 1979; Rudd, Joiner, & Rajab, 2001). To better account for the multitude of symptoms reported by psychiatric patients, Beck (1996) proposed a theory of "modes" to explain suicide attempts, which takes into account not only cognitions but also additional psychological factors such as cognitive, behavioral, affective, motivational, and physiological schemas that are activated by internal and external events (see the detailed discussion of the suicidal mode in Chapter 4).

An empirically based theoretical framework is essential for sound conceptualization, treatment planning, and psychoeducation. For instance, the cognitive behavioral model of suicide can be used by the clinician to identify and interpret core beliefs, behaviors, and maladaptive coping strategies that may precede a suicidal episode. This, in turn, will help to identify the most appropriate points of intervention and prevention. The theoretical model can also be used as a clinical tool, which provides the patient with an easy-to-understand explanation of why he or she made a suicide attempt and what he or she should do to keep it from happening again. For instance, in the initial phase of BCBT, an outline of the suicide mode (Rudd et al., 2014) is used in collaboration with the patient to establish a conceptualization of the unique predispositions, triggers, coping behaviors, physiological reactions, emotional reactions, and suicidal belief system that interact during a suicidal crisis. This gives the patient the all-important understanding of his or her pathological behaviors. This knowledge, paired with newly learned abilities to manage emotional distress, serves as the basis of effective self-management. An important added benefit in the use of a theoretical framework to guide treatment is the ability to ensure that treatment progresses in a logical and consistent manner while minimizing diversions.

Skill Building

Central to effective therapies is the establishment of adaptive coping skills that may serve to mitigate a potential suicidal crisis. The most common skills include emotional regulation, problem solving, anger management, interpersonal communication skills, and cognitive restructuring. A significant proportion of time is spent in session and out of session to practice and master these techniques so that they can generalize to diverse settings, contexts, and situations. This is done in the name of the overarching goal of self-management. Hence, the patient is not only able to identify what has gone awry but is also capable of engaging the appropriate skill set to alleviate distress and manage the situation without turning to self-directed violence.

Crisis Management Services

Effective treatments consistently address the vital need for a written crisis response plan and easy access to emergency support services both during and after the intervention to aid during suicidal crises. A crisis response plan (also referred to as a safety plan) clearly delineates the steps an individual should take to keep him- or herself safe during a suicidal crisis. Important components include previously identified self-management strategies (e.g., coping cards or pleasant activities), detailed list of social support sources (e.g., family or friends) that previously agreed to be of assistance during a suicidal crisis, as well as a specific listing of professionals or resources whom the patient can contact (i.e., primary mental health provider, mental health clinic, emergency department, and the National Suicide Prevention Hotline at 1-800-273-TALK [8225]) if deemed necessary. Each crisis response plan should include a clear plan of action that begins with self-management strategies in order to minimize hospitalization and then includes external sources of support later in the crisis response plan. The clinician and patient collaborate to develop a tailored and effective crisis management plan while practicing its implementation and troubleshooting potential barriers and limitations. The patient is given the knowledge and autonomy to appropriately identify what does and does not constitute a crisis and implement the correct level of intervention, thereby shifting from a clinician-only to patient–clinician collaboration in responsibility for preventing suicide. The crisis response plan/safety plan is described in detail in Chapter 8.

Means Restriction

Few suicide prevention strategies are as effective as the restriction of access to potentially lethal means for suicide (Yip et al., 2012), as the risk of engaging in a suicide attempt decreases dramatically if the preferred method is unavailable (Daigle, 2005). Means restrictions also capitalizes on the often short-lived nature of most suicidal crises and the significant ambivalence regarding the wish to live and die that is often present among those contemplating suicide (Daigle, 2005). Limited access to a preferred method can serve as an important obstacle to suicide attempts even among individuals with very high levels of suicidal intent and intense psychiatric distress. Means restriction therefore reduces the risk for lethal suicide attempts without necessarily targeting suicidal intent directly. Although some patients may decide to use an alternative means for suicide, the alternative method is oftentimes less lethal and/or more likely to enable an opportunity for rescue. Modification of the environment in order to decrease or eliminate access to lethal means should take place at the outset of treatment, and all patients be asked about their access to firearms given the high rate of fatality associated with this method. In most cases, the clinician and patient collaborate to secure both high (e.g., firearms) and low lethality (e.g., pills) until the patient no longer feels suicidal. If needed, significant others such as family members, friends, supervisors, and other sources of support can be asked to limit or remove access to means. Means restriction counseling is described in detail in Chapter 9.

Personal Responsibility

Each of the above strategies requires that the patient become self-aware and self-reliant in order to adopt a sense of personal responsibility for his or her well-being and safety. The assumption is that, with appropriate knowledge and coping skills, the patient will be fully capable of addressing the emotional distress associated with certain events and any potential suicidal urges that may follow. In effective treatments, all interventions emphasize the patient's personal responsibility for his or her safety and provide them with considerable autonomy. This is in contrast to traditional therapeutic approaches in which the responsibility for maintaining the safety of the patient is assumed to be largely controlled by the clinician. In effective treatments, the expectation is that the responsibility for safety that is shared among the clinician and patient is likely to promote a sense of empowerment, motivation, and treatment compliance, with improved outcomes.

Patient Compliance

Evidence indicates that greater treatment adherence is associated with better outcomes in both psychological and medical studies (Horwitz & Horwitz, 1993). This is particularly salient for cognitive behavioral approaches, which are skill based, thereby assuming active patient participation in order to acquire the proficiencies necessary for therapeutic change (Schmidt & Woolaway-Bickel, 2000). Based on this evidence, effective treatments emphasize treatment compliance both directly and consistently. This is particularly salient when dealing with high-risk individuals. Studies consistently demonstrate that patients are more likely to remain actively engaged in effective treatments. This finding extends to the family members of suicidal patients who are invited to participate in treatment as well (Esposito-Smythers & Spirito, 2004; Linehan, 2005). Higher compliance rates among suicidal patients enrolled in effective treatments may be attributed to those cognitive behavioral tenets that target poor motivation for treatment with clear plans about what to do if noncompliance emerges. This is essential given the improved outcomes associated with greater treatment compliance (Burns & Spangler, 2000).

Treatment Adherence and Competence

Effective interventions display a high level of treatment competence and fidelity on behalf of the therapist. This is perhaps unsurprising in light of evidence that treatment outcomes improve among clinicians with high levels of treatment fidelity (Durlak & DuPre, 2008). All of the effective treatments for reducing suicide attempts were manual driven with clear expectations regarding necessary material and order in which the information was presented. Each study clearly outlined extensive training and supervision procedures, which typically involved formal training and ongoing review and feedback from recorded sessions. Several studies utilized formal therapy assessment rating scales such as the Cognitive Therapy Rating Scale (CTRS; Young & Beck, 1980) to provide ongoing measurement of treatment fidelity (Brown et al., 2005; Esposito-Smythers & Spirito, 2004; Rudd et al., 2014). These procedures ensured that the patient received the appropriate "dose" of therapy and that the therapist covered the essential material in a competent manner, thereby limiting treatment disruption by peripheral issues.

What Doesn't Work

With knowledge about "what works" in suicide prevention comes a greater understanding of what does not work. A solid understanding of less efficacious or counterproductive suicide prevention strategies is equally important given the potentially dire consequences of poorly managed patients at high risk for suicide. Suicide prevention guidelines recommend treating the underlying disorder through psychotherapy and/or pharmacotherapy, with the use of hospitalization for the most severe cases (WHO, 2012). The clinical trials described above indicate that traditional approaches to treating suicidal patients, in which the associated psychiatric disorder is emphasized as the primary treatment goal is not ideal. Interestingly, targeting suicidal ideation and risk for suicide attempts not only leads to improvement in suicide-related outcomes but also in related psychiatric symptoms (Esposito-Smythers & Spirito, 2004).

Research also suggests that treatment as usual, in comparison to cognitive behavioral approaches, may insufficiently manage suicide risk over time. Treatment as usual is difficult to characterize given the many treatment modalities it can represent. It is conceivable, and indeed highly likely, that therapists providing traditional mental health care under routine conditions are using some of the very same interventions that characterize effective therapies. Unfortunately, studies to date are unable to provide sufficient information about what specific techniques and interventions are being provided in treatment as usual to more clearly differentiate between essential and nonessential (and possibly harmful) elements of therapy. Despite this limitation, the fact that treatment as usual was provided by typical clinicians under routine conditions suggests that treatments that are primarily supportive or insight oriented may be inferior to brief cognitive behavioral methods.

One final common practice that lacks empirical support is the use of no-suicide contracts. No-suicide contracts are agreements made between the clinician and patient in which the patient agrees to not harm him- or herself, but rather to seek professional help if in a crisis. Despite the lack of evidence supporting the use of no-suicide contracts, they continue to be utilized as an intervention for high-risk patients in psychiatric hospitals and outpatient settings (Farrow & O'Brien, 2003). No-suicide contracts provide a false sense of safety and security for the clinician or facility concerned with maintaining the safety of the high-risk patient. As such, the no-suicide contract is not perceived by the patient to be particularly therapeutic or useful. In direct response to the potentially ineffective no-suicide contract is the commitment to treatment statement and crisis response plan/safety plan, which is a common element of treatments that work and are discussed in Chapter 8 of this volume. Preliminary support suggests that this approach may be more useful than no-suicide contracts in reducing the incidence of suicide attempts and other forms of self-directed violence.

Summary

The treatment of suicidal ideation and suicide attempts is one of the most complex clinical challenges faced by mental health providers. Although the empirical literature on efficacious interventions for suicide risk is limited, this situation is rapidly changing, with converging evidence of efficacy emerging across a number of recent clinical trials of brief suicide-focused cognitive behavioral treatments. As will be discussed in the following chapters, brief cognitive behavioral treatments consistently contribute to significantly reduced suicide attempt rates compared to other treatment modalities. As discussed in this chapter, these treatments share a collection of common elements and characteristics: an emphasis on suicide risk as the primary objective, use of theory-driven interventions, skill set development, crisis response plans and means restriction, patient responsibility, and treatment compliance and adherence. These studies provide evidence supporting the outpatient treatment of individuals at elevated risk for suicide, thereby providing a viable and empirically supported alternative to inpatient psychiatric hospitalization. As will be discussed in greater detail later (Chapter 6), no randomized controlled trials have been conducted as yet that support the efficacy of inpatient hospitalization for the prevention of suicide attempts (Goldsmith, Pellmar, Kleinman, & Bunney, 2002), although a number of studies to date suggest that high-risk individuals, including those who have recently made a suicide attempt, can be successfully treated on an outpatient basis.

While these suicide-specific interventions show great promise, it is unclear as to which component or combination of components account for the decrease in suicide attempt rates. Identifying which "ingredients" are most helpful would help improve existing treatments and aid in the development of new treatments for other populations of interest. In addition, the nature and degree of participation bias among individuals who attempt suicide and agree to participate in clinical trials is unclear (Arensman et al., 2001). As indicated in at least one study (Linehan et al., 2006), a significant proportion of suicidal individuals refuse to participate or dropped out of treatment. As such, the generalizability of effective therapies may be limited to a small subgroup of patients who are willing to participate in research studies. The consistency of findings associated with brief cognitive behavioral therapies characterized by similar approaches, interventions, and models of care across a range of populations (e.g., urban residents, active duty military, women with borderline personality disorder, and adolescents with substance use disorders) nonetheless speaks to the robust nature of these treatments.

References

Arensman, E., Townsend, E., Hawton, K., Bremner, S., Feldman, E., Goldney, R., . . . & Träskman-Bendz, L. (2001). Psychosocial and pharmacological treatment of patients following deliberate self-harm: The methodological issues involved in evaluating effectiveness. *Suicide and Life-Threatening Behavior, 31*(2), 169–180.

Beck, A. T. (1979). *Cognitive therapy and the emotional disorders.* New York: Penguin.

Beck, A. T. (1996). Beyond belief: A theory of modes, personality, and psychopathology. In P. M. Salkovskis (Ed.), *Frontiers of Cognitive Therapy* (pp. 1–25). New York, NY: Guilford Press.

Brown, G. K., Ten Have, T., Henriques, G. R., Xie, S. X., Hollander, J. E., & Beck, A. T. (2005). Cognitive therapy for the prevention of suicide attempts. *JAMA: The Journal of the American Medical Association, 294*(5), 563–570.

Burns, D. D., & Spangler, D. L. (2000). Does psychotherapy homework lead to improvements in depression in cognitive–behavioral therapy or does improvement lead to increased homework compliance? *Journal of Consulting and Clinical Psychology, 68*(1), 46.

Carkhuff, R. R. (1969). *Helping and Human Relations, Vol. 1.* New York, NY: Holt, Rinehart, & Winston.

Centers for Disease Control and Prevention (2012). *Suicide: Facts at a glance 2012.* Retrieved from www.cdc.gov/violenceprevention/pdf/Suicide_DataSheet-a.pdf

Cipriani, A., Pretty, H., Hawton, K., & Geddes, J. R. (2005). Lithium in the prevention of suicidal behavior and all-cause mortality in patients with mood disorders: A systematic review of randomized trials. *American Journal of Psychiatry, 162*(10), 1805–1819.

Clinical Care and Intervention Task Force to the National Action Alliance for Suicide Prevention (2011). *Suicide Care in Systems Framework.* Retrieved December 3, 2014 from http://actionallianceforsuicideprevention.org/sites/actionallianceforsuicideprevention. org/files/taskforces/ClinicalCareInterventionReport.pdf

Comtois, K. A., & Linehan, M. M. (2006). Psychosocial treatments of suicidal behaviors: A practice-friendly review. *Journal of Clinical Psychology, 62*(2), 161–170.

Cotgrove, A., Zirinsky, L., Black, D., & Weston, D. (1995). Secondary prevention of attempted suicide in adolescence. *Journal of Adolescence, 18*(5), 569–577.

Daigle, M. S. (2005). Suicide prevention through means restriction: assessing the risk of substitution: A critical review and synthesis. *Accident Analysis & Prevention, 37*(4), 625–632.

Durlak, J. A., & DuPre, E. P. (2008). Implementation matters: A review of research on the influence of implementation on program outcomes and the factors affecting implementation. *American Journal of Community Psychology, 41*(3–4), 327–350.

Esposito-Smythers, C., & Spirito, A. (2004). Adolescent substance use and suicidal behavior: A review with implications for treatment research. *Alcoholism: Clinical and Experimental Research, 28*(S1), 77S–88S.

Evans, K., Tyrer, P., Catalan, J., Schmidt, U., Davidson, K., Dent, J., . . . & Thompson, S. (1999). Manual-assisted cognitive-behaviour therapy (MACT): A randomized controlled trial of a brief intervention with bibliotherapy in the treatment of recurrent deliberate self-harm. *Psychological Medicine, 29*(1), 19–25.

Farrow, T. L., & O'Brien, A. J. (2003). 'No-suicide Contracts' and Informed Consent: An analysis of ethical issues. *Nursing Ethics, 10*(2), 199–207.

Fergusson, D., Doucette, S., Glass, K. C., Shapiro, S., Healy, D., Hebert, P., & Hutton, B. (2005). Association between suicide attempts and selective serotonin reuptake inhibitors: Systematic review of randomised controlled trials. *British Medical Journal, 330*(7488), 396.

Gelder, M., Mayou, R., & Cowen, P. (2001). Suicide and deliberate self-harm. *Shorter Oxford Textbook of Psychiatry*, 507–532.

Goldsmith, S. K., Pellmar, T. C., Kleinman, A. M., & Bunney, W. E. (Eds.). (2002). *Reducing suicide: A national imperative*. Washington, DC: National Academies Press.

Gunnell, D., Saperia, J., & Ashby, D. (2005). Selective serotonin reuptake inhibitors (SSRIs) and suicide in adults: Meta-analysis of drug company data from placebo controlled, randomised controlled trials submitted to the MHRA's safety review. *British Medical Journal, 330*(7488), 385.

Hawton, K., Arensman, E., Townsend, E., Bremner, S., Feldman, E., Goldney, R., . . . & Träskman-Bendz, L. (1998). Deliberate self harm: Systematic review of efficacy of psychosocial and pharmacological treatments in preventing repetition. *British Medical Journal, 317*(7156), 441–447.

Hawton, K., Townsend, E., Arensman, E., Gunnell, D., Hazell, P., House, A., & Van Heeringen, K. (1999). Psychosocial and pharmacological treatments for deliberate self harm. *Cochrane Database of Systematic Reviews,* Issue 4.

Henriksson, S., Boëthius, G., & Isacsson, G. (2001). Suicides are seldom prescribed antidepressants: Findings from a prospective prescription database in Jämtland County, Sweden, 1985–1995. *Acta Psychiatrica Scandinavica, 103*(4), 301–306.

Horwitz, R. I., & Horwitz, S. M. (1993). Adherence to treatment and health outcomes. *Archives of Internal Medicine, 153*(16), 1863–1868.

Kerkhof, A. J. F. M., & Arensman, E. (2001). Pathways to suicide: The epidemiology of the suicidal process. In K. van Heeringen (Ed.), *Understanding suicidal behaviour: The suicidal process approach to research, treatment and prevention* (pp. 15–39). Chichester: John Wiley.

Linehan, M. M. (2008) Suicide interventional research: A field in desperate need of development. *Suicide and Life Threatening Behavior, 38*, 483–485.

Linehan, M. M., Armstrong, H. E., Suarez, A., Allmon, D., & Heard, H. L. (1991). Cognitive-behavioral treatment of chronically parasuicidal borderline patients. *Archives of General Psychiatry, 48*(12), 1060.

Linehan, M. M., Comtois, K. A., Murray, A. M., Brown, M. Z., Gallop, R. J., Heard, H. L., . . . & Lindenboim, N. (2009). Two-year randomized controlled trial and follow-up of dialectical behavior therapy vs. therapy by experts for suicidal behaviors and borderline personality disorder. *Archives of General Psychiatry, 63*(7), 757.

Linehan, M. M., Heard, H. L., & Armstrong, H. E. (1993). Naturalistic follow-up of a behavioral treatment for chronically parasuicidal borderline patients. *Archives of General Psychiatry, 50*(12), 971.

Mann, J.J., Apter, A., Bertolote, J., Beautrais, A., Currier, D., Haas, A., . . . & Hendin, H. (2005). Suicide prevention strategies. *JAMA: The Journal of the American Medical Association, 294*(16), 2064–2074.

Meltzer, H.Y., Alphs, L., Green, A.I., Altamura, A., Anand, R., Bertoldi, A., . . . & Potkin, S. (2003). Clozapine treatment for suicidality in schizophrenia: international suicide prevention trial (InterSePT). *Archives of General Psychiatry, 60*(1), 82.

Montgomery, S. A., Montgomery, D. B., Rani, S. J., Roy, P. H., Shaw, P. J., & McAuley, R. (1979). Maintenance therapy in repeat suicidal behavior: A placebo-controlled trial. Paper presented at the Xth International Congress for Suicide Prevention and Crisis Intervention, Ottawa, Canada.

Nock, M.K., Borges, G., Bromet, E.J., Alonso, J., Angermeyer, M., Beautrais, A., . . . & Williams, D. (2008). Cross-national prevalence and risk factors for suicidal ideation, plans and attempts. *The British Journal of Psychiatry, 192*(2), 98–105.

Oquendo, M.A., Galfalvy, H.C., Currier, D., Grunebaum, M.F., Sher, L., Sullivan, G.M., . . . & Mann, J.J. (2011). Treatment of suicide attempters with bipolar disorder: A randomized clinical trial comparing lithium and valproate in the prevention of suicidal behavior. *American Journal of Psychiatry, 168*(10), 1050–1056.

Rudd, M. D. (2012). Brief cognitive behavioral therapy (BCBT) for suicidality in military populations. *Military Psychology, 24*, 592–603.

Rudd, M. D., Bryan, C. J., Wertenberger, E. G., Peterson, A. L., Young-McCaughan, S., Mintz, J., Williams, S. R., Arne, K. A., Breitbach, J., Delano, K., Wilkinson, E., & Bruce, T. O. (2014). Brief cognitive behavioral therapy reduces post-treatment suicide attempts in a military sample: results of a 2-year randomized clinical trial. *American Journal of Psychiatry.*

Rudd, M. D., Bryan, C. J., Wertenberger, E. G., Peterson, A. L., Young-McCaughan, S., Mintz, J., Williams, S. R., Arne, K. A., Breitbach, J., Delano, K., Wilkinson, E., & Bruce, T. O. (in press). Brief cognitive behavioral therapy reduces post-treatment suicide attempts in a military sample: Results of a 2-year randomized clinical trial. *American Journal of Psychiatry.*

Rudd, M. D., Joiner, T. E., & Rajab, M. (2001). *Treating Suicidal Behavior: An Effective, Time-Limited Approach.* New York, NY: Guilford Press.

Salkovskis, P. M., Atha, C., & Storer, D. (1990). Cognitive-behavioural problem solving in the treatment of patients who repeatedly attempt suicide. A controlled trial. *The British Journal of Psychiatry, 157*(6), 871–876.

Schmidt, N.B., & Woolaway-Bickel, K. (2000). The effects of treatment compliance on outcome in cognitive-behavioral therapy for panic disorder: Quality versus quantity. *Journal of Consulting and Clinical Psychology, 68*(1), 13.

Turner, R.M. (2000). Naturalistic evaluation of dialectical behavior therapy-oriented treatment for borderline personality disorder. *Cognitive and Behavioral Practice, 7*(4), 413–419.

World Health Organization (2012). *Public health action for the prevention of suicide: A framework.* Retrieved from http://apps.who.int/iris/bitstream/10665/75166/1/9789241503570_eng.pdf?ua=1

Yip, P.S., Caine, E., Yousuf, S., Chang, S.S., Wu, K.C.C., & Chen, Y.Y. (2012). Means restriction for suicide prevention. *The Lancet, 379*(9834), 2393–2399.

Young, J., & Beck, A.T. (1980). Cognitive therapy scale: Rating manual. *Unpublished manuscript, University of Pennsylvania, Philadelphia.*

Part II

The Cognitive Behavioral Model of Suicide

four
A Cognitive Behavioral Model of Suicide Risk

Tracy A. Clemans

NATIONAL CENTER FOR VETERANS STUDIES AND
THE UNIVERSITY OF UTAH

Traditionally, self-directed violence has been classified according to its topographical characteristics and/or the symptoms of associated psychiatric disorders (Nock & Prinstein, 2004; Jobes, 2006), an approach that has been referred to as the psychiatric *syndromal model* (Hayes, Wilson, Gifford, Follette, & Strosahl, 1996). An alternative approach for categorizing self-directed violence is the *functional model*, wherein self-directed violence is organized according to the functional processes that initiate and maintain the behavior over time. These functional processes are generally understood to be antecedent and consequent contextual influences (Hayes et al., 1996), which impact suicide ideation and attempts despite the associated psychiatric disorder(s). Regardless of how this functional framework has aided our understanding of psychological and behavioral disorders, this approach has not been widely utilized in examining self-directed violence in general and suicide attempts in particular. Unfortunately, this means that some of the reasons for *why* individuals think about suicide and/or make suicide attempts have yet to be fully explored or understood (Bryan, Rudd, & Wertenberger, 2013).

Nock and Prinstein (2004) applied the functional approach in their studies of non-suicidal self-injury, which is a related yet distinct type of self-directed violence from suicide attempts. They devised four primary functions of non-suicidal self-injury across two dimensions of reinforcement: type of reinforcement (i.e., positive versus negative reinforcement) and source of reinforcement (i.e., automatic versus social contingencies). Positive reinforcement occurs when a behavior is followed by a pleasant stimulus, whereas negative reinforcement occurs when an unpleasant stimulus is removed following behavior. Automatic contingencies are internally focused, while social contingencies are externally focused. By employing a functional framework, *automatic-negative reinforcement* occurs when an individual makes a suicide attempt as a way to alleviate or reduce tension or unpleasant psychological and affective states. Thus, the suicide attempt functions as an escape or avoidance of intense psychological pain (e.g., "to stop feeling bad" or "to get away from my thoughts"), which is consistent with several leading theories of suicide (Joiner, 2005; Linehan, 1993; Schneidman, 1993). In contrast, *automatic positive reinforcement* occurs when the function of the suicide attempt is to generate or create a particular emotional or psychological state, sometimes transpiring as a way "to punish myself" or "to feel something . . . even if it is pain."

Social contingencies occur as a way to regulate or modify an individual's social or externally focused environment. Thus, *social negative reinforcement* refers to suicide attempts that occur with the purpose of avoiding interpersonal tasks or demands (e.g., "to avoid doing something unpleasant" or "to escape punishment from others"), whereas *social positive reinforcement* refers to suicide attempts that occur for the purpose of obtaining or creating a desired environmental condition (e.g., "to get help" or "to let others know how unhappy/desperate I am"). Sometimes mental health professionals refer to this latter function as "attention seeking behavior" or "manipulation"; however, the accuracy and/or utility of this perception has received very little empirical support (Nock & Prinstein, 2004), although it is often negatively received by the suicidal individual because it insinuates malintent or deception on the part of the suicidal individual.

In a study of active duty soldiers who had made suicide attempts, Bryan, Rudd, and Wertenberger (2013) established that, of the four functions proposed by Nock and Prinstein (2004), the primary function of suicide attempts is automatic negative reinforcement, or the reduction or avoidance of uncomfortable and aversive internal emotional states. These findings provide further support of the functional model of self-directed violence (Nock & Prinstein, 2004) and align with leading theories of suicide, which posit that suicidal individuals make suicide attempts to reduce or escape psychological pain and suffering (Joiner, 2005; Linehan, 1993; Schneidman, 1993). Results of Bryan et al.'s study further suggests that even when individuals attempt suicide for socially oriented reasons (e.g., "to get out of doing a task"), escape from emotional pain frequently co-occurs and/or is the more prominent motivation for the suicide attempt. Clinically, these findings have serious implications for the assessment and treatment of individuals who make suicide attempts for socially oriented reasons, as these individuals are sometimes viewed in a negative manner (e.g., "manipulative" or "attention seeking") by clinicians, potentially resulting in suboptimal clinical judgment (Bryan et al., 2013).

Fluid Vulnerability Theory of Suicide and the Suicidal Mode

Multiple risk assessment models have been developed over the years with the majority emphasizing the evaluation of risk and protective factors for suicide (Clark & Fawcett, 1992; Hirschfeld & Russell, 1997; Joiner et al., 1999). Although these models provide useful clinical information, they were not developed using a coherent theory that explains the distinction between risk categories (e.g., low, moderate, high) and how and why risk levels for individuals change over time. Likewise, risk assessment models have failed to adequately describe the differences between individuals who present with an acute suicidal crisis compared to individuals who exhibit chronic suicide ideation and/or repetitive suicide attempts (Rudd, Joiner, & Rajab, 1996; Rudd & Joiner, 1998). Despite these limitations, mental health professionals are obligated and responsible for conducting effective suicide risk assessments and utilizing this information to inform treatment planning and intervention. Consequently, a theory of suicide risk assessment that integrates acute versus chronic suicide risk; clearly defines fundamental assumptions of suicidal self-directed violence; and includes risk and protective factors from existing, broader models of suicide risk assessment is imperative.

The *fluid vulnerability theory* (FVT; Rudd, 2006) is one such theory of suicide that incorporates these essential elements into a comprehensive model that aides in understanding the process of suicide risk over the short and long term. According to the FVT, suicide risk is best conceptualized as an interaction of two dimensions of suicide risk: baseline and acute. Baseline risk entails the individual's predisposing vulnerabilities (e.g., genetic predispositions, trauma exposure) that elevate his or her overall likelihood for experiencing suicidal crises and making suicide attempts over the long term. Because these vulnerabilities tend to be static and/or historical in nature, they contribute to enduring and persistent risk over time. Acute risk, in contrast, corresponds to short-term fluctuations in the environmental context (e.g., life stressors) and internal psychological states (e.g., psychiatric symptoms, suicidal intent, insomnia) that manifest as suicidal episodes. The FVT has several fundamental assumptions that help to explain the onset, length, and severity of acute suicidal episodes over time (Rudd, 2006):

1. Suicidal episodes are time limited in nature (Litman, 1991; Rudd, 2006).
2. The baseline risk for suicide, or the threshold at which a suicidal episode is activated, varies among individuals. For example, some individuals have a higher threshold, in that their suicidal mode is never activated, whereas other individuals have a lower threshold, such that a particular stressor (e.g., loss of a relationship) can easily trigger a suicidal crisis.
3. Upon resolution of an acute suicidal episode, individuals will return to their baseline risk level (Rudd, 2006). For example, individuals with high baseline risk levels (e.g., chronically suicidal individuals) will remain at relatively elevated risk for suicide despite the resolution of their acute suicidal episode.
4. The baseline risk for patients with a history of multiple (i.e., two or more) suicide attempts is higher and endures for a longer period of time compared to individuals with only one or zero previous suicide attempts (Rudd, 2006; Rudd, Joiner, & Rajab, 1996; Clark & Fawcett, 1992). Clinically, the increased risk among individuals who have made multiple suicide attempts is noteworthy because, in addition to having more risk factors for suicide, they also

have fewer available protective factors (e.g., positive family support) that can reduce the risk of suicide attempts (Rudd, 2006).

5. Suicide risk increases when individuals experience internal or external stressors, also known as aggravating factors. These stressors include situations such as the recent loss of a job or ending of a relationship (external stressors) or thoughts of being a failure (internal stressor). Once activated by a stressor, a suicidal crisis is influenced by cognitive, affective, physiological, and behavioral factors referred to as the *suicidal mode* (described below).

6. The severity of a suicidal episode will be dependent on the interaction between baseline predispositions and the severity of aggravating or acute risk factors (Rudd, 2006). For example, an individual with a history of trauma and psychiatric disorders who experiences a reemergence of anxiety symptoms may interpret the return of these symptoms as an indication he or she is broken and will never get better, which can activate a suicidal crisis. In contrast, an individual without this same history may interpret the reemergence of anxiety symptoms as an indicator of transient distress.

7. Suicide risk activated by stressors or other aggravating factors will naturally resolve over time, although individuals with higher baseline risk will take longer to experience this resolution.

8. Acute suicide risk will resolve once stressors and aggravating risk factors are effectively targeted and/or protective factors are enhanced. Specifically, this final assumption suggests that the primary target for treatment should be symptoms and behaviors that directly contribute to and maintain the suicidal crisis.

The Suicidal Mode

The FVT is rooted in cognitive behavioral theory and incorporates at its core a cognitive behavioral model for conceptualizing suicide ideation and suicide attempts. This conceptual model is referred to as the *suicidal mode* (Rudd, Joiner, & Rajab, 2004) and is proposed to be comprised of four integrated systems: 1) *cognition*, also known as the "suicidal belief system," which includes suicidogenic automatic thoughts, assumptions, and core beliefs such as hopelessness, shame, self-hatred, and perceived burdensomeness; 2) *emotion*, which includes negative affects states such as depression, guilt, and anxiety; 3) *physiology*, which includes the physical/somatic experiences associated with suicidal crises such as insomnia, concentration and problem solving deficits, and physical pain; and 4) *behavior*, which includes maladaptive coping strategies including substance use, social withdrawal, and non-suicidal self-injury. From the perspective of the suicidal mode, when individuals experience triggering stressors, they engage in maladaptive behaviors and experience emotional distress, suicide-specific beliefs, and physiological arousal. Triggers range from thoughts, images, and perceptions (internal stressors) to circumstances, people, and situations (external stressors). It is these internal or external stressors that activate the suicidal mode in sufficiently vulnerable

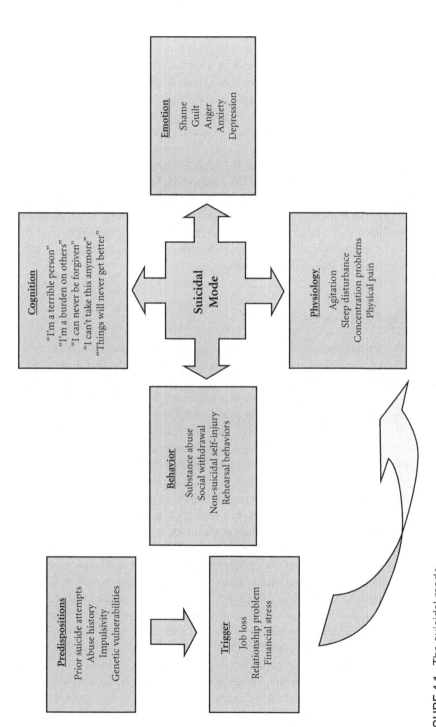

FIGURE 4.1. The suicidal mode

individuals (Rudd, Joiner, & Rajab, 2004). In other words, a stressor might activate a suicidal crisis in Person A but not Person B because the former has more vulnerabilities (i.e., higher baseline risk) than the latter.

Once the suicidal mode is triggered by a stressor, the suicidal belief system becomes active and can include active thoughts of death by suicide (e.g., "I want to kill myself"), unlovability (e.g., "I am worthless"), helplessness (e.g., "I am never going to solve this problem"), incompetence and self-hatred (e.g., "I cannot stand this pain anymore"), perceived burdensomeness (e.g., "Others would be better off without me"), and hopelessness (e.g., "There is no hope for my life"). The suicidal belief system is proposed to be the central domain of the suicidal mode, as these negative and self-critical identity-based thoughts magnify emotional distress including sadness, anger, guilt, shame, humiliation, and anxiety and motivate the individual to pursue maladaptive behavioral responses such as social withdrawal/isolation and substance abuse, which, in turn could potentially result in non-suicidal self-injury, preparatory and rehearsal behaviors (e.g., buying a gun or writing a suicide note), and suicide attempts.

Suicide Risk Assessment

One of the main objectives of a suicide risk assessment is to identify when a patient has reached a heightened state of risk for suicide and to implement appropriate interventions to modify and reduce their risk level (American Psychiatric Association, 2003). It is important for suicide risk assessments to be based on scientifically supported evidence while also being practical for the clinical setting. In other words, the risk assessment not only needs to be feasible within clinical settings but must also function as a way for clinicians to gather critical information based on empirical evidence, which can be used to modify patient suicide risk levels and inform treatment decisions.

In most cases, the suicide risk assessment will begin with a conversation of the patient's current stressors and/or recent problems that prompted him or her to seek out mental health care ("What brings you in today? Has anything in particular been especially stressful for you recently?"). This not only helps to establish rapport by prioritizing the patient's primary concerns, but it also helps to provide important information about the context and circumstances within which the patient's current crisis has emerged. Clinicians can then transition from identifying individuals' current stressors to assessing their current symptom presentation ("Have you been feeling depressed lately? How has this been affecting your life?") and their level of hopelessness ("Oftentimes people who are depressed will feel like things aren't going to get better for them. Do you ever feel this way?"), and then finally inquiring about the nature of their current suicidal thinking ("It's not uncommon for people who are depressed and feeling hopeless to experience suicidal thoughts. Do you ever have thoughts about your own death, or specifically thoughts of wanting to kill yourself?"). This gradual progression from current stressors to symptoms to suicide ideation allows the clinician to establish rapport with the patient while also helping to manage and reduce any potential anxiety or agitation that is sometimes present during the interview process. Likewise, risk assessment questions sequenced in this manner can help to normalize the individuals' experience of hopelessness and suicidal thoughts as being a part of a depressive episode or other presenting psychiatric condition (Bryan & Rudd, 2006). This hierarchical approach to risk assessment therefore creates an environment in which the patient feels safe disclosing suicidal thoughts and urges.

Another important consideration for suicide risk assessment is clarifying the difference between explicit and implicit suicidal intent (Beck & Lester, 1976). Explicit (or subjective) intent is the patient's stated intent and motivation, or what he or she actually tells the clinician during the assessment process. Conversely, implicit (or objective) intent is based on the individual's current and past behaviors, along with the lethality of the method he or she has chosen or implemented. In clinical settings, patients will frequently verbalize conflicting reports of explicit and implicit suicidal intent. For instance, a patient who held a firearm to his head while intoxicated the night before might later report to a clinician that he was "just drunk and being dumb" and state "I'm not going to kill myself." Where discrepancies between explicit and implicit intent exist, it is necessary for the clinician to weigh the objective markers of intent (e.g., holding a firearm to one's head) relative to the subjective markers of intent (e.g., denial of suicidal desire), and to inquire about any discrepancies by gently pointing out the discrepancy to their patients and gather more information, with the ultimate goal being to resolve the discrepancy. For example, clinicians might say, "You mentioned earlier that you have no plans to kill yourself, but you also indicated to me that you have been collecting some of your medication over the past few days. Let's talk about this and together we can figure out what's going on here." As illustrated in this example, the clarification process of an individual's implicit versus explicit intent allows the clinician to gather more accurate risk assessment data and to make better clinical decisions as a result.

It can also be helpful for clinicians to inquire a minimum of two times about the methods for suicide that a patient might be considering, as it is not uncommon, especially among patients who are chronically suicidal, to omit telling clinicians about the most lethal method or most accessible method they are considering. For example, clinicians might ask, "Have you considered any other methods to kill yourself?" Along these same lines, clinicians should also make a point to specifically ask about access to firearms, even if self-inflicted gunshot wound is not an explicitly stated method being considered. As will be discussed in detail in Chapter 9, the high lethality of firearms as a suicide method warrants particular attention during suicide risk assessment interviews, so that appropriate safety interventions (i.e., means restriction counseling) can be implemented.

A final strategy that can be beneficial for clinicians to use during the risk assessment process is to ask patients to rank specific emotions or symptoms (e.g., hopelessness, depression) and subjective suicidal intent on a Likert rating scale.

For example, clinicians might ask a patient, "What is your intention to kill your-self on a scale of 1 to 10, where 1 indicates no intention at all and 10 indicates very strong intent?" By utilizing such rating scales, clinicians can quantify patients' emotional experiences, objectively make comparisons of symptomatology over time, and monitor fluctuations in symptoms and overall improvement across treatment. With the ongoing use of these ratings, patients may also find it help-ful to understand what they are doing themselves (e.g., getting out of the house or exercising) that is contributing to fluctuations (especially decreases) in suicide ideation, suicidal intent, and other symptoms that contribute to suicide attempts. Tracking improvements over time can be empowering for patients and contribute to their sense of mastery and self-control, which is especially relevant for patients and clinicians as they work together to reduce their suicide risk.

Components of the Suicide Risk Assessment

Based on current empirical findings and consistent with the notion of the suicidal mode, there are several key areas to be assessed within the suicide risk interview. First, static risk factors that comprise predispositions to suicide such as previous suicide attempts and impulsivity (Rudd, Joiner, & Rajab, 2004; Bryan & Rudd, 2006) should be assessed, as these variables constitute the patient's baseline suicide risk. Second, aggravating variables such as precipitating stressor(s), symptomatic presentation (e.g., emotions and physical symptoms), presence of hopelessness, and the nature of suicidal ideation (to include the suicidal belief system) are key areas comprising the patient's acute risk. Finally, in addition to risk factors for suicide, clinicians should also examine protective factors, as these variables help to keep the patient alive (Rudd, Joiner, & Rajab, 2004; Bryan & Rudd, 2006).

Predispositions to Suicide

Clinicians may want to begin the risk assessment by assessing any predispositions to suicide or preexisting vulnerabilities within their history that are known to increase baseline suicide risk. These variables include past psychiatric diagnoses (especially chronic or agitated depression), history of abuse/trauma, family history (a proxy for genetic-based risk), history of suicide attempts, and recent discharge from inpatient psychiatric treatment. When conceptualizing psychiatric diagnos-tic history, it is beneficial for clinicians to evaluate whether diagnoses are recurring or chronic in nature (e.g., recurrent depressive episodes) and/or if comorbidities exist, as both of these factors are associated with increased risk for suicide. Consis-tent with the FVT, any patient who reports a history of multiple suicide attempts should be considered to have higher baseline risk suggesting long-term vulner-ability to make suicide attempts. Individuals who have previously utilized highly lethal means and methods for suicide attempts should also be considered to have especially high baseline risk even during periods of relative calm (Rudd, 2006; Rudd et al., 1996; Clark & Fawcett, 1992). Clinicians should also keep in mind that patients who have made multiple suicide attempts also have fewer available protective factors (e.g., problem-solving skills, support), which can further contribute to elevated risk (Bryan & Rudd, 2006).

When assessing previous suicide attempts, clinicians should ask about the intent of each of these attempts, which can be accomplished by asking questions such as:

- "What did you hope you would happen?"
- "Did you want to die?"
- "Were you happy to be alive afterward?"

Clinicians should always assess whether patients have a history of multiple attempts and then gather information about each individual attempt. For patients who have made multiple suicide attempts, clinicians can focus their attention on assessing the first suicide attempt, the worst-point suicide attempt, and the most recent suicide attempt using an open-ended question like, "Tell me the story of the first time you tried to kill yourself," and then probing for needed details to establish suicidal intent. The worst-point suicide attempt entails the suicide attempt during which the patient experienced the greatest amount of suicidal intent or most wanted to die; it does not indicate the most lethal or life-threatening suicide attempt. Focusing on the worst-point suicide attempt is an important risk assessment component because data indicate that the worst-point suicidal episode is a better predictor of suicide attempts than any other suicidal episode, including the current or most recent suicide attempt (e.g., Beck, Brown, Steer, Dahlsgaard, & Grisham, 1999).

For each suicide attempt, clinicians should determine the frequency and context of the suicide attempt (e.g., "How often have you attempted to kill yourself in the past? What was going on at this time in your life?"), perceived lethality and outcome (e.g., "Why did you choose that particular method?"), opportunity for rescue and help seeking (e.g., "Did you know your [family member, friend] would come home and find you?"), and suicide preparatory behaviors ("Have you done anything to practice the method we talked about earlier? Have you taken any steps to prepare to kill yourself such as writing a suicide note, giving your things away, driving to location where you want to kill yourself, or anything else like this?"). In this way, using the first-worst-most-recent approach to assessing suicide attempt history enables clinicians to identify trajectories of intent and lethality over time (e.g., increasing versus stable lethality), as well as to establish patterns in behaviors (e.g., similar contextual triggers, similar methods), in a manner that is practical and time efficient.

Precipitant Stressors

Clinicians should also aim to identify aggravating variables that contribute to the individual's acute suicide risk level. Precipitant stressors are those internal or external variables that "aggravated" or triggered the individual's acute suicidal crisis.

Specifically, clinicians should query about any current stressors such as relationship conflicts and interpersonal problems, legal or disciplinary issues, financial problems, and physical injuries, as all of these variables are known to increase the risk for suicide attempts and death by suicide (Bryan & Rudd, 2012). Clinicians may inquire about the precipitating stressor by asking questions like, "Is there anything in particular that happened that may have triggered you wishing to be dead or having suicidal thoughts?"

Symptomatic Presentation

Following an inquiry about precipitant stressors, clinicians should explore the patient's symptoms associated with this event, such as emotions, physical symptoms, and cognitions. Clinicians should ask questions that elicit details about the patient's current emotional state such as, "Can you tell me how you have been feeling lately?" or "Have you been feeling [nervous, anxious, worried, down, low, blue] recently?" Important symptom clusters to examine within the risk assessment are depressive symptoms (e.g., anhedonia, low self-esteem, fatigue) and symptoms of agitation (e.g., racing thoughts, irritability, restlessness, impulsivity). Combined agitation with depression is associated with especially increased risk. Other emotions that can increase suicide risk are guilt and shame (Bryan et al., 2013), which can be assessed by asking, "Have you (or do you) feel bad about an action or decision you have made?" (guilt) or "Do you ever find yourself feeling bad about who you are as a person?" (shame) or "Do you consider yourself to be [worthless, broken, damaged]?" (shame).

Related to agitation, it is important for clinicians to evaluate the presence of arousal symptoms more globally, as many have of these symptoms are correlated with increased risk for suicide risk. For example, symptoms such as insomnia, restlessness, and impaired attention and concentration may be indicative of physiological arousal and can be rated using the 1 to 10 Likert scale mentioned previously ("How difficult has it been to fall or stay asleep on a scale of 1 to 10?"). Finally, it is also beneficial for clinicians to note any signs of increased physiological arousal observed during the assessment interview (e.g., agitation, restlessness, difficulty with concentrating).

Nature of Suicidal Thinking (Cognitions)

Clinicians should also assess the frequency, intensity, and duration of the individual's wishes for death, suicidal ideation, and any specific thoughts about a suicide plan. Utilizing the hierarchical approach described above, clinicians can start by asking about desire for death ("Do you ever experience thoughts of wanting to die or wishing life would stop?") and then proceed to asking about more specific thoughts of suicide ("Have you ever thoughts about suicide?"). Other useful data to collect are the frequency, intensity (use the 1 to 10 scale), and duration of the patient's wishes to be dead or suicide ideation. When assessing the current suicidal episode, clinicians should always ask about the presence of any current suicide plans ("Have you thought about how you might kill yourself?"), recent preparatory behaviors ("Have you practiced [method] in anyway or done anything to prepare for your death?"), and suicidal intent ("Do you have any intention at all, even if only a little bit, to follow through on the plan you just described?") Finally, questions that directly ask about the accessibility of potentially lethal means for suicide (e.g., firearm in the home) are crucial during the risk assessment, as means restriction is an effective suicide prevention strategy (Beautrais, 2000; Mann et al., 2005) that can easily be implemented by clinicians (see Chapter 9).

In addition to suicide ideation, other suicide-related cognitions to be assessed by clinicians include the perception that the individual is a burden on others ("Do you feel like a burden on anyone, or that others would be better off without you?"), thinking no one cares about them ("Do you ever feel disconnected or isolated from others?"), and feelings of defectiveness ("Do you feel like a failure in life?"). Recent research suggests that these components of the suicidal belief system are not only significant predictors of suicide ideation and suicide attempts (e.g., Bryan, 2011; Bryan, Clemans, & Hernandez, 2012; Bryan, McNaughton-Cassill, Osman, & Hernandez, 2013; Bryan, Morrow, Anestis, & Joiner, 2010; Bryan et al., 2014; Van Orden, Witte, Gordon, Bender, & Joiner, 2008), but they also predict future suicide attempts better than current suicide ideation (Bryan et al., 2014).

Presence of Hopelessness

Another suicide-specific cognition that clinicians should assess for is the presence of hopelessness, which is an individual's belief that his or her situation is hopeless or unchangeable. Clinicians should inquire about the severity and duration of their hopelessness, as this particular risk factor is found in the majority of suicidal patients (Bryan & Rudd, 2006). Recent data also indicate that the risk associated with situational hopelessness is increased among individuals who lack an optimistic or hopeful disposition (Bryan, Ray-Sannerud, Morrow, & Etienne, 2013).

Protective Factors

A final component of the suicide risk assessment is probing about variables that are associated with *reducing* the risk for suicide attempts, or protective factors. Questions assessing for protective factors may include:

- "Do you have access to family or friends whom you can talk to and depend on?"
- "What reasons do you have for living?"
- "What keeps you from making a suicide attempt?"

Common protective factors to assess for include social support, presence of hope, children being present in the home, religious engagement, fear of social disapproval (of dying by suicide), fear of death, active participation and commitment to treatment, and presence of effective problem-solving or coping skills. Although risk factors have a stronger relationship with suicide attempts than protective factors, interventions that focus on increasing protective factors while reducing risk factors are more effective than interventions focused on reducing only risk factors (Bryan & Rudd, 2006).

Summary

The benefits of completing a thorough and accurate suicide risk assessment are considerable within clinical settings, as clinicians who approach suicide risk assessment based on the most important domains relevant to suicide risk are likely to make clinical decisions with much greater confidence in terms of their clinical decision making. Likewise, clinicians can transition the information obtained during the risk assessment process for use to develop subsequent treatment recommendations designed to reduce both short-term (acute) and long-term (chronic) suicide risk.

References

American Psychiatric Association (2003). Practice guideline for the assessment and treatment of patients with suicidal behaviors. *Official Journal of the American Psychiatric Association, 160*, 1–60.

Beautrais, A. L. (2000). Restricting access to means of suicide in New Zealand: A report prepared for the Ministry of Health on methods of suicide in New Zealand 1997–1996. Wellington, New Zealand: New Zealand Ministry of Health. Retrieved from www.moh.govt.nz/moh.nsf/pagesmh/1244

Beck, A. T., Brown, G. K., Steer, R. A., Dahlsgaard, K. K., & Grisham, J. R. (1999). Suicide ideation at its worst point: A predictor of eventual suicide in psychiatric outpatients. *Suicide and Life-Threatening Behavior, 29*, 1–9.

Beck, A. T., & Lester, D. (1976). Components of suicidal intent in completed and attempted suicides. *Journal of Psychology: Interdisciplinary and Applied, 92*, 35–38.

Bryan, C. J. (2011). The clinical utility of a brief measure of perceived burdensomeness and thwarted belongingness for the detection of suicidal military personnel. *Journal of Clinical Psychology, 67*, 981–992.

Bryan, C. J., Clemans, T. A., & Hernandez, A. M. (2012). Perceived burdensomeness, fearlessness of death, and suicidality among deployed military personnel. *Personality and Individual Differences, 52*, 374–379.

Bryan, C. J., Clemans, T. A., Hernandez, A. M., & Rudd, M. D. (2013). Loss of consciousness, depression, posttraumatic stress disorder, and suicide risk among deployment military personnel with mild traumatic brain injury. *Journal of Head Trauma Rehabilitation, 28*, 13–20.

Bryan, C. J., Gartner, A. M., Wertenberger, E., Delano, K., Wilkinson, E., Breitbach, J., & Rudd, M. D. (2012). Defining treatment completion according to patient competency: A case example using Brief Cognitive Behavioral Therapy (BCBT) for suicidal patients. *Professional Psychology: Research & Practice, 43*(2), 130–136.

Bryan, C. J., Jennings, K. W., Jobes, D. A., & Bradley, J. C. (2012). Understanding and preventing military suicide. *Archives of Suicide Research, 16*(2), 95–110.

Bryan, C. J., McNaughton-Cassill, M., Osman, A., & Hernandez, A. M. (2013). The association of physical and sexual assault with suicide risk in nonclinical military and undergraduate samples. *Suicide and Life-Threatening Behavior, 43,* 223–234.

Bryan, C. J., Morrow, C. E., Anestis, M. D., & Joiner, T. E. (2010). A preliminary test of the interpersonal psychological theory of suicidal behavior in a military sample. *Personality and Individual Differences, 48,* 347–350.

Bryan, C. J., Morrow, C. E., Etienne, N., & Ray-Sannerud, B. (2013). Guilt, shame, and suicidal ideation in a military outpatient clinical sample. *Depression and Anxiety, 30,* 55–60.

Bryan, C. J., Ray-Sannerud, B. N., Morrow, C. E., & Etienne, N. (2013). Optimism reduces suicidal ideation and weakens the effect of hopelessness among military personnel. *Cognitive Therapy and Research, 37,* 996–1003.

Bryan, C. J., & Rudd, M. D. (2006). Advances in the assessment of suicide risk. *Journal of Clinical Psychology, 62*(2), 185–200.

Bryan, C. J., & Rudd, M. D. (2012). Life stressors, emotional distress, and trauma-related thoughts occurring within 24 h of suicide attempts among active duty U.S. soldiers. *Journal of Psychiatric Research, 46*(7), 843–848.

Bryan, C. J., Rudd, M. D., & Wertenberger, E. (2013). Reasons for suicide attempts among active duty soldiers: A functional approach. *Journal of Affective Disorders, 144,* 148–152.

Bryan, C. J., Rudd, M. D., Wertenberger, E., Etienne, N., Ray-Sannerud, B. N., Peterson, A. L., & Young-McCaughon, S. (2014). Improving the detection and prediction of suicidal behavior among military personnel by measuring suicidal beliefs: An evaluation of the Suicide Cognitions Scale. *Journal of Affective Disorders, 159,* 15–22.

Clark, D. C., & Fawcett, J. (1992). Review of empirical risk factors for evaluation of the suicidal patient. In B. Bongar (Ed.), *Suicide guidelines for assessment, management, and treatment* (pp. 16–48). New York: Oxford University Press.

Hayes, S. C., Wilson, K. G., Gifford, E. V., Follette, V. M., & Strosahl, K. (1996). Experiential avoidance and behavioral disorder: A functional dimensional approach to diagnosis and treatment. *Journal of Consulting and Clinical Psychology, 64,* 1152–1168.

Hirschfeld, R. M., & Russell, J. M. (1997). Assessment and treatment of suicidal patients. *New England Journal of Medicine, 337,* 910–915.

Jobes, D. A. (2006). *Managing suicidal risk: A collaborative approach.* New York: Guilford Press.

Joiner, T. E. (2005). *Why people die by suicide.* Cambridge, MA: Harvard University Press.

Joiner, T. E., Walker, R. L., Rudd, M. D., & Jobes, D. A. (1999). Scientizing and routinizing the assessment of suicidality in outpatient practice. *Professional Psychology: Research and Practice, 30,* 447–453.

Linehan, M. M. (1993). *Cognitive Behavioral treatment of borderline personality disorder.* New York, NY: Guilford Press.

Litman, R. E. (1991). Predicting and preventing hospital and clinic studies. *Suicide and Life-Threatening Behavior, 21,* 56–73.

Mann, J. J., Apter, A., Bertolote, J., Beautrais, A., Currier, D., Haas, A. . . . Hendin, H. (2005). Suicide prevention strategies: A systematic review. *JAMA: Journal of the American Medical Association, 294,* 2064–2074.

Nock, M. K., & Kessler, R. C. (2006). Prevalence of and risk factors for suicide attempts versus suicide gesture: Analysis of the National Comorbidity Survey. *Journal of Abnormal Psychology, 115*(3), 616–623.

Nock, M. K., & Prinstein, M. J. (2004). A functional approach to the assessment of self-mutilative behavior. *Journal of Consulting and Clinical Psychology, 72,* 885–890.

Rudd, M.D. (2006). Fluid vulnerability theory: A cognitive approach to understanding the process of acute and chronic suicide risk. In Ellis, T.E. (Ed.), *Cognition and suicide: Theory, research, and therapy* (pp. 355–368). Washington, DC: American Psychological Association.

Rudd, M. D., & Joiner, T. E. (1998). The assessment, management, and treatment of suicidality: Toward clinically informed and balanced standards of care. *Clinical Psychology; Science and Practice, 5,* 135–150.

Rudd, M.D., Joiner, T.E., & Rajab, M.H. (1996). Relationships among suicide ideators, attempters, and multiple attempters in a young-adult sample. *Journal of Abnormal Psychology, 105*(4), 541–550.

Rudd, M.D., Joiner, T. E., & Rajab, M. H. (2004). *Treating suicidal behavior: An effective, time-limited approach.* New York, NY: Guilford Press.

Schneidman, E. S. (1993). *Suicide as psychache: A clinical approach to self-destructive behavior.* Lanham, MD: Rowan & Littlefield Publishers, Inc.

Van Orden, K. A., Witte, T. K., Gordon, K. H., Bender, T. W., & Joiner, T. E. (2008). Suicidal desire and the capability for suicide: Tests of the interpersonal-psychological theory of suicidal behavior among adults. *Journal of Consulting and Clinical Psychology, 76,* 72–83.

five
Cognitive Therapy for Suicide Prevention

An Illustrative Case Example

Kelly L. Green and Gregory K. Brown

THE UNIVERSITY OF PENNSYLVANIA

Cognitive Therapy for Suicide Prevention (CT-SP) is a brief, targeted, and evidence-based psychotherapy that aims to reduce the risk of suicide in high-risk individuals by teaching them cognitive and behavioral skills for managing suicidal ideation and preventing suicide attempts (Wenzel, Brown, & Beck, 2009). CT-SP is *brief* in that it is comprised of approximately ten 50-minute sessions that may be provided as a stand-alone treatment or in conjunction with other mental health treatment. CT-SP is *targeted* in that the explicit focus of the treatment is on suicide prevention, as opposed to targeting psychiatric disorders that may also comprise the clinical picture. CT-SP is *evidence based* in that a landmark study of CT-SP in psychiatric outpatients recruited individuals from emergency departments and inpatient units following a suicide attempt (Brown et al., 2005). Participants were randomly assigned to receive either 10 sessions of CT-SP or usual care enhanced by case management and followed prospectively for 18 months. This study found that CT-SP led to a 50% reduction in repeat suicide attempts compared to enhanced usual care. As a follow up to this study, the developers are currently conducting a clinical trial evaluating an adaptation of CT-SP for older men with suicidal ideation.

The treatment progresses in three phases. In the beginning phase, the therapist and patient work together in order to identify triggers and warning signs for suicidal crises; to develop an individualized, cognitive case conceptualization; and to identify specific and measurable treatment goals. In the middle phase of treatment, the therapist assists the patient in learning and implementing specific cognitive and behavioral skills that are selected to target the treatment goals. In the later phase of treatment, the therapist and patient review the skills that were learned over the course of the therapy, and a guided imagery relapse prevention task is completed to assess the patient's readiness for ending treatment.

In this chapter, the three phases of the CT-SP treatment, along with a subset of core features and intervention strategies, will be briefly described and illustrated using a case vignette. The case description and examples used in this chapter are fictional and represent the types of issues addressed by this treatment. For a full description of the CT-SP intervention and additional case illustrations, please refer to the published treatment manual (Wenzel et al., 2009).

Case Vignette

John is a 67-year-old man who was referred to psychotherapy by his psychiatrist after disclosing that his suicidal ideation had increased in severity over the past several months and that he had been considering potential plans for suicide that included carbon monoxide poisoning with his car or overdosing on his prescription pain medications. John has chronically struggled with suicidal ideation for the past 10 years, since sustaining a back injury at his job as a mechanic, which has led to chronic pain that ultimately prevented him from continuing to work. Since leaving work 5 years ago, John has experienced financial difficulties, which has caused a strain on his relationship with his wife. John also has a daughter and three grandchildren.

John grew up in what he described as a "strict Catholic" household. His mother was a housewife and his father worked in a factory to provide for the family. He stated that while his mother had a warm demeanor, his father was distant and had high expectations of him. His father would often treat him coldly when he made a mistake or failed to live up to these expectations. John reported that these experiences made him strive to be the best that he could be and that he holds himself to the same high standards as his father. He reported that his parents also instilled a high value of work in him and that he started working when he was 13 (delivering newspapers), and has been employed since that time until 5 years ago.

He was hospitalized 1 year ago after his wife walked in to find him with a gun to his head and convinced him to go to the hospital. This was the first time he had received mental health treatment, and he has been seeing his psychiatrist as an outpatient since his discharge. He has recently been distressed about his financial situation and told his psychiatrist that he has been talking to his wife about selling their house, as they can no longer afford the property taxes. His relationship with his wife has continued to be strained, and John reports that they fight all the time.

Beginning Phase of Treatment

The goal of the introductory phase of CT-SP is to orient the patient to treatment and begin to instill hope for the future. The following tasks are completed in the beginning phase of treatment: 1) conducting a suicide risk assessment; 2) providing a treatment rationale and obtaining informed consent; 3) completing a narrative interview of recent suicidal crises; 4) developing a Safety Plan; 5) exploring reasons for living and dying; and 6) developing a case conceptualization and collaboratively identifying treatment goals.

Suicide Risk Assessment

Because individuals experiencing suicidal ideation (and those who have a history of past suicide attempts) are at an increased risk for suicide, a necessary component of the beginning phase of treatment is conducting a comprehensive suicide risk assessment. This can be incorporated into standard intake procedures that occur prior to the commencement of treatment. Risk is then continually assessed and updated over the course of therapy. Such an assessment should include questions about the content, frequency, duration, and severity of current suicidal ideation, as well as about past suicidal ideation and behavior (including suicide attempts). Plans for suicide, intent to make a suicide attempt, and access to potentially lethal means are particularly important components of suicide risk to thoroughly assess. In addition, the clinician should assess both risk factors (e.g., level of hopelessness, recent losses, etc.) as well as protective factors (e.g., strong social support, fear of suicide, etc.).

During his intake, John describes that over the past several months, he has experienced suicidal ideation more days than not, with the thoughts lasting for between half an hour to an hour at a time. He stated that, most often, he experiences thoughts such as, "I should just end it now" and "My death will make everything better." He endorsed thinking about methods for suicide about once per week. He described that he sometimes thinks about how many pills it would take to bring about his death and that he has also considered how he could use carbon monoxide from his car to poison himself. On a 1 to 10 scale, with 10 being the highest, he rated both the intensity of his ideation and the desire to act on the thoughts when he has them at a 6 and 5, respectively.

John reported that he has never followed through with a suicide attempt before but did endorse an interrupted attempt a year ago prior to his hospitalization. He stated that he had planned to shoot himself but that his wife walked in on him while he was contemplating pulling the trigger and stopped him. He stated that his ideation was at its worst during that time; he was having thoughts of suicide continuously throughout the day, with a strong desire to act on these thoughts. He stated that he believes he would have attempted suicide if his wife had not come home early and discovered him. John no longer has access to a gun; his wife gave it to a relative while he was hospitalized. However, he does have ready access to prescription pain medications, as well as his car. Other risk factors that John's therapist identified include ongoing interpersonal conflicts, hopelessness about the future, presence of major depressive disorder, chronic physical pain, and his perceptions that he is a burden on his loved ones.

The risk assessment also elucidated protective factors. John was able to identify reasons for living including his grandchildren and his dog. He further reported that while their relationship is conflicted, he feels a responsibility to support his wife. He ultimately believes that suicide is wrong and immoral, due to his Catholic faith and regular church attendance. Based upon weighing the relative strengths of the risk and protective factors, John was assessed to be at moderate risk for suicide. It is important to conduct an ongoing assessment of suicide risk at each therapy session. As part of the usual structure of each session (see Wenzel et al., 2009), the therapist asks the patient if he or she has been thinking about suicide since the last session or provides the patient with a self-report measure of depression, such as the *Beck Depression Inventory-II* (Beck, Steer, & Brown, 1996), that includes questions about hopelessness and suicidal thinking.

Treatment Rationale and Informed Consent

Hopelessness is a key clinical characteristic of suicidal patients (Brown, Beck, Steer, & Grisham, 2000) and may affect the patient's expectations about the effectiveness of treatment, leading some patients to drop out of treatment prematurely. Thus, it is important to not only orient patients to the process and structure of CT-SP, in addition to the potential risks and benefits of treatment (e.g., Rudd et al., 2009), but also to obtain the patient's consent and commitment to participate in the therapy. John and his therapist have the following conversation at the beginning of their first therapy session together:

Therapist: Before we get started, first I would like to discuss the treatment I am suggesting and answer any questions you may have about it so that you can make an informed decision about whether this is a treatment you would like to receive. How does that sound?

John: I'd appreciate that. I haven't really done much therapy before, except for when I was in the hospital. It was a lot of talking about the past, which I didn't really like. Is that what this will be like, too?

Therapist: Well, not exactly. The treatment I would like to use with you is called Cognitive Therapy. This type of therapy is based on the idea that it's hard to have direct control over your feelings, but that the way you think and the things you do have a big impact on the way you feel. So the goal of the therapy is for us to work together to take a look at your thoughts and behaviors and come up with some new strategies that you can use to decrease thoughts of suicide and to feel better. We may talk about the past at times, but we will focus most of our efforts on how you're doing now and how to improve things for you in the present. How does that sound compared to therapy you've had before?

John: It sounds a lot different. Before, I talked a lot about my feelings and what landed me in the hospital and that I needed to cope better. You're saying that in this therapy, we'll actually talk about how to cope better?

Therapist: Yes, that's exactly right. The goal of this therapy is to give you skills to cope with, and hopefully overcome, suicidal thoughts. Research has

	shown that this approach is effective in preventing suicide attempts, and I've used it with good success for many patients.
John:	All right, well, that sounds good so far.
Therapist:	I'm glad to hear that. Let me tell you a little bit more about what the therapy will look like. Our sessions together will have a structure to them. At the beginning of session, we will check in about your mood that day and about how your thoughts of suicide have been over the last week. We'll review what we talked about at the last session, and we'll make an agenda of the things that you would like to talk about and address that day in session.
John:	So we'll talk about how I'm doing and then I can talk about whatever I want? You won't tell me what the best thing to talk about is?
Therapist:	Well, I want us to work together as a team so that we can make sure we are talking about the problems and situations that are the most important to you. I can help out with suggestions for topics if you are stuck, but I really need your input on the things you feel are important to talk about.
John:	That's fair, I guess.
Therapist:	We will spend the majority of our sessions talking about these important problems that you bring in and working together to come up with things that you can try to improve them. Each session, we'll come up with something that you can do in between sessions to practice the strategies that we talk about in session and test them out in your everyday life.
John:	You keep talking about strategies. Can you explain that more? I just don't know what I can do to get rid of these thoughts I have. I feel like I've tried everything. I see my doctor, I take the meds, I try to talk about it and nothing seems to work.
Therapist:	Let me use an analogy. You worked as a mechanic, right?
John:	Yeah, that's right.
Therapist:	Well, let's say your car needed an oil change and the only tools you had on hand were a hammer and a screwdriver.
John:	I'd be up a creek; those aren't the right tools. I'd need a funnel and a wrench set at least. I'd probably have to jack the car up to get under it too.
Therapist:	Exactly, you wouldn't have the tools you needed to fix it. That's what I mean when I say "strategies". The goal of therapy is to identify the tools that you already have in your toolkit that can be helpful for you and to also give you new tools to use that you may not already have.
John:	So you're saying that maybe I need some new tools to deal with the stuff that's been going on.
Therapist:	Yes, that's one of the things we'll work to figure out. How does this treatment approach sound to you?
John:	Well, it's something that I haven't tried yet. The way you describe it sounds like maybe it could help. I'm willing to give it a try.

Therapist: I'm glad to hear that. Before you make a final decision about it, I also want to make sure that we discuss the potential risks of therapy. One of the main risks is that therapy will involve talking about topics that may be very upsetting to you and may cause you some discomfort. We will work together to manage any potential discomfort.

John: Yeah, talking about all this is definitely not something I'm looking forward to. But I know I probably need to do it.

Therapist: The other main risk is that that the treatment may not reduce or eliminate your suicidal thinking, and it is possible that you could make a suicide attempt during treatment. I may also have to break our confidentiality in order to keep you safe. If I think there is a need to do this, I will do my best to discuss it with you first.

John: Yeah, my psychiatrist says the same thing. I feel like I've been good about keeping it from going too far down that road lately. I'd tell you if it were like last year again.

Therapist: I appreciate that, John. Do you think that you would still like to give this therapy a try?

John: Yep. I'll try my best with it.

In this conversation, the therapist oriented the patient to the CT-SP treatment and briefly to the cognitive model. The therapist actively engaged the patient in this conversation, asking him about his past therapy experience and also asking questions to assess his understanding of and reactions to the treatment being proposed. Importantly, before allowing the patient to consent to the treatment, the therapist made sure to discuss the potential risks. After gaining informed consent, the therapist would then have a conversation about the patient's expectations for treatment as a way of instilling hope both in the treatment and in the future. After these important conversations, the therapist would then begin obtaining more information about the motivations for the patient's suicidal crises by conducting the narrative interview.

Narrative Interview of the Suicidal Crisis

The next step of CT-SP is to conduct what is called the narrative interview. This interview allows the patient to tell the story of a recent suicidal crisis, including the thoughts, feelings, and behaviors that occurred prior to, during, and after the crisis. The narrative interview helps to develop the therapeutic relationship, in addition to providing information for the cognitive case conceptualization. The narrative interview also assists with the identification of warning signs for suicidal crises and thus provides a natural segue into the collaborative development of the Safety Plan.

Therapist: John, I'd like to hear more about the specifics that lead to you thinking about suicide. Sometimes people can become upset when they describe the thoughts and feelings they have recently experienced in detail. If this happens to you, would you let me know and then we can decide how best to proceed?

John: Okay.

Therapist: Good. So, can you tell me what happened that led you to think about suicide, including when these thoughts were at the worst point?

John: Yeah, about a couple weeks ago I had a really bad day. I sat for hours playing out different scenarios in my head, about how I could do it and make sure it would work.

Therapist: What led up to that?

John: Well, the day had started out okay, but then when I checked the mail, I saw that we had another notice that the taxes on the house were overdue. We've already gotten two of them. So I saw that letter and everything just went downhill.

Therapist: Uh-huh.

John: I was thinking there was no way I could pay it. It's hard enough keeping up with all the other bills, you know? So, I went inside and my wife was in the kitchen. I told her that we got the notice. She started worrying and wondering what we were going to do about it. She suggested that maybe we ask my daughter and her husband for help. That made me mad and I told her it was a stupid idea. Then that started another fight like always. She got mad and went to go do something else.

Therapist: What made you so mad about her suggestion?

John: I'm not going to ask the kids for money. It's my job to take care of the family and not theirs. And I was mad that my damn back keeps me from doing it like I used to.

Therapist: It sounds like you were feeling pretty angry and discouraged at this point. What happened next?

John: Yes, I was feeling pretty beat down at this point. I decided to go sit in the garage so I could get away from my wife for a while. I have a chair and a radio out there. I remember I was sitting there just thinking about things: all the money problems. And I was looking at my tools, wishing I could just go back to work and get back to the way things used to be instead of being so useless.

Therapist: I understand.

John: I just kept coming back to the fact that I can't do the things I used to do and support my wife like I'm supposed to. I was feeling pretty useless to her and everyone else. Then I thought that maybe they would all be better off if I just ended it and that I would be better off as well. After thinking about this for a while, I started mapping out in my head how I could do it. Trying to figure out how many pills it would take if I used my pain pills. I also thought about how I could close up the garage and let the car exhaust run; how I could do it without tipping my wife off so she couldn't stop me.

Therapist: And how were you feeling while you were thinking about all of these scenarios?

John: Sad, I guess. Exhausted. Just really beat down.

Therapist: I can understand that. So to summarize, things started to go badly on this day when you got the notice in the mail about the taxes. You started worrying about how you could pay them. Then your wife found out about the notice and she suggested that you ask your daughter for money, which made you really angry and you got into an argument with her. After that, you went into the garage to get away for a while and you started mulling over these financial problems and had the thought that you were useless and would be better off dead. That got you started with thinking about potential ways that you could kill yourself and trying to figure out a good plan to do it. Do I have that right?

John: That's what happened. I don't contribute anymore. I just don't see the point in living that way. So when I get to feeling that way, yeah, I usually think about ending it.

Therapist: But you didn't try to end it that day. What happened?

John: Like I said, I sat there for a good 3 or 4 hours. Then, my cell phone rang and it was my daughter. She said my granddaughter wanted to talk to me, and she put her on the phone, and she was telling me all about how she lost her first tooth. She's 6 and she was so excited to find the dollar under her pillow that morning. That really knocked me out of it, I think, when I heard her on the phone.

Therapist: Your grandkids are really important to you.

John: Definitely. That helped me to feel better enough to get out of the garage and stop thinking those thoughts that day.

Therapist: I think this is good information. Maybe one of the things we should work on together is these thoughts you have about being useless. And we have some information about something that really helps to distract you from thoughts about suicide: talking to your grandkids. Let's think about this a little more and try to identify other things that commonly trigger thoughts of suicide and also other things that may be helpful to you to distract you from those thoughts.

As can be observed from this interview, it is important for the therapist to carefully listen to the patient and to empathize with his or her situation and feelings. You'll also notice that the therapist asked a few questions to prompt John to describe the situation in greater detail and then summarized John's story. Although the therapist may have helped John to identify his thoughts, feelings, and behaviors (i.e., the cognitive model), the point of this part of the therapy is not to do problem solving or teach strategies. Rather, the aim of the interview is to establish a strong therapeutic alliance and to understand what contributed to the suicidal thoughts and what helped them to dissipate.

John and his therapist then reviewed what led to his interrupted suicide attempt in order to further identify other triggers and warning signs for suicide. John described that on that day, he tried to do some yard work but was unable to complete it due to severe back pain. His wife then yelled at him for trying to do too much and hurting himself. When she left the house to run errands, he was thinking about ending his pain, which led to him going to get his gun. The narrative interview resulted in the identification of several warning signs for suicide and led naturally into the introduction and first step of the Safety Plan.

Safety Plan

The Safety Planning Intervention (SPI: Stanley & Brown, 2012) is a brief intervention that can be used as either a stand-alone intervention or incorporated into ongoing treatment. The purpose of the SPI is to assist individuals in decreasing their risk for suicide by consulting a predetermined set of potential coping strategies and resources to use during a crisis. The Safety Plan is created by both the therapist and patient as a collaborative process and involves six steps. The first step is recognizing warning signs for suicidal crises that may serve to cue the patient to use the Safety Plan. The second step involves identifying internal coping strategies that the patient may use on his or her own to distract from suicidal thoughts, while the third step identifies other people or social settings that may aid in distraction. In the fourth step, the patient identifies individuals whom he or she can ask for help. Similarly, in the fifth step, professionals or agencies (including emergency numbers) that can be contacted for help are identified. Finally, in the sixth step, the therapist and patient work together to make the patient's environment safe via means restriction.

The Safety Plan is used in the beginning of CT-SP as a front-line intervention strategy to mitigate suicide risk early in treatment and is updated over the course of therapy to incorporate learned skills. Figure 5.1 depicts the Safety Plan that John created with his therapist. For a more thorough description of the intervention, please see Chapter 8 of this volume.

Reasons for Living and Dying

Suicidal individuals often vacillate between wanting to live and wanting to die, and an individual can have both wishes simultaneously to differing degrees (Harris, McLean, Sheffield, & Jobes, 2010; Kovacs & Beck, 1977). Thus, a discussion about reasons for living and dying can be a useful strategy for instilling hope for the future (Jobes, 2006). Asking the patient to identify reasons for dying is often the best place to start, as this is where they may be the most focused and allows them to feel heard. Once reasons for living and dying have been listed out, asking the patient to rank them in order of importance is also a helpful strategy in order to examine the relative strength of the reasons in each list. Identifying reasons for living and dying can also be useful for the development of treatment goals. That

SAFETY PLAN	

Step 1: Warning signs for when I should use the plan:

1. When I have a fight with my wife
2. Thoughts about not being able to pay the bills
3. Thoughts about being useless
4. When I can't do something I want because of back pain

Step 2: Internal coping strategies—Things I can do to take my mind off my problems without contacting another person:

1. Watch ESPN on TV
2. Play fetch with the dog in the yard
3. Take a nap

Step 3: People and social settings that provide distraction:

1. My friend Pete   Phone: 555-555-5555
2. Go to church
3. Go to the diner down the street for a coffee

Step 4: People whom I can ask for help:

1. Name: My daughter, Jane   Phone: 555-555-5556

Step 5: Professionals or agencies I can contact during a crisis:

1. Clinician Name: My therapist, Dr. Doe   Phone: 555-555-5558

   Clinician Pager or Emergency Contact #: 555-555-5559

2. Clinician Name: My psychiatrist, Dr. Deer   Phone: 555-555-5566

   Clinician Pager or Emergency Contact #: 555-555-5577

3. Local Emergency Room: Regional Hospital

   Urgent Care Services Address: 555 Main St., City, ST 55555

   Urgent Care Services Phone: 555-555-5550 or 911

4. National Lifeline: 1-800-273-TALK (8255)

Step 6: Making the environment safe:

1. Organize my medications by day into a pill box each week
2. Keep my medication bottles locked in the kitchen drawer

©Stanley & Brown (2012). Reprinted with permission.

http://www.suicidesafetyplan.com

FIGURE 5.1. Safety Plan for John

is, goals of treatment may be framed around strengthening and increasing reasons to live, while decreasing or eliminating reasons to die. The following conversation between John and his therapist illustrates the process by which these lists may be generated.

Therapist: John, last time we talked about past situations where your suicidal thoughts have gotten really bad and about some of the things that led to these thoughts, like thoughts that you are useless. I'm wondering if today we can talk more about the reasons that factor in to your wanting to die and also explore any reasons that you have for living. Would that be okay?

John: I guess we can do that. I can think of lots of reasons why ending it makes sense. It's hard to think about reasons to keep going.

Therapist: I can understand that. You've been dealing with a lot of difficulties. How about we just start with reasons for wanting to die right now?

John: Those are easy. I can't work with my back the way it is, and it has caused a lot of financial problems. My wife shouldn't have to worry about this; the man is supposed to provide for the family and I can't, so I'm obviously less of a man now, just useless.

Therapist: I would like to write some of these things down so we can refer to them later. Would you like to do it, or do you want me to do it?

John: I would rather you do it.

Therapist: (*starts writing a list*) Okay. We've talked about the financial problems you've been having, and I know they're an important part of this. You also mentioned that you feel like you're less of a man and you're useless; is that part of the financial problems or a separate reason?

John: It relates, but it's separate. I also can't stand that I'm not able to do things that I used to do because of my back, like helping around the house.

Therapist: Okay, let's add that to the list too. What other reasons should we add?

John: Well, the only other one is that I feel like me and my wife are growing apart with all these fights we've been having.

Therapist: These all sound like important reasons that are contributing to these thoughts you have about dying. Are there any others?

John: Not that I can think of.

Therapist: Okay. If you think of others, we can always add them to the list later. I'm interested in knowing how these reasons rank for you; what order would they go in if we were to list them starting with the most important reason?

John: The first one would definitely be feeling useless, like I'm not a man anymore. Then, the second would be all the fighting with my wife, and third, probably the financial problems. The last one would be not being able to do things anymore like I used to do.

Therapist: (*Writes down the ranks on the list*) All right. Now looking at this list, do you think there's anything else that's important to add?

John: Nope, that about covers it.

Therapist: All right. I really appreciate your willingness to talk about these reasons. I know it can be hard for you.

John: Yeah, well, that's why I'm here.

Therapist: Would it be all right if we changed tracks and discussed potential reasons for staying alive?

John: Those are harder to come up with. I guess my family is the main reason to hang in there, especially those grandkids. I don't want to hurt them with my death.

Therapist: (*starts list*) Your family is an important reason for living then.

John: Yeah. My dog is too.

Therapist: Are there any other reasons that you can think of?

John: Not really. That's what has kept me alive so far.

Therapist: I remember last session when we were creating the Safety Plan, you listed church as something that helps distract you from your suicidal thoughts. Is there anything about your religion or faith that creates a reason to live for you?

John: Now that you mention it, I guess another reason would be to not go to hell. I know God doesn't want me to kill myself.

Therapist: Which of these reasons would you say is the most important?

John: Definitely family. Then God, then the dog is number three.

Therapist: Let's take a look at these two lists, side by side. Do you have any thoughts about what we've come up with?

John: Huh. I ended up coming up with more for living than I thought I would. The ones on the dying side are still bad, but I guess it's good that the living side has more than I think about sometimes.

Therapist: It sounds like doing these lists has made you realize that perhaps you have more reasons to live than may come to mind when you're feeling really badly. Is that right?

John: I would say so.

Therapist: That's good. Would it be okay if we transitioned into starting to talk about potential goals for our work together? I think these lists will give us some good ideas about the best things to work on in order to decrease the reasons for dying and increase the reasons for living.

John: Okay.

In this example, the therapist assisted the patient in identifying and ranking his reasons for living and dying. The therapist used follow-up questions to elicit additional reasons for living that the patient did not immediately think about, based upon things that the therapist already knew about the patient. While the therapist ended up writing in this example, it can sometimes be helpful if the patient does the writing. An important component of the intervention is asking the patient for feedback. In this example, examining reasons for living and dying helped to foster more hope in the patient. Using this and other information obtained from the patient, the therapist will then develop a cognitive case conceptualization and collaborate with the patient on establishing goals for treatment.

Cognitive Case Conceptualization and Identification of Treatment Goals

After discussing reasons for living and dying, the therapist and patient work together to develop mutually agreeable goals for the treatment. One of the core components and guiding principle of CT-SP is the development of a cognitive case conceptualization. The treatment goals, in turn, are guided by the cognitive case conceptualization. The conceptualization is based upon the narrative interview and discussion about reasons for living and dying. It is then continually updated and refined over the course of therapy, as more information about the patient and his or her beliefs is learned. The key components of the case conceptualization include automatic thoughts, intermediate beliefs, and core beliefs that are activated during suicidal crises, in addition to compensatory behaviors that may maintain or promote these crises. The case conceptualization is the cornerstone of the therapy; it informs the selection of cognitive and behavioral strategies that are most likely to reduce suicidal ideation and prevent future suicide attempts. Figure 5.2 illustrates the cognitive case conceptualization that was developed based on information obtained from the interview with John. For more details about the construction of the conceptualization, refer to the CT-SP manual (Wenzel et al., 2009).

The beginning phase of therapy concludes with the therapist and patient identifying and agreeing upon goals for treatment. The narrative interview, review of reasons for living and dying, and development of the cognitive case conceptualization sets the stage for the development of treatment goals by elucidating the problems and processes most proximal to a suicidal crisis. Treatment goals should encapsulate the targets that are most relevant to reducing suicide risk and prioritized in order of importance. When discussing treatment goals, it is also important to discuss how progress toward the goals will be measured, preferably in objective and behavioral terms.

John and his therapist agreed upon three primary goals for treatment. The first was to decrease thoughts of uselessness and increase meaning in John's life. He stated that he would know he had accomplished this goal if he were engaged in at least one activity every day that allowed him to feel a sense of accomplishment or meaning. The second treatment goal was to improve John's problem-solving ability such that he would face and engage in problem solving right away instead of avoiding his problems. Finally, John also wanted to improve his relationship with his wife by decreasing the number of fights they have.

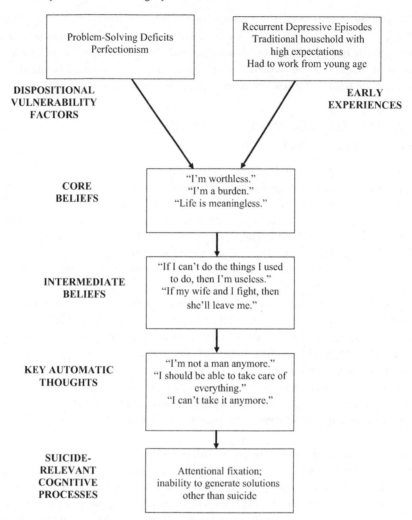

FIGURE 5.2. John's Cognitive Case Conceptualization

Wenzel, Beck, & Brown (2009). Adapted with permission.

Middle Phase of Treatment

The middle phase constitutes the majority of the therapy sessions and involves implementing cognitive and behavioral strategies to target the treatment goals and teach the patient new skills. While there are a wide variety of cognitive and behavioral strategies that may be employed with suicidal patients, in this chapter, we focus on a few key strategies: the Hope Kit, activity monitoring and scheduling, cognitive restructuring, problem solving, and coping cards. The published treatment manual includes descriptions and examples of these and other CT-SP strategies (Wenzel et al., 2009).

Hope Kit

The Hope Kit is a unique strategy that is specific to the CT-SP treatment protocol and involves a collection of reminders about a patient's reasons for living that can then be used during a suicidal crisis to instill hope and distract from suicidal thinking (Wenzel et al., 2009). The Hope Kit can take any form, such as a box, a folder, or a bulletin board. Patients can then collect items in one place to remind them of their ties to life (e.g., pictures, religious scriptures, small mementos, etc.). At the beginning of the middle phase of treatment, John's therapist introduces the idea of the Hope Kit.

Therapist: John, can you remember what we talked about the last couple of sessions in terms of something this treatment is meant to help with?

John: Yeah, you said that we would work together to help me have more tools to use to make things better and solve problems. And that hopefully, I'd have less reason to die and more reason to live.

Therapist: That's right. One of the strategies that I've found that can be particularly helpful with reasons to live is to have a visual reminder of them to look at when you're thinking of suicide. So I thought today we could talk about creating this reminder that's called the Hope Kit.

John: That sounds kind of hokey. What do you mean?

Therapist: Well, I know we've talked about how it's hard for you to focus on the reasons you have to live, especially when the reasons for suicide are on your mind.

John: Yeah, that's true.

Therapist: The Hope Kit is meant to be a place where you can store reminders of your reasons for living, like pictures, writing, or objects, in order to look through when you think about suicide to remind you of your reasons for living in that moment. The kit can be a shoebox, a drawer, or anything you want.

John: When you put it that way, I guess it could be helpful. It does make me feel better when I look at pictures of my grandkids.

Therapist: That sounds like a good start for what you might put in your kit. Could we talk more about putting one together?

John: Okay, but I don't know if I want like a box of stuff. My wife would wonder what that's about, and I don't think I'd want to explain it. What if I put things in a folder? I could keep it in the storage flap of my armchair where I keep the Safety Plan.

Therapist: That sounds like a great idea. Besides pictures of your grandchildren, what else do you think would be good to put in the folder?

John: I've also got other family photos that I like to look at: my wedding photo, pictures of my daughter when she was growing up, and maybe a picture of my dog.

Therapist: Sounds like there are a lot of visual reminders of family you could put in.

John: Yeah. You also mentioned writings for an idea. Both my daughter and my wife gave me really nice cards for my birthday a few weeks ago. They said some nice things in them, and they would be good to keep and put in there.

Therapist: Definitely. One of your other reasons for living that we haven't covered yet is your religious faith. Is there something you could put in the folder to remind you about that?

John: I have an extra rosary that could probably fit in a folder.

Therapist: That sounds like a great idea. Are there any other things you can think of that would be good to add?

John: Not that I can think of right now.

Therapist: That's okay. I think we've created a good list so far. As you start to gather things, you may think of other things at that time that you can add. What do you think would be a good action plan over the next week to start putting this together?

John: Well, I already have a folder to use, I think. I can start going through old photographs to pull the ones I want to use. And put the cards I saved in it and the rosary. It shouldn't be too hard to put together.

Therapist: Great. And do you understand the purpose of the Hope Kit?

John: It's to remind me of everything I have to live for. I forget about those things when it gets bad and I think of ending it. The Hope Kit will help me remember.

Therapist: Exactly. When should you use the Hope Kit?

John: Definitely when I'm thinking about suicide. Maybe also at other times when I'm feeling badly to give myself a boost.

John's therapist will then check in with John about the creation of his Hope Kit at the next session. At this time, they can evaluate how helpful the Hope Kit is during times that John is thinking about suicide and troubleshoot any obstacles to using the Hope Kit. They can also discuss other ideas for things that can be added to the Hope Kit.

Activity Monitoring and Scheduling

Activity monitoring and scheduling is a common behavioral strategy that first involves monitoring the current activity level of the patient in order to identify patterns between activities and the patient's mood throughout a given week (Beck & Greenberg, 1974). Once patterns have been identified, activity scheduling then typically involves the identification of activities that bring about a sense of pleasure or accomplishment. In our work, we have found that, especially for suicidal older adults, a focus on activities that are *meaningful* is especially important.

John has had thoughts of uselessness since he had to stop working as a mechanic. He reports that currently, he does not do very many things that make him feel productive, largely because he feels inhibited by his chronic back pain. He reported that he also does not spend as much time with his wife as he used to and now tries to avoid her so as not to get into arguments with her. After discussing the potential relationship between his activity level and his mood, John agrees to monitor his activities over the next week. At their next session, he and his therapist review this and work to schedule activities that will improve John's perceptions of his usefulness and improve his relationship with his wife.

John: I filled out that form you gave me about what I did last week and how I felt.

Therapist: That's great, John. Let's take a look at it together and see what we can learn from how your week was. Can you review how you rated your mood for the days last week?

John: Well, most of the days last week, my mood wasn't that great at the end of the day; usually a 4 or 5. But last Sunday, it was pretty good. I rated it a 7.

Therapist: Can you tell me about what you did that day?

John: Well, I got my check last week, so I was able to pay some of the bills for the month. That made me feel pretty good. I also decided to go to Mass instead of skipping it like I have been doing. Then, when my wife made dinner, instead of eating it in front of the TV, I ate at the kitchen table with her. That was nice. We talked about the grandkids and my daughter's new job, and we didn't argue about anything. Then I did the dishes since she cooked. She thanked me for doing it, and I felt like I had contributed.

Therapist: That sounds like a really nice day. How was that day different than the other days where you rated your mood a 4 or 5?

John: Well, I just didn't do much those days, just the same old, watching TV and sitting around the house.

Therapist: I see. So what do you make of why your mood was so different on Sunday?

John: Well, Sunday was just really different. I did some productive things. I went to church and spent a little time with my wife. It reminded me of how things used to be.

Therapist: So you're saying that the things you did on Sunday really had an effect on your mood that day.

John: Yeah, it was a nice change.

Therapist: It sounds like you learned something really important by tracking these things last week. It confirmed that maybe we should spend some time focusing on how you can do more things that make you feel useful or that are meaningful for you.

John:	That's true. I guess I didn't really realize that just sitting around watching TV all day wasn't really helping me.
Therapist:	How would you feel about taking this a step farther and talking about some activities that you could put on a schedule to do over the next week to see how changing it up even more might impact your mood?
John:	I guess I could do that. Some days it's just really hard to get motivated to do much of anything, though. My back sure doesn't help either.
Therapist:	I know you just don't feel like doing things sometimes. Going from not doing a lot to starting to do many things in a day may also feel overwhelming to you. What if we focused on identifying just one thing per day that you could do?
John:	I think I could manage that.
Therapist:	So first let's just brainstorm a list of things that you could do. Then we'll figure out what you'd like to do next week and when. We want to focus on activities that you think are useful or that give you meaning.
John:	Okay, let's see. Well, I guess I can try to do more around the house. It's hard to come up with what. The yard needs mowed, but there's no way I can do that with my back.
Therapist:	Yes, that sounds like a big job. I wonder if there are smaller jobs around the house that might be easier for you to do, given your back pain. Like how you did the dishes last week.
John:	Yeah, I usually don't think of those. I could probably take out the trash on trash day. It's usually not too heavy, and the outdoor cans have wheels on them.
Therapist:	That sounds manageable. What other things do you think you'd like to try?
John:	I'd like to go to Mass again. I really need to start going every week again. Um, I could also go out back and throw the ball for the dog. I feel bad that I don't play with him like I used to.
Therapist:	Both of those sound like great ideas. What else?
John:	I could bring my grandkids over one day to spend time with them and give the kids a break for a while. Maybe also do something with my wife, rent a movie or something. How many things is that now?
Therapist:	That's five things so far. Should we think of more, or would you like to schedule what days you'd like to do what and maybe do a couple of the things you came up with on two different days?
John:	It's hard to keep coming up with things. It would be easier to repeat some for the first time I try to do this.
Therapist:	That sounds good. (*pulls out activity schedule*) Let's figure out when you'll do these things over the next week.

John and his therapist will then work together to pick the day and time that he will complete his chosen activities over the course of the next week. They will also discuss any barriers that may get in the way of completing activities and things that

John can do to overcome perceived barriers. At the next session, they will discuss how the week went and examine the effect of the activities both on John's mood and also his perceptions about himself. Future sessions will focus on assisting John to continue to identify and implement activities that will provide evidence against the idea that he is useless, in addition to activities that are meaningful to him and that may serve to improve his relationship with his wife.

Cognitive Restructuring

Cognitive restructuring is the process by which the therapist assists the patient in identifying, evaluating, and changing untrue and unhelpful automatic thoughts. This can be a difficult skill for patients to learn and is often best taught in components. First, the therapist will help patients to identify automatic thoughts by teaching them to recognize sudden shifts in their mood that can serve as a cue to ask what is running through their minds in that moment. Next, patients will learn to evaluate their automatic thoughts by examining the evidence for and against the thought. Finally, patients will learn to create what is called a rational response that they can think about to counteract the automatic thought. After learning the different components of cognitive restructuring, John and his therapist put them together in order to target automatic thoughts about uselessness that John often experiences.

Therapist: So John, you were telling me about the day this week where your back pain was really bad and you were thinking of suicide. It seems like right before, you were thinking about being useless again.

John: Yeah, just like usual.

Therapist: Can you identify the specific automatic thought that you were having in that situation?

John: Yeah, it was the same thing as always. I was thinking that I'm useless because my back pain keeps me from contributing anything productive to the house.

Therapist: On our 0 to 100 scale, how much did you believe that thought?

John: At the time, 100. It made me feel pretty sad.

Therapist: All right. So we've identified the thought and how you were feeling. Do you remember the next step of the process of trying to turn the thought around?

John: Yeah, looking at the evidence.

Therapist: Okay, how about you take me through that and I'll write down what you come up with so we can look at it.

John: Well the evidence that it's true is that I don't do the things that I used to because I just can't due to my back. Also, I'm not making the money anymore to support my wife. If I can't do those things, then what use am I?

Therapist: So there are things that certainly make that thought seem true sometimes. I wonder about the other side of that, though. Is there any evidence against the idea that you're useless and not contributing?

John: Yeah, I guess there is. I still am able to do some things. I've been taking the trash out and helping with the dishes. I also feed the dog. I've been better at asking my wife what I can do to help her.

Therapist: Is there any other evidence against we should consider?

John: I'm not working, but I am still managing the money. Trying to keep everything paid. I guess that counts for something.

Therapist: It definitely does. Is there anything else you'd like to do to evaluate this thought?

John: No, that's about it.

Therapist: So what's the next step of the process?

John: Now I need to come up with a thought to say back to myself when I think I'm useless.

Therapist: Exactly. So looking at the evidence for and against that you've come up with, what would be a good thing to say to yourself that summarizes the reality of the situation?

John: I do what I can to keep contributing. It's not the same as it was before, but I'm not useless.

The therapist and John will then review his level of belief in the automatic thought in light of his new rational response. The therapist also asked John to summarize the steps in identifying and evaluating his negative thoughts so that he is more likely to use this skill between sessions. It will also be important to discuss how John can remember to use his rational response in response to automatic thoughts of uselessness, perhaps by creating coping cards (discussed in the next section). This technique will be used throughout the course of therapy for other automatic thoughts that contribute to John's suicidal ideation.

Coping Cards

Another useful strategy in CT-SP is the development of coping cards that patients can review to reinforce or remind them to use therapy skills in times of crisis. An advantage of coping cards is that they are small and easy for patients to keep with them (e.g., in a purse or wallet) so that they are always available. Some patients also like to create coping cards using free flashcard apps on their smartphones. We have found that creating and then laminating coping cards during session increases the odds that a patient will keep them and use them.

There are a variety of different types of coping cards that can be created and utilized. For example, coping cards can assist patients in remembering an adaptive response to common types of automatic thoughts. Coping cards can also be used to enhance problem solving, particularly if the solution is complex and might involve several steps to implement. Other examples of coping cards that could be created include a smaller version of the Safety Plan, listing reasons for living, or listing potential strategies patients may use when they are thinking of suicide or experiencing a crisis. Figure 5.3 depicts some of the coping cards that John and his therapist created together over the course of therapy.

FRONT	BACK
Automatic Thought: My wife is probably going to divorce me.	Response: We've been going through a hard time, but my wife is still here trying to work through it. Things are not all bad, and I know she loves me.

Steps to setting up a payment plan with city hall:

1. Go to the city office and get an application
2. Sit down with my wife to fill out the application
3. Make copies of disability check stubs and bank statements to go with the application
4. Turn in the application and documents to city hall office
5. Call to followup about the application in 2 weeks

Therapy Skills

1. Safety Plan
2. Hope Kit folder
3. Schedule productive or meaningful activities
4. Problem solving
5. Create responses for automatic thoughts

FIGURE 5.3. John's Coping Cards

Problem Solving

Suicidal patients often have deficits in problem-solving ability (e.g., Pollock & Williams, 1998). Thus, teaching effective problem-solving skills is a core component of the CT-SP intervention. The skill of problem solving is taught as a series of sequential steps. First, the specific problem to be solved is identified. Next, the therapist assists the patient in brainstorming as many possible solutions to the problem as possible, while reserving judgment on the perceived helpfulness of each potential solution. After brainstorming, the therapist and patient will then work together to evaluate the possible solutions by discussing their consequences and the advantages and disadvantages. After evaluating the generated solutions, the therapist will then ask the patient to choose the one that he or she feels is likely to be the most helpful in solving his or her problem in order to try it out and see how it works.

Over the course of therapy, John's therapist noticed that he tended to avoid his problems rather than facing them. His therapist shared this observation when he was discussing his financial problems one session. John agreed that has not been solving problems effectively, and they decided to begin working to improve his problem-solving skills. John identified the problem as being behind on property taxes and not having money to pay them. He and his therapist brainstormed the following solutions: ignore the payment notices, try to sell the house, ask someone to borrow the money, take out a loan, get a job, and set up a payment plan with the city.

After evaluating each potential solution, John ultimately decided that trying to set up a payment plan with the city was the best solution to try first. He and his therapist then discussed the various steps that he would need to take in order to implement this solution, in addition to discussing how John could overcome perceived obstacles to completing the steps. John's therapist assisted him in continuing to practice problem solving in future sessions for other problems related to suicidal crises that he brought into session.

Later Phase of Treatment

Skill Consolidation and the Relapse Prevention Task

Once patient has mastered new skills such that he or she is able to prevent suicidal crises and has reduced his or her suicidal thinking, the therapist will help the patient to consolidate and practice skills learned over the course of therapy. Skill consolidation will include a review of all the strategies the patient can use, as well as writing them down for a patient to refer to in the future. This written list can then be used as a part of a "Toolkit" for preventing future suicidal crisis. It can also be helpful to update the Safety Plan to include new distracting strategies that the patient can do alone and with others. This Toolkit, Safety Plan, and other written documents, such as coping cards, can remind patients of their new skills.

After this is done, the therapist will guide the patient through the Relapse Prevention Task, in order to help him or her to practice preventing relapse in suicidal thinking or a future suicide attempt (Wenzel et al., 2009). The Relapse Prevention Task is a guided imagery exercise in which the patient will imagine both situations from the past and potential situations in the future that have the potential to trigger a suicidal crisis. The patient will then imagine and describe how he or she will use his or her skills to prevent a suicidal crisis from occurring in response to the given situation. The patient's degree of success in completing the task serves as a useful indicator for whether or not the patient is ready to terminate therapy.

It is important to obtain the patient's informed consent prior to conducting the Relapse Prevention Task, as it often involves experiencing upsetting memories and emotions. In our experience, some patients choose not to complete the task. For these patients, we recommend modifying the protocol to instead discuss how a patient may apply his or her therapy skills in the future rather than having him or her imagine specific scenarios. John completes the following Relapse Prevention exercise during his last therapy session:

Therapist: John, I'd like to sit back and get comfortable. Close your eyes and imagine the situation you identified where you have a fight with your wife and she accuses you of being lazy. Take me through this. How you would be thinking and feeling in this situation, and what you would do?

John: I can imagine her yelling at me. Telling me that I would help her more if I wasn't so lazy. That makes me really mad. I'm yelling back at her and telling her to shut up. That I try and do as much as I can. At that point, she would probably just walk away like she always does.

Therapist: How are you feeling at the point she walks away?

John: Mad as hell. Also sad. Kind of worthless because she called me lazy.

Therapist: And what are you thinking?

John: As I start to think about the fight, I start to wonder if maybe I really am just useless and good for nothing.

Therapist: What happens next?

John: Well, I know this is one of those hot spots for me. And I need to do something instead of just sitting and thinking about it. So I'm going to go to my chair and pull out that hope folder.

Therapist: What do you see when you look in your hope folder?

John: Pictures of my grandkids. I have my dog's picture in there and one of his collars from when he was a puppy. I have the rosary in my hand, feeling the beads. That calms me down a little.

Therapist: So you're feeling a little calmer now. What are you thinking about?

John: I'm still wondering whether my wife is right. That thought that I'm not a man keeps creeping into my head.

Therapist: So your hope folder has helped a little, but it sounds like you're still having that thought. What are you going to do next?

John: I'm going to look at my coping card. This is the one that has the evidence against the thought that I'm useless. And I'm reading the response to use: that even though I can't do the things I used to, I do still do things to help and I'm not useless.

Therapist: How are you feeling as you read over the card?

John: I'm starting to feel better. Now I'm just mad at her for calling me lazy. But this is reminding me that I'm not really useless.

Therapist: What do you think you should do next?

John: I should probably get away from the situation for a while. Maybe schedule to go see my daughter or help my friend Pete. I can hand him his tools while he works on his car.

Therapist: How do you think the rest of the day would go if you did one of those things?

John: Probably better. I know it wouldn't go down the road of me wanting to end it if I did those things.

After this exercise, John and his therapist will debrief and review his success in practicing skills during the imagined situation. As they prepare to end therapy, John's therapist will discuss scheduling booster therapy sessions in the future to prevent relapse and to help John to identify the situations in which he might call to schedule another session. Usually, patients are not discharged from therapy until they can successfully accomplish this task during the session.

Summary

In this chapter, Cognitive Therapy for Suicide Prevention was illustrated by following the case of John through the key components of the treatment. Core features of the intervention include the case conceptualization and development of treatment goals in the beginning phase, targeted interventions such as the Hope Kit and coping cards during the middle phase, and completion of the Relapse Prevention Task in the later phase prior to terminating treatment. Additional case examples and a more thorough description of the full intervention can be found in the published treatment manual (Wenzel et al., 2009).

References

Beck, A.T., & Greenberg, R.L. (1974). *Coping with depression*. New York: Institute for Rational Living.

Beck, A.T., Steer, R.A., & Brown, G.K. (1996). *Manual for the Beck Depression Inventory-II*. San Antonio, TX: Psychological Corporation.

Brown, G.K., Beck, A.T., Steer, R.A., & Grisham, J.R. (2000). Risk factors for suicide in psychiatric outpatients: A 20-year prospective study. *Journal of Consulting and Clinical Psychology, 68*, 371–377.

Brown, G.K., Have, T.T., Henriques, G.R., Xie, S.X., Hollander, J.E., & Beck, A.T. (2005). Cognitive therapy for the prevention of suicide attempts: A randomized controlled trial. *JAMA: Journal of the American Medical Association, 294*, 563–570.

Harris, K.M., McLean, J.P., Sheffield, J., & Jobes, D. (2010). The internal suicide debate hypothesis: Exploring the life versus death struggle. *Suicide and Life-Threatening Behavior, 40*, 181–192.

Jobes, D. (2006). *Managing suicidal risk: A collaborative approach*. New York, NY: Guilford.

Kovacs, M., & Beck, A.T. (1977). The wish to die and the wish to live in attempted suicides. *Journal of Clinical Psychology, 33*, 361–365.

Pollock, L.R., & Williams, J.M. (1998). Problem solving and suicidal behavior. *Suicide and Life-Threatening Behavior, 28*, 375–387.

Rudd, M.D., Joiner, T., Brown, G.K., Cukrowicz, K., Jobes, D.A., Silverman, M., & Cordero, L. (2009). Informed consent with suicidal patients: Rethinking risks in (and out of) treatment. *Psychotherapy: Theory, Research, Practice, Training, 46*, 459–468.

Stanley, B., & Brown, G.K. (2012). Safety planning intervention: A brief intervention to mitigate suicide risk. *Cognitive and Behavioral Practice, 19*, 256–264.

Wenzel, A., Brown, G.K., & Beck, A.T. (2009). *Cognitive therapy for suicidal patients: Scientific and clinical applications*. Washington, DC: APA Books.

Part III

Suicide Prevention in Different Settings

Part III

Suicide
Prevention
In Different
Settings

six
Treating Risk for Self-Directed Violence in Inpatient Settings

Marjan Ghahramanlou-Holloway, Laura L. Neely, and Jennifer Tucker

UNIFORMED SERVICES UNIVERSITY OF
THE HEALTH SCIENCES (USUHS)

Disclaimer: *The opinions or assertions contained herein are the private views of the authors and are not to be construed as official or as reflecting the views of the Department of Defense.*

This chapter describes a novel inpatient psychotherapeutic approach aimed at the reduction of risk for suicide attempts. The intervention, titled Post Admission Cognitive Therapy (PACT; Ghahramanlou-Holloway, Cox, & Greene, 2012; Neely et al., 2013), is designed for delivery by trained providers to adults hospitalized in a psychiatric setting due to suicide-related ideation and/or behaviors. PACT has been adapted from an empirically supported outpatient cognitive behavioral protocol for the prevention of suicide (Brown, Henriques, Ratto, & Beck, 2002; Brown et al., 2005; Ghahramanlou-Holloway, Brown, & Beck, 2008; Wenzel, Brown, & Beck, 2009). The designed intervention has undergone pilot and feasibility testing and is currently under empirical evaluation in a well-powered multisite randomized controlled trial (RCT). A history of the process of development for PACT and a description of its theoretical rationale along with its evidence-based components are provided here. The purpose of this chapter is to introduce the PACT model as a targeted and enhanced strategy for delivering inpatient psychiatric care for individuals following hospitalization for a suicide attempt.

Prevalence of Psychiatric Hospitalizations Due to Self-Directed Violence

For every suicide, there are 31 Emergency Department (ED) visits and five inpatient hospitalizations due to suicide ideation and suicide attempts—resulting in over 1 million self-directed violence-related hospital visits per year (Hoyert, Kung, & Smith, 2005). The 2012 National Survey on Drug Use and Health (NSDUH) (Substance Abuse and Mental Health Services Administration, 2013) indicates that 9 million adults (3.9%) experienced serious suicide ideation, 2.7 million made a suicide plan, and 1.3 million attempted suicide in the previous year. Approximately 1.9 million adults received inpatient mental health treatment in the United States in 2012, and approximately 500,000 adults stayed one night or longer in a US hospital setting after a suicide attempt. An additional 729,000 adults received medical attention after a suicide attempt in 2012 (Substance Abuse and Mental Health Services Administration, 2013).

Due to differences in diagnostic and treatment procedures, unit specialties, and reimbursement considerations, suicidal individuals may be assigned either a primary diagnosis of suicide behavior (i.e., suicide ideation, attempts, and self-injurious behaviors) or, more likely, a primary diagnosis of a mood disorder with a secondary diagnosis of suicide behavior during their hospitalization. For those discharged with a primary diagnosis of suicide behavior (n = 2,048), the average length of stay in a US community hospital in 2011 was 2.7 days with an average overall cost of $3,192 (Healthcare Cost and Utilization Project [HCUP], 2010). For those discharged with a primary diagnosis of a mood disorder and a secondary diagnosis of suicide behavior (n = 341,258), the average overall charges (which are charged to the primary payer but not necessarily fully reimbursed) for the entire stay were $15,646 (HCUP, 2010). The Centers for Disease Control and Prevention (2013) has estimated that each suicide in the United States costs approximately $1.1 million dollars in medical costs and lost wages, which amounts to a total annual cost of $35 billion.

The newly released report entitled "A Prioritized Research Agenda for Suicide Prevention" (National Action Alliance for Suicide Prevention: Research Prioritization Task Force, 2014, p. 35) recommends that short-term research objectives must be to "[i]dentify feasible and effective, fast acting interventions . . ." and to "[f]ind interventions for the highest risk groups in care settings or community settings . . . that reduce the risk of suicide." Moreover, even though the national average length of psychiatric stay has declined from 421 days in 1969 to our current estimates of 6 to 7 days, the relationship between the length of hospital stay and subsequent prognosis remains unclear—and this may be partially explained by a lack of existing evidence-based approaches in inpatient psychiatric care (Desai, Dausey, & Rosenheck, 2005; Ho, 2003; Sokolov, Hilty, Leamon, & Hales, 2006). For instance, an examination of a decade's treatment impacts indicated that "[d]espite a dramatic increase in treatment, no significant decrease occurred in suicidal thoughts, plans, gestures, or attempts in the United States during the 1990s"

(Kessler, Berglund, Borges, Nock, & Wang, 2005, p. 2487). Given the emotional, economic, and societal costs associated with suicide attempts, an evidence-based and standardized strategy for treating suicidal individuals who present to inpatient settings is desperately needed.

Background and History of the Development of PACT

Limited Empirical Support for Effective Inpatient Interventions for Suicide Prevention

Psychiatric hospitalizations remain the standard of care for those at imminent risk of suicide, as well as for those who actually attempt suicide, even though the necessity of psychiatric hospitalizations for these individuals has been called into question by clinicians and researchers alike (Goldsmith, Pellmar, Kleinman, & Bunney, 2002; Larkin, Smith, & Beautris, 2008). In fact, a 2002 Institute of Medicine report on reducing suicide concluded that "the effectiveness of brief hospitalization is questionable" (Institute of Medicine, 2002). The utility of the practice has been disputed in part because there continue to be no published RCTs that measure the efficacy of hospitalization on subsequent suicide risk (Goldsmith et al., 2002). Given that hospitalization continues despite little to no evidence supporting the value of the practice, the development of effective inpatient treatments for preventing suicide attempts is considered a significant national suicide prevention objective.

The importance of developing an effective inpatient treatment for suicide prevention is underscored by post-hospitalization suicide risk statistics. While many individuals are generally safe under inpatient medical supervision, they often face multiple stressors upon returning to their home environment, where they also regain the opportunity to engage in self-directed violence (Goldsmith et al., 2002). The period of highest risk for a subsequent suicide attempt is 1 week post-discharge (Qin & Nordentoft, 2005). Within 1 year of discharge for a suicide attempt, approximately 15% of patients will make another attempt (Owens, Horrocks, & House, 2002). Additionally, 20–25% of those hospitalized for an attempt will engage in a subsequent attempt at some point in their lives (Owens et al., 2002). A meta-analytic study indicated that individuals with a history of a suicide attempt are 38 times (95% CI 34.03–43.08) more likely to die by suicide than those who never attempted suicide (Harris & Barraclough, 1997). Finally, in the 12 months following an attempt, approximately 1.8% of individuals will die by suicide (Jenkins, Hale, Papanastassiou, Crawford, & Tyrer, 2002). While the lack of empirical support for interventions offered to suicidal individuals constitutes a notable gap in the field of suicidology (Linehan, 2008), the PACT intervention, as described below, is aimed at addressing this research and clinical gap.

History of Development of Post Admission Cognitive Therapy (PACT)

Only two published studies have evaluated an inpatient intervention for individuals recently hospitalized following a suicide attempt (Liberman & Eckman, 1981; Patsiokas & Clum, 1985). In the first study (Liberman & Eckman, 1981), two treatment interventions, insight-oriented therapy and behavior therapy, were evaluated for effectiveness with patients admitted with a recent suicide attempt. Patients in both groups received 4 hours of treatment per day for 8 days. Significantly reduced levels of depression, suicide ideation, and subsequent suicide attempts were observed in both groups; however, participants in behavior therapy maintained improvements for a longer period of time. The second study was conducted by Patsiokas and Clum in 1985. Hospitalized patients admitted for a suicide attempt were randomized to one of three groups: cognitive restructuring (Beck, 1976), problem-solving therapy (D'Zurilla & Goldfried, 1971), or nondirective control. Participants received 10 individual therapy sessions over a 3-week period. All participants, regardless of their group assignment, improved on hopelessness, suicide ideation, and intent.

Even though the studies mentioned above were published almost 3 decades ago, the scientific community continues to lack an inpatient treatment RCT that targets recurrent suicide attempts. In a recent report commissioned by the Suicide Prevention Resource Center (SPRC) and the Substance Abuse and Mental Health Services Administration (SAMHSA; Knesper, American Association of Suicidology, & Suicide Prevention Resource Center, 2010), the following is noted: "[d]espite the centrality of hospitalizing seriously ill psychiatric patients, the research base for inpatient hospitalization for suicide risk is surprisingly weak. This review could not identify a single randomized trial about the effectiveness of hospitalization in reducing suicide acts after discharge." While psychiatric inpatient units currently offer a variety of services including group therapy, medication management, art therapy, physical therapy, recreation therapy, and individual therapy, none of these services directly target suicidal ideation and/or suicide attempts.

In regard to outpatient treatments that target recurrent suicide attempts, cognitive behavioral therapy (CBT) for the treatment of individuals with a recent suicide attempt has demonstrated favorable results (Bilsker & Forster, 2003; Hawton et al., 1998; Rotheram-Borus, Piacentini, Cantwell, Belin, & Song, 2000; Rush, Beck, Kovacs, Weissenburger, & Hollon, 1982; van der Sande, Buskens, Allart, van der Graaf, & van Engeland, 1997). More recently, an outpatient cognitive therapy protocol (Brown et al., 2005) has proven effective in preventing subsequent suicide attempts among adults. An average of 9 hours of individual outpatient CBT is reported to reduce the likelihood of repeat suicide attempts by approximately 50% (Brown et al., 2005).

However, the efficacy of this new intervention in other settings (e.g., inpatient) is unknown. Given the short-term nature of outpatient CBT for suicide prevention and its module-based plan of delivery in combination with the obvious lack of evidence-based inpatient interventions directly targeted at the unique needs of hospitalized suicidal individuals, the first author of this chapter prepared a treatment development grant application that was subsequently submitted to the National Institute of Mental Health (NIMH) in 2006. While undergoing revisions requested by NIMH reviewers, the proposal to adapt and test the Brown et al. (2005) CBT protocol in an inpatient setting (i.e., PACT) was enthusiastically received by reviewers at the National Alliance for Research on Schizophrenia and Depression (NARSAD) and the Congressionally Directed Medical Research Program (CDMRP). With generous funding provided by these two organizations for variations on pilot and feasibility studies of PACT, the plans to adapt and pilot test the PACT protocol were underway in early 2008 and completed in 2013.

Description of PACT

Theoretical Foundation

Theoretically, PACT is based on the cognitive model of depression and emotional disorders (Beck, 1976; Beck, Rush, Shaw, & Emery, 1979) and suicide (Beck, 1996). Suicidal individuals, from the perspective of this model, have a unique combination of biological, psychological, and/or social vulnerability factors. Once thoughts about suicide have been activated, these individuals experience automatic thoughts, associated images, and core beliefs that, if not altered, can result in suicide attempts. For example, one may have the automatic thought, "My life is too painful, and I am so tired of living," along with an image involving seeing oneself as being at peace and pain-free following death. A core belief activated due to suicide-related cognitions and images can be related to one's sense of helplessness.

The biopsychosocial vulnerability factors in combination with suicide-related cognitive activity, as described above, eventually lead to the formation, maintenance, and exacerbation of what Beck (1976) termed the *suicide-specific mode* (see also Chapter 4 for a detailed discussion and description). Beck (1976, p. 123) explains that once a suicide-specific mode has been activated, suicide appears as the *only* option and may even be considered a rational course of action by the individual. At times, the suicidal individual may experience cognitive rigidity and attentional fixation (Wenzel et al., 2009) such that he or she is no longer able to problem solve effectively (Ghahramanlou-Holloway, Bhar, Brown, Olsen, & Beck, 2012) other than seeing death as the only and most reasonable solution for one's pain. An information-processing bias further elevates suicide risk as the individual interprets ambiguous information negatively and overgeneralizes memories about the past (Wenzel et al., 2009). For instance, a suicidal man may distort his wife's anger toward him as a sign that she would be better off and even happier without him, leading to selective rumination about times when she had told him that he was not a necessity in her life and that she could do perfectly well without him.

Using cognitive therapy terminology, a mode refers to the structural and operational components of personality. A mode is defined by an amalgam of unified, functionally synchronous cognitive, affective, motivational, and behavioral systems. Once a suicide-specific mode is formed during the course of one's life, it can become activated following exposure to selective internal (e.g., "I am worthless to everyone around me") and/or external (e.g., argument with spouse) stressors. The activation of a suicide-specific mode leads to the simultaneous reactivity of corresponding maladaptive schemas within the cognitive, affective, motivational, and behavioral systems (Rudd, Joiner, & Rajab, 2001).

For example, consider an individual who experiences the thought, "I have disappointed everyone around me, and there is no way out for me" and as a result feels extreme levels of hopelessness. Motivationally, this individual may begin to isolate him- or herself even further and begin preparing for suicide. Additionally, a suicide mode can be activated when a person, for instance, experiences loss-related cognitions (e.g., "I don't deserve to live because I could not save him"), sad or angry affect (e.g., "Finally, they will all see how much pain I truly feel"), and/or increased impulsivity (e.g., "Do it—do it right now").

For some individuals, risk factors may outweigh protective factors, in which case the frequency and severity of activation of the suicide-specific mode may increase over time. In particular, patients who have attempted suicide in the past are expected to require minimal internal and/or external triggers for a reactivation of their existing suicide-specific mode. Moreover, some individuals may chronically experience an activated suicide mode and therefore remain at ongoing elevated risk for suicide attempts.

In PACT, the step-wise approach to the treatment of suicide attempts is to first deactivate the suicide mode, subsequently modify its structure and content, and finally to construct and practice more adaptive structural modes. PACT providers guide patients through the process of challenging distorted cognitions, such as their excessive pessimism and high estimations for future negative outcomes. In addition, patients are engaged in problem-solving skills and assisted in either developing or improving existing coping strategies so that suicide is no longer the *only* available option worth considering. Suicide modes can be formed independently of psychiatric diagnoses. Therefore, the PACT treatment is transdiagnostic and directly targets the suicide mode.

Treatment Objectives

The overall objectives of PACT are: 1) to reduce the likelihood of the recurrence of suicide attempts; 2) to reduce the severity of established psychological risk factors for suicide, which include depression, suicide ideation, and hopelessness; 3) to bolster problem-solving and coping skills, especially regarding the problems and stressful life events that preceded and triggered the most recent suicide attempt; 4) to improve one's adaptive use of an existing social support network or to help one establish a new network; 5) to increase use of and compliance with adjunctive medical, substance abuse, psychiatric, and social interventions during and after hospitalization; and 6) to plan for safety and management of future suicide-related crises with patients, family members, and/or friends.

Structure of Treatment

Brown et al.'s (2005) original cognitive therapy protocol for the prevention of suicide, described in detail in Chapter 5, consists of 10 individual therapy outpatient sessions (averaging 45 minutes per session, totaling approximately 7.5 hours). The adapted PACT intervention consists of approximately six to eight individual therapy inpatient sessions (averaging 60–90 minutes per session, totaling approximately 7 to 12 hours). In addition, PACT offers a maximum of 4 telephone booster sessions, each lasting up to 60 minutes, within the first 3 months following psychiatric discharge in order to maximize the likelihood of linkage to aftercare. In general, PACT patients receive two sessions of psychotherapy each day for, preferably, 3–5 consecutive days.

Therapist Education and Training

Similar to other forms of cognitive behavioral therapy, PACT may be offered by a trained mental health provider with either a master's or doctoral degree in social work, psychology, or related field or by a psychiatric nurse, resident, or physician who has received adequate training and supervision in the delivery of both CBT and PACT. Training in CBT is traditionally obtained via coursework, clinical experience, and continuing education workshops. Training in PACT is generally provided in the form of a 2–3 day workshop consisting of didactics, video demonstrations, and role-playing sessions. Supervision, particularly on the initial cases to be treated with PACT, is a must, and ongoing team consultation (similar to what is practiced in Dialectic Behavior Therapy) is an expected component of effective delivery. Competency in treatment delivery can be measured by the Cognitive Therapy Rating Scale (CTRS; Young & Beck, 1980). An adapted version of the CTRS is currently under development for PACT.

Three Stages of PACT Delivery and Booster Sessions

The delivery of PACT has been formulated to involve three distinct phases in addition to a series of face-to-face inpatient and telephone booster sessions following psychiatric discharge. In phase 1 (early sessions 1–2), a PACT provider engages the patient in treatment and first plans for the safety of the patient within the inpatient milieu. Next, the patient is asked to provide a suicide narrative (or story) that outlines the details about the most recent suicide crisis that triggered hospitalization. The PACT provider then collaboratively develops a cognitive conceptualization based on a review of patient's suicide attempt narrative (or story) and gains a better understanding of underdeveloped (e.g., inability to ask for help) and/or overdeveloped (e.g., overreliance on self and stoicism) skills that are most likely to precipitate a patient's suicide mode. In phase 2 (middle sessions 3–4), a PACT provider teaches cognitive behavioral coping strategies targeted at addressing the underdeveloped and overdeveloped skills most likely to activate a future suicide crisis.

In phase 3 (late sessions 5–6), a PACT provider collaboratively adapts the patient's existing safety plan for usage following discharge from the hospital and reviews relapse prevention strategies in order to prevent the recurrence of suicide attempts. Finally, up to two face-to-face booster sessions may be provided during the inpatient stay, and up to four telephone booster sessions are provided during the 3-month post-discharge period with the major emphasis placed on linkage to aftercare. The goal of this phase is to solidify patients' emerging cognitive behavioral skills and to enhance their motivation and behavioral intention to engage in recommended aftercare treatments. In the sections below, a more detailed description of each phase of treatment is provided.

Early Phase

The major objectives of the early phase of treatment are: 1) to build a strong therapeutic relationship with the patient; 2) to develop a safety plan such that the patient is best equipped in terms of handling a suicide crisis during the inpatient stay; 3) to ask the patient to describe the narrative associated with the suicide attempt or ideation episode that precipitated hospitalization; 4) to gain a better understanding of the patient's motivation to live and overall readiness for change; and 5) to develop a cognitive conceptualization based on the patient's narrative.

In PACT, relationship building is a rather quick process because of the short-term nature of the intervention—therefore, it is very important that the provider be skilled in demonstrating empathy, genuineness, and unconditional positive regard. The intake assessment is intentionally designed to be conducted by the same provider who delivers the PACT intervention, in order to ensure continuity of care, enhance his or her own knowledge of the patient's history, and to strengthen rapport. Flexible scheduling, therapist matching when possible, adherence to PACT protocol yet flexibility in its delivery, consultation with expert advisors and/or peers, as well as the involvement of significant others where feasible are strategies that can potentially strengthen overall rapport and patient engagement and compliance.

The telling of the suicide story is another aspect of treatment that allows for an opportunity to build a relationship with the patient and to understand his or her trajectory for suicide. The patient is asked to tell a story with a beginning, a middle, and an end to fully describe the circumstances, thoughts, and feelings that resulted in the suicide attempt. The PACT provider explains that the purpose of telling the story is to collaboratively gain a better perspective on how suicidal ideation and the decision to make a suicide attempt came about. As much as possible, the provider remains quiet so that the patient has an opportunity to tell his or her story—to be truly heard and understood. This story serves as the foundation for the cognitive case conceptualization that then drives the personalized treatment plan for the patient. Therefore, similar to what happens in a prolonged exposure session for traumatized patients, the PACT therapist guides the patient through the process of sharing his/her experiences on the day of the suicide attempt.

It is also important to note that during the first PACT session, heavy emphasis is placed on psychoeducation. The patient is socialized to the PACT treatment format, structure, delivery, and content. In addition, the following domains are covered: 1) introducing the patient to the course and rationale for treatment and his or her role as a treatment seeker—with the important reminder that PACT's primary aim is to prevent future suicide attempts; and 2) familiarizing the patient with the high dropout rates in psychotherapy and problem-solving strategies to maximize engagement in treatment.

Throughout the delivery of the intervention, the provider gauges the patient's readiness for change, assesses for emotional and cognitive responses to the recent suicide attempt (e.g., automotive thought, "I regret that my suicide attempt did not work."), which may serve as a risk factor for eventual death by suicide (Henriques, Wenzel, Brown, & Beck, 2005) and pays close attention to motivational factors (i.e., reasons for living) that may best advance the patient toward engagement in and compliance with treatment. The PACT provider is familiar and comfortable with the usage of motivational interviewing (MI) skills and checks for the patient's attitudes and expectations regarding inpatient therapy in order to help the individual move closer to the decision to live (Miller & Rollnick, 2002). Additionally, past experiences with therapy, the patient's perceived obstacles for living, and strategies to address these obstacles are discussed.

During the second session, the patient is encouraged to again describe the sequence of events that resulted in his or her decision to die. The PACT provider's task is to help the patient, through the use of Socratic questioning, gain a better understanding of the automatic thoughts, associated images, emotions, and behaviors that collectively resulted in the decision to die by suicide. Particular attention is paid to the specific life events (e.g., loss of relationship), automatic thoughts and images (e.g., "I am alone again"), and emotions (e.g., sense of being rejected) that activated core beliefs (e.g., "I am unlovable") and furthermore the suicide mode (e.g., "My life is such a waste—I must end my pain"). The provider guides the patient in the process of better understanding and articulating his/her problem-solving approach (e.g., avoidant by isolating herself) in response to the activating event (e.g., husband having an extramarital affair). In addition, the patient's cognitive appraisal of reasons for dying and reasons for living shortly before the suicide attempt are reviewed. All of this information is then used for the purposes of generating a cognitive case conceptualization and subsequently sharing it with the patient. A cognitive conceptualization is based on a careful narrative review or chain analysis of life events and associated automatic thoughts, images, emotions, and behaviors leading to the suicide attempt.

Middle Phase

The sessions offered during the middle phase of PACT are personalized to the unique needs of each suicidal individual. The information obtained from the baseline assessment as well as during the early phase of treatment (via both the suicide narrative and the associated collaborative conceptualization) is used to determine the patient's underdeveloped and overdeveloped skills that specifically result in the activation of the suicide mode. For example, the patient may have demonstrated poor emotion regulation skills (i.e., underdeveloped ability to regulate intense emotions) and strong obsessional skills (i.e., overdeveloped ability to ruminate over negative emotions).

Overall, the middle phase of treatment targets one or more of the following domains that reflect underdeveloped or overdeveloped skills commonly observed in suicidal individuals: 1) coping strategies, self-efficacy, and problem solving; 2) emotion regulation; 3) hopelessness where reasons for dying outweigh reasons for living; 4) perceived or actual lack of social support or inadequate use of existing social support; 5) learned capability for self-directed violence and motivation to repeat; and/or 6) compliance-related problems associated with medical and/or psychiatric care. While it is beyond the scope of this chapter to outline the cognitive behavioral treatment strategies associated with each of these domains, several therapeutic areas are highlighted below.

For instance, one of the strategies to instill hope during the delivery of PACT is to guide the patient through the construction of a Hope Kit (see Chapter 5), which consists of a collection of positive life experiences and future aspirations that serve to remind the patient why his or her life is valuable and worth living. The hope box can take many forms, such as an actual physical box that the patient decorates with inspiring words and fills with pictures and memorabilia, a collection of wallet-sized cards that list important achievements and personal strengths, or a homemade video that depicts positive memories and encounters with loved ones. Other examples of hope box contents include a medal received after Vietnam (a reminder of a previous success), a picture of a daughter's wedding (a reminder of a joyous time), the phone number of a therapist (a reminder of available support), a picture of oneself at a younger age (a reminder of a more fulfilling and/or carefree time—hope for one's future), and the names of grandchildren (a current reason for living). The process of constructing the hope box helps the patient to modify worthless, helpless, and unlovable core beliefs while the act of looking through the hope box serves to remind patients of reasons for living. Ultimately, the hope box functions as a physical representation of the patient's reasons for living that gives the patient something tangible to do and reflect upon while suffering through a period of extreme distress, such as a suicidal crisis.

Another PACT strategy is to help the patient strengthen his or her problem-solving strategies since effective problem solving is one of the best ways to cope with life problems. For this goal to be met in treatment, the PACT provider first educates the patient about the direct relationship between one's perceived inability to solve life problems and one's decision to use suicide as a permanent solution for these problems. The patient is further educated about how disruptive and/or extreme emotions can result in irrational, avoidant, and/or impulsive problem-solving patterns that precipitate or exacerbate suicide attempts. The provider and patient then use the cognitive case conceptualization corresponding to the most recent suicide attempt to identify methods and patterns of problem solving that were ineffective or only partially effective during the most recent suicide crisis. Through this sequence of lessons, the patient is brought, more or less gently, to the realization that the most recent suicide attempt was a nonfunctional method of solving a life problem. Ideally, accompanying this realization for the patient is the understanding that effective problem-solving skills are essential for preventing a future suicide attempt.

In teaching patients about the process of problem solving, providers outline and review the following steps: 1) identifying and listing problems; 2) prioritizing problems; 3) generating alternatives and plans (with emphasis on variety and quantity); 4) weighing pros and cons of proposed solutions; 5) working out discrete tasks to achieve the goal; and 6) carrying out the chosen solution and assessing its outcome (Nezu, Nezu, & D'Zurilla, 2007). In addition to teaching the patient about the process of problem solving and the effects of the emotions on problem solving, providers teach patients that external circumstances also affect one's ability to effectively problem solve. For example, the concept of distancing (Wright et al., 1993) is used to demonstrate that one's problem-solving skills may improve while in a safe and therapeutic inpatient environment. To illustrate this concept, the patient is encouraged to think about how being away from the environmental stressors that precipitated the suicide attempt is an important benefit of hospitalization because it gives the patient some distance from and a different perspective on the stressors. With a different perspective, the patient may think of different ways (i.e., alternative plans) to cope with the stressors. Additionally, in thinking about the positives associated with inpatient treatment, the patient may view the hospitalization from a more positive, healing perspective, which enables more positive coping.

In summary, the most important message to be conveyed in the middle phase of treatment is that suicide is only one option for coping with life stressors and that alternative options deserve consideration as well. Patients can be provided with a copy of the book *Choosing to Live* (Ellis & Newman, 1996) as a self-help resource highlighting similar issues discussed during therapy.

Final Phase

The objectives of the final phase of treatment (prior to psychiatric discharge) are twofold: 1) to review relapse prevention strategies and to successfully complete a relapse prevention task (i.e., by demonstrating one's ability to utilize the skills learned and/or practiced in earlier sessions); and 2) to plan for safety following departure from the hospital.

To begin with the relapse prevention segment of therapy, the PACT provider provides psychoeducation about the meaning and purpose of relapse prevention. Using MI strategies, the PACT provider asks for permission to proceed with this final phase of treatment. In the first stage of the relapse prevention task, the patient is instructed to recall and retell the suicide narrative that was covered in the first phase of treatment. The patient can be told that the purpose of retelling the story is to refresh both the patient's and the provider's memories about what was discussed during the earlier phase of treatment. The PACT provider carefully listens to this story and takes notes. Next, the patient is asked to tell the story again but this time to stop along the way to collaboratively explore alternative strategies that could have been implemented and alternative choices that could have been made to change the outcome of the suicide story.

The purpose of this exercise is to show the patient that with even the slightest change in thoughts, emotions, and/or behaviors, different outcomes are possible other than suicide. Another therapeutic aim is to improve patients' perceived self-efficacy and problem solving during a future suicide crisis. For example, a patient may be experiencing emotional pain and in order to cope, he may self-medicate with alcohol. Feeling guilty for yet again slipping up and drinking, the patient starts having the following thought: "My family would be better off without me." The feelings of guilt and shame activate the negative emotions of despair and hopelessness, and coupled with negative automatic thoughts in the context of the core belief that "I am weak," the suicide mode becomes activated. Utilizing distress tolerance or self-soothing skills could have been a small change with a big impact, possibly preventing the activation of the suicide mode. For example, the patient could have restructured the automatic thought to the following instead: "Some of my family members would be better off without me, but my young daughter cannot grow up without her father."

The last step to the relapse prevention task is for the patient to imagine a future suicide crisis scenario so that he or she can demonstrate, through the usage of the learned skills, effective crisis management skills. Basically, the patient is being asked to engage in self-exposure such that he or she can plan and prepare effectively, with the assistance of the PACT provider, for a future suicide crisis scenario. If the patient is avoidant and/or unable to generate a hypothetical story involving the activation of the suicide mode, the PACT provider can actively assist with the task. Treatment is often viewed as complete when the patient is able to show an adequate ability to cope with a future imagined suicidal episode.

Finally, during this phase of treatment, the patient is assisted with the formulation of a written safety plan that is collaborative and feasible. To begin, the therapist explores the patient's prior attempts and challenges in maintaining safety. Then the therapist guides the patient to develop a list of coping strategies (including the ones learned during the middle phase of therapy) to utilize in the event of a future suicidal crisis. The safety plan should include important phone numbers, including the contact information for a provider, an on-call provider if available, a local 24-hour emergency psychiatric hospital, and at least one crisis hotline such as 1-800-273-TALK (8255), the National Suicide Prevention Lifeline. The patient and the PACT provider may sign the safety plan, and multiple copies are made in order to share with family members and/or friends, if desired.

Upon completion of the inpatient sessions, it is made clear that the PACT intervention is only a first step in recovery and that additional support and services are needed. Therefore, the importance of following up with outpatient care after discharge is continually emphasized. Engaging in aftercare is one more important step in preventing relapse. Aftercare services and resources are made available with guidance from the inpatient treatment team. Services are tailored to the patient's level of readiness for change. Perceived barriers to care are explored, and seeking help in times of need is highly encouraged.

Extension of Inpatient Therapy: Booster Sessions and Aftercare

Often, psychiatric stays for suicidal individuals are very brief, and therefore there may be no opportunity to provide inpatient booster sessions as needed, following the completion of the three phases of PACT. However, in situations where feasible, the PACT provider may offer inpatient booster sessions in order to further help the patient to practice learned skills. Given the manualized format of PACT, up to two booster sessions are generally offered; however, the decision about the number of booster sessions to offer outside of the context of a research study is ultimately left to the PACT provider.

Following discharge, the PACT provider maintains communication with the patient for up to 3 months via regularly scheduled telephone booster sessions. The purpose of these calls is to maintain therapeutic contact during a high-risk period, solidify individuals' emerging cognitive behavioral skills, and enhance motivation and behavioral intention to engage in recommended aftercare treatments and services. Because patients often continue to experience severe psychiatric symptoms and impaired functioning at the time of hospital discharge, engagement in follow-up treatment may be critical to address unresolved symptoms. At this time, MI principles are used as a core strategy for enhancing the utilization of mental health services post-hospitalization.

Originally described by Miller (1983) and more fully discussed in a seminal text by Miller and Rollnick (2002, p. 25), MI is a "client-centered, directive method for enhancing intrinsic motivation to change by exploring and resolving ambivalence." The MI approach is aimed at removing internal barriers to getting help. PACT providers establish a nonconfrontational and supportive climate where individuals feel comfortable considering their own reasons for and against change or treatment seeking and how their current behavior or health status affects their ability to achieve their life goals or live out their core values.

Common Clinical Challenges and Implementation Barriers

Clinical Challenges

Emotional Avoidance

A common clinical challenge occurs when the patient remains emotionally distant from the thoughts and feelings that precipitated the suicide attempt. Of course, it is understandable that the decision to kill oneself and the experience of attempted suicide are traumatic life events with associated memories that are generally painful and thus avoided. To address this challenge, the PACT provider asks the patient to describe the specific thoughts and emotions experienced immediately prior to attempting suicide. If the patient talks in generalities or moves off topic, the PACT provider proceeds to take the patient step by step through the suicide narrative, asking for the precise thoughts and feelings experienced in each moment. The patient is educated about the role of avoidance in the processing of painful memories and the therapeutic function of "digesting" (i.e., processing) the experience by revisiting it in the safe therapeutic environment.

Maintaining the Treatment Focus on Preventing Suicide

Another clinical challenge in the delivery of PACT is related to its targeted focus on suicide prevention. As stated previously, the primary objective of the intervention is to prevent a future suicide attempt by directly treating factors that contribute to suicide attempts (as opposed to treating indirectly related psychiatric symptoms such as a depressed mood). However, despite being educated from the start about the targeted focus of the treatment, the chaotic nature of some patients' lives leads them to discuss additional issues, which may or may not be related to their suicide attempt—e.g., marital issues, substance-related disorders, conflict with work supervisors and/or inpatient treatment team. While some of these issues may relate to the activation of a patient's suicide mode and would therefore be appropriate fodder for a PACT session, the limited time available in PACT sessions necessitates that the provider redirect patients back to relevant suicide-related material when they start to veer off topic. The provider can gently remind the patient of the scope of the treatment and encourage the patient to discuss any unrelated issues during inpatient group sessions or in another type of mental health treatment.

Denial of Suicide Attempt

There may be times during treatment when the patient denies or is dismissive of the seriousness of the suicide attempt. In this situation, the PACT provider could educate the patient about how a suicide attempt is generally defined, yet still meet with resistance in having the patient accept the event as a suicide attempt. For example, consider the story of a patient who had decided to kill himself by shooting himself in the head. Although he had made his decision to die by suicide and had even pointed the gun toward his head, he changed his mind and decided to abort the attempt before pulling the trigger. Unfortunately, the gun discharged as he was in the process of putting it away and he accidentally shot himself in the face. During treatment, this particular patient refused to consider the fact that his story clearly indicated an aborted suicide attempt.

In such cases, providers are advised to initially match the patient's language when referring to the reason for psychiatric hospitalization (e.g., "your recent accidental shooting"). Referring to the event as a "suicidal crisis" may also be appropriate and more palatable to patients uncomfortable with the term "suicide attempt." In addition, it may help to change language when discussing the rationale for the suicide story activity. For example, if the patient explains that he or she did not actually mean to kill him- or herself, it may be helpful to frame the telling of the story as needing to understand the circumstances that triggered the patient's hospitalization (as opposed to suicide attempt), in order to help prevent future hospitalization or suicide-related crises in the future.

Throughout treatment, it is important to be aware of changes in the client's language regarding the suicide attempt as well as his or her reported level of intent to die. It is not uncommon for a patient who strongly denies an attempt at the initial session to admit some level of intent by the end of the treatment, when a more trusting relationship between the patient and the provider has been established. Therefore, although it is important to match the patient's language regarding the attempt initially, it can also be constructive and healing to help the patient gain insight into any true intent to die that was experienced and to encourage the use of language that accurately reflects the intent at the time.

Barriers in Implementation

There are several complex and multifaceted barriers to implementing the PACT protocol in inpatient settings. The first category of barriers concerns those who implement the treatment: the inpatient staff members. Behavioral health providers in inpatient settings may vary significantly from one another in terms of educational level, discipline, training, and clinical exposure to suicide (Bongar & Harmatz, 1989; Feldman & Freedenthal, 2006). Providers may have different approaches and techniques for providing services to suicidal inpatients that are not fully congruent with the techniques used in PACT. Additionally, the multidisciplinary approaches of inpatient milieus, staff attitudes and opinions related to manualized treatments, beliefs regarding suicidal individuals, professional burnout, anxiety surrounding suicide risk and liability, and provider expertise and experience could all impact the implementation of this new treatment. Hence, upon dissemination, PACT may require some tailoring in order to make it accessible and relevant to the multiple disciplines and educational levels of providers in a typical psychiatric inpatient setting.

The second category of barriers to PACT implementation concerns the feasibility of treatment delivery on the inpatient milieu. Patients may have limited availability to engage in the treatment protocol due to their daily programming schedules. Patients may have impaired alertness and subsequent poor engagement in treatment as a side effect of necessary medications. It is important to address these feasibility and delivery concerns by consulting with inpatient staff and obtaining their feedback and suggestions regarding the best delivery method and timing. Increasing the communication between inpatient staff and PACT providers on how to best fit PACT into the existing treatment program may increase staff awareness and support for the intervention. Reactions of inpatient staff to the PACT protocol can also be processed during team meetings in order to increase motivation, engagement, and overall adherence to the protocol. The involvement in a supportive consultation group may serve as a motivating factor for the implementation of PACT, especially for those providers who are experiencing professional burnout.

The third category of PACT implementation barriers concerns the patient's engagement in treatment. Patients who are admitted involuntarily may experience higher suicide rates and may be more difficult to engage in treatment due to poor readiness for change. Providers should pay particular attention to each patient's level of engagement in treatment because early engagement can have a profound effect on minimizing relapse. Difficulties engaging in treatment could be due to a variety of reasons, including problems in adapting to the inpatient milieu and a low level of readiness for change, which is itself associated with factors like reaction to the suicide attempt, perceived self-efficacy, level of social support, reasons for living, hopefulness, and available and appropriate resources.

In addition to the three types of implementation barriers discussed in this section, it is important to note that PACT may not be an appropriate treatment option for all suicidal inpatients. PACT may not adequately address the needs of actively psychotic patients, patients experiencing severe medical incapacitation, or patients with severe cognitive impairment. Other types of patients with different symptom presentations may also not be appropriate for PACT. For example, a patient who does not show motivation for change or who regrets surviving the suicide attempt may display a less favorable response to PACT, especially compared to a patient who regrets making the suicide attempt. Furthermore, the accelerated delivery and brevity of the PACT treatment may not adequately address a severely entrenched suicide-specific mode, such as would be found in an individual who had multiple attempts combined with severe levels of depression and hopelessness. To account for entrenched suicide modes, as well as to provide patients with maximum levels of support post-discharge, PACT providers work to encourage and motivate all patients to link to outpatient aftercare services immediately following discharge.

Summary

Post Admission Cognitive Therapy (PACT) is a comprehensive yet brief cognitive behavioral inpatient treatment program that has been specifically designed for patients admitted due to suicidal ideation and/or suicide attempt. PACT is adapted from an efficacious outpatient cognitive behavioral treatment for the prevention of suicide that was originally developed by Aaron Beck and Gregory Brown at the University of Pennsylvania. PACT is a promising, novel, and feasible approach that capitalizes in providing immediate individual psychotherapy to at-risk patients following their hospitalization. In addition, PACT aims to increase linkage to after-care within the first 3 months post–psychiatric discharge by delivering a series of telephone booster sessions. PACT is currently under evaluation in a multisite randomized controlled trial, but it is important to note that the treatment components associated with PACT are based on evidence-based CBT practices previously found to be effective for suicidal patients. In the meantime, inpatient providers are encouraged to consider implementation of PACT or, at the very least, some of its evidence-based treatment components.

Acknowledgements

We would like to thank military service members and their family members who kindly agreed to participate in our research studies, during their hospitalization, in order to assist with the development and dissemination of Post Admission Cognitive Therapy. In addition, we are grateful for the support provided to our research team by the Walter Reed National Military Medical Center and the Ft. Belvoir Community Hospital, particularly due to the leadership of Lt Col Geoffrey Grammer and Dr. Jennifer Weaver. Finally, we would like to acknowledge the research assistance of Kacie Armstrong and Katheryn Ryan.

References

Beck, A. T. (1976). *Cognitive therapy and the emotional disorders.* New York: Meridian.

Beck, A. T. (1996). Beyond belief: A theory of modes, personality, and psychopathology. In M. Salkovskis (Ed.), *Frontiers of cognitive therapy* (pp. 1–25). New York: Guilford Press.

Beck, A. T., Rush, A. J., Shaw, B. F., & Emery, G. (1979). *Cognitive therapy of depression.* New York: Guilford Press.

Bilsker, D., & Forster, P. (2003). Problem-solving intervention for suicidal crises in the psychiatric emergency service. *Crisis, 24*(3), 134–136.

Bongar, B., & Harmatz, M. (1989). Graduate training in clinical psychology and the study of suicide. *Professional Psychology: Research and Practice, 20,* 209–213.

Brown, G. K., Henriques, G. R., Ratto, C., & Beck, A. T. (2002). *Cognitive therapy treatment manual for suicide attempters.* Philadelphia: University of Pennsylvania.

Brown, G. K., Ten Have, T., Henriques, G. R., Xie, S. X., Hollander, J. E., & Beck, A. T. (2005). Cognitive therapy for the prevention of suicide attempts: A randomized controlled trial. *Journal of the American Medical Association, 294,* 563–570.

Centers for Disease Control and Prevention, National Center for Injury Prevention and Control (2013, December 31). *Suicide: Consequences.* Retrieved from www.cdc.gov/violenceprevention/suicide/consequences.html

D'Zurilla, T. J., & Goldfried, M. R. (1971). Problem-solving and behavior modification. *Journal of Abnormal Psychology, 78,* 107–126.

Desai, R. A., Dausey, D. J., & Rosenheck, R. (2005). Mental health service delivery and suicide risk: The role of individual patient and facility factors. *American Journal of Psychiatry, 162,* 311–318.

Ellis, T. E., & Newman, C. F. (1996). *Choosing to live: How to defeat suicide through cognitive therapy.* Oakland, CA: New Harbinger Publications.

Feldman, B. N., & Freedenthal, S. (2006). Social work education in suicide intervention and prevention: An unmet need? *Suicide and Life-Threatening Behavior, 36*(4), 467–480.

Ghahramanlou-Holloway, M., Bhar, S., Brown, G., Olsen, C., & Beck, A. T. (2012). Changes in problem-solving appraisal after cognitive therapy for the prevention of suicide. *Psychological Medicine, 42,* 1185–1193.

Ghahramanlou-Holloway, M., Brown, G. K., & Beck, A. T. (2008). Suicide. In M. Whisman (Ed.), *Adapting cognitive therapy for depression: Managing complexity and comorbidity* (pp. 159–184). New York: Guilford Press.

Ghahramanlou-Holloway, M., Cox, D., & Greene, F. (2012). Post-Admission Cognitive Therapy: A brief intervention for psychiatric inpatients admitted after a suicide attempt. *Cognitive and Behavioral Practice, 19,* 233–244.

Goldsmith, S. K., Pellmar, T. C., Kleinman, A. M., & Bunney, W. E. (2002). *Reducing suicide: A national imperative.* Washington, DC: National Academies Press.

Harris, E. C., & Barraclough, B. (1997). Suicide as an outcome for mental disorders: A meta-analysis. *British Journal of Psychiatry, 170,* 205–228.

Hawton, K., Arensman, E., Townsend, E., Bremner, S., Feldman, E., Goldney, R. et al. (1998). Deliberate self harm: Systematic review of efficacy of psychosocial and pharmacological treatments in preventing repetition. *British Medical Journal, 317,* 441–447.

Healthcare Cost and Utilization Project (HCUP) (2010). HCUP Nationwide Inpatient Sample (NIS). Rockville, MD: Agency for Healthcare Research and Quality.

Henriques, G., Wenzel, A., Brown, G. K., & Beck, A. T. (2005). Suicide attempters' reaction to survival as a risk factor for eventual suicide. *American Journal of Psychiatry, 162,* 2180–2182.

Ho, T.-P. (2003). The suicide risk of discharged psychiatric patients. *Journal of Clinical Psychiatry, 64,* 702–707.

Hoyert, D. L., Kung, H. C., & Smith, B. (2005). Deaths: Preliminary data for 2003. *National Vital Statistics Reports, 53*(15), 1–48.

Institute of Medicine (2002). *Reducing suicide: A national imperative.* Washington, DC: National Academies Press.

Jenkins, G. R., Hale, R., Papanastassiou, M., Crawford, M. J., & Tyrer, P. (2002). Suicide rate 22 years after parasuicide: Cohort study. *British Medical Journal, 325,* 1155.

Kessler, R. C., Berglund, P., Borges, G., Nock, M., & Wang, P. S. (2005). Trends in suicide ideation, plans, gestures, and attempts in the United States, 1990–1992 to 2001–2003. *Journal of the American Medical Association, 293*(20), 2487–2495.

Knesper, D. J., American Association of Suicidology, & Suicide Prevention Resource Center (2010). *Continuity of care for suicide prevention and research: Suicide attempts and suicide deaths subsequent to discharge from the emergency department or psychiatry inpatient unit.* Newton, MA: Education Development Center, Inc.

Larkin, G. L., Smith, R. P., & Beautris, A. L. (2008). Trends in US emergency department visits for suicide attempts, 1992–2001. *Crisis, 29*, 73–80.

Liberman, R. P., & Eckman, T. (1981). Behavior therapy vs. insight-oriented therapy for repeated suicide attempters. *Archives of General Psychiatry, 38*, 1126–1130.

Linehan, M. (2008). Suicide intervention research: A field in desperate need of development. *Suicide and Life-Threatening Behavior, 38*(5), 483–485.

Miller, W. R. (1983). Motivational interviewing with problem drinkers. *Behavioural Psychotherapy, 11*, 147–172.

Miller, W. R., & Rollnick, S. (2002). *Motivational interviewing: Preparing people to change addictive behavior* (2nd ed.). New York: Guildford Press.

National Action Alliance for Suicide Prevention: Research Prioritization Task Force (2014). *A prioritized research agenda for suicide prevention: An action plan to save lives.* Rockville, MD: National Institute of Mental Health and the Research Prioritization Task Force.

Neely, L., Irwin, K., Carreno Ponce, J. T., Perera, K., Grammer, G., & Ghahramanlou-Holloway, M. (2013). Post Admission Cognitive Therapy (PACT) for the prevention of suicide in military personnel with histories of trauma: Treatment development and case example. *Clinical Case Studies, 12*(6), 457–473.

Nezu, A. M., Nezu, C. M., & D'Zurilla, T. J. (2007). *Solving life's problems: A 5-step guide to enhanced well-being.* New York: Springer Publishing.

Owens, D., Horrocks, J., & House, A. (2002). Fatal and non-fatal repetition of self-harm: Systematic review. *British Journal of Psychiatry, 181*, 193–199.

Patsiokas, A. T., & Clum, G. A. (1985). Effects of psychotherapeutic strategies in the treatment of suicide attempters. *Psychotherapy, 22*, 281–290.

Qin, P., & Nordentoft, M. (2005). Suicide risk in relation to psychiatric hospitalization. *Archives of General Psychiatry, 62*, 427–432.

Rotheram-Borus, M. J., Piacentini, J., Cantwell, C., Belin, T. R., & Song, J. (2000). The 18-month impact of an emergency room intervention for adolescent female suicide attempters. *Journal of Consulting and Clinical Psychology, 68*, 1081–1093.

Rudd, D. M., Joiner, T. E., & Rajab, M. H. (2001). *Treating suicidal behavior: An effective, time-limited approach.* New York: Guilford Press.

Rush, A. J., Beck, A. T., Kovacs, M., Weissenburger, J., & Hollon, S. D. (1982). Comparison of the effects of cognitive therapy and pharmacotherapy on hopelessness and self-concept. *American Journal of Psychiatry, 139*, 862–866.

Sokolov, G., Hilty, D. M., Leamon, M., & Hales, R. E. (2006). Inpatient treatment and partial hospitalization. In R. E. Hales (Ed.), *The American Psychiatric Publishing textbook of suicide assessment and management* (pp. 401–419). Washington, DC: American Psychiatric Publishing.

Substance Abuse and Mental Health Services Administration (2013). *Results from the 2012 National Survey on Drug Use and Health: Mental health findings.* Rockville, MD: Substance Abuse and Mental Health Services Administration.

van der Sande, R., Buskens, E., Allart, E., van der Graaf, Y., & van Engeland, H. (1997). Psychosocial intervention following suicide attempt: A systematic review of treatment interventions. *Acta Psychiatrica Scandinavica, 96*, 43–50.

Wenzel, A., Brown, G. K., & Beck, A. T. (2009). *Cognitive therapy for suicidal patients: Scientific and clinical applications.* Washington, DC: American Psychological Association.

Wright, J. H., Thase, M. E., Beck, A. T., & Ludgate, J. W. (1993). *Cognitive therapy with inpatients: Developing a cognitive milieu.* New York: Guilford Press.

Young, J., & Beck, A. T. (1980). *Cognitive Therapy Rating Scale Manual.* Philadelphia: University of Pennsylvania.

seven
Preventing Suicide Attempts in Military Settings

Craig J. Bryan

NATIONAL CENTER FOR VETERANS STUDIES AND
THE UNIVERSITY OF UTAH

M. David Rudd

NATIONAL CENTER FOR VETERANS STUDIES AND
THE UNIVERSITY OF MEMPHIS

Suicides among members of the US Armed Forces have more than doubled since 2004, with suicide now ranking as the second-leading cause of death among military personnel (Ramchand, Acosta, Burns, Jaycox, & Pernin, 2011). Historically, suicide rates among military personnel have been lower than the suicide rate among the US general population, although direct comparisons of the military suicide rate to the civilian suicide rate are complicated by a number of factors. First, there are considerable demographic differences between the military and general populations: the military as a whole is younger, and has a larger proportion of men and Caucasians, than the general population. Because age, gender, and race are important risk factors for suicide, appropriate adjustments must be made before comparisons can be made. Second, the procedures for reporting suicide-related data vary between geographic regions and states, and between states and the Department of Defense (DOD). As a result, available statistics for suicide attempts are not derived from standardized surveillance methods or databases. Related to this, suicide statistics are often reported on a monthly basis by the military in "real time," whereas suicide statistics for the general population tend to lag a few years (i.e., the 2013 suicide numbers for the US general population will not be available until at least 2015 or 2016). Contextualizing recent trends in military suicides relative to the US general population is therefore difficult. Finally, because military personnel are included as a part of US general population statistics, military suicides may be counted twice, both in the military suicide rate and in the general population rate. Because of these issues, direct comparisons of the "military versus civilian" suicide rates are generally not feasible.

Despite these limitations, there is little doubt that the historical gap between the military and general population suicide rates has closed during the past decade. When adjusting for demographic differences (i.e., age, gender, race), the adjusted suicide rate for the US general population has traditionally hovered around 19 per 100,000, while the military suicide rate has hovered around 10 per 100,000 (Ramchand et al., 2011). Beginning in 2004, however, the military suicide rate started to rise and surpassed the adjusted general population rate in 2008; it has remained above 20 per 100,000 since (Department of Defense, 2011). Suicides have increased across all branches of service, although the Army and the Marines have experienced a relatively larger increase. During the same time, the suicide rate of the US general population has increased as well (Centers for Disease Control, 2013), most likely due to the sustained economic downturn in the United States, although this overall increase has been much smaller in magnitude as compared to that seen in the military.

No single reason accounts for the sudden rise in military suicides; rather, a complex interaction of multiple factors and variables contributes to suicide attempts in the military. Recent research focused on military suicidal ideation and suicide attempts has revealed that many of the risk and protective factors that have been established for self-directed violent thoughts and behaviors in the general population also apply to the military and can be conceptualized using the suicidal mode, as described in detail in Chapter 4. In terms of predisposing factors, suicide deaths in the military occur primarily among Caucasian men, with firearms being the most frequently used method (DOD, 2011). Previous self-directed violence, especially suicide attempts that occurred prior to military service, are associated with significantly increased risk for suicide attempts while in the military (Bryan, Bryan, Ray-Sannerud, Etienne, & Morrow, in press). Military personnel who have been the victim of interpersonal violence such as sexual assault or domestic battery are more likely to experience suicidal thoughts and make suicide attempts, with repeated victimization incrementally increasing risk (Bryan, McNaughton-Cassill, Osman, & Hernandez, 2013). Similarly, traumatic brain injury (TBI), especially two or more lifetime TBIs, is associated with increased likelihood of lifetime and recent suicidal ideation (Bryan & Clemans, 2013). Consistent with the fluid vulnerability theory, these predisposing factors escalate service members' likelihood to become suicidal, especially when experiencing acute stressors.

Interpersonal problems such as relationship failures or conflicts with others are the most common stressors immediately preceding suicide attempts and suicide deaths in military personnel, although financial problems, physical injury, and legal or disciplinary issues are also very common (Bryan & Rudd, 2012; DOD, 2011). Following a return from deployment, reintegration and readjustment issues such as family conflict or financial problems are similarly associated with increased likelihood for suicidal ideation (Kline, Ciccone, Falca-Dodson, & Black, C. M., &

Losonczy, M., 2011). Acute stressors such as these are proximally related to suicide attempts in military personnel and serve as activators of the suicidal mode.

In terms of the active suicidal mode, similarities between military and non-military populations have also been noted. In the emotional domain, severe depression, posttraumatic stress, and guilt are associated with increased risk for suicide attempts (Bossarte et al., 2012; Bryan, Clemans, Hernandez, & Rudd, 2013; Bryan, Morrow, Etienne, & Ray-Sannerud, 2013; Rudd, Goulding, & Bryan, 2013). In the behavioral domain, over one-quarter of military personnel who die by suicide were intoxicated or abusing substances at the time of death (Logan, Skopp, Karch, Reger, & Gahm, 2012), and non-suicidal self-injury is overrepresented in military personnel with suicidal ideation and suicide attempts (Bryan & Bryan, in press). In the physical domain, insomnia and very short sleep duration are associated with both suicidal ideation and future suicide attempts (Luxton et al., 2011; Ribeiro et al., 2012). Finally, in the cognitive domain, perceived burdensomeness (Bryan, 2011; Bryan, Clemans, & Hernandez, 2012; Bryan, Morrow, Anestis, & Joiner, 2010), the perception that no one cares about him or her (Bryan, 2011; Bryan, McNaughton-Cassill, & Osman, 2013), and hopelessness (Bryan, Ray-Sannerud, Morrow, Etienne, 2013a) have been reported.

The relationship of deployments in general, and combat exposure in particular, with self-directed violence is not as straightforward as often assumed, however. In some studies, combat exposure is directly associated with increased risk for suicidal ideation and suicide attempts among military veterans, although the relationship is generally very small in magnitude (Fontana, Rosenheck, & Brett, 1992; Rudd, in press; Maguen et al., 2012; Sareen et al., 2007; Thoresen & Mehlum, 2008). In contrast, military data suggests that deployment and combat exposure are not risk factors for suicide attempts or suicide deaths among military personnel (DOD, 2011), and some studies have failed to find a direct relationship of combat exposure with suicidal ideation and suicide attempts among active military personnel (Bryan et al., 2013; Griffith & Vaitkus, 2013; LeardMann et al., 2013). Furthermore, less than one in six military personnel who have made a suicide attempt report thinking about combat on the day they attempted suicide (Bryan & Rudd, 2012), and the strongest predictor of suicidal ideation after a deployment is suicidal ideation that occurred *prior* to a deployment (Griffith & Vaitkus, 2013). This latter finding suggests that deployment and combat exposure may contribute relatively less to self-directed violence than other preexisting vulnerabilities.

A recently conducted narrative review and meta-analysis provides some clarity to the issue of deployment- and combat-related predictors of suicide-related outcomes among military personnel and veterans (Bryan et al., 2014). In this review, Bryan et al. noted that studies utilizing deployment history as a predictor variable generally resulted in very small effect sizes with null findings, whereas studies utilizing combat exposure as a predictor variable generally resulted in somewhat larger (although still small) effects with mixed findings. Those studies that specifically assessed for exposure to killing, death, and atrocity found the largest effect sizes and consistently reported statistically significant findings. Bryan et al. concluded that differences in measurement schemes likely accounted for seemingly disparate results across studies. More critically, they noted that exposure to very specific types of deployment-related traumas—killing and death—were consistently related to suicide death, suicide attempts, and suicidal ideation. Taken together, these findings suggest that certain types of combat exposure may serve as long-term predispositions for suicide risk, similar to other traumatic events, but they probably do not serve as acute triggers for suicidal crises. Combat exposure may serve as a long-term or relatively distal risk factor for suicide by sensitizing or increasing service members' vulnerability to other risk factors, such as guilt or self-deprecation (Bryan, Morrow, Etienne, & Ray-Sannerud, 2013), which increase the likelihood of suicidal mode activation.

Understanding Self-Directed Violence Within the Context of the Military

Although the risk factors for suicidal ideation and suicide attempts are similar for military and nonmilitary groups, the cultural context within which these thoughts and behaviors occur differs considerably. Understanding these cultural dynamics and issues can be critical to the treatment process, as a patient's cultural background can influence how he or she experiences emotional distress, and his or her social environment can shape the trajectory of recovery over time. The culture of the US military differs in many ways from the culture of the US general population (Bryan, Jennings, Jobes, & Bradley, 2012). The military, for instance, highly values and explicitly reinforces strength, elitism, resilience, mental toughness, self-sacrifice, and self-sufficiency. In the military, an explicit and implicit expectation exists for personnel to be able to manage their emotions, solve problems on their own, and to minimize the impact of these issues on their coworkers and work duties. Within such a culture, individuals who are unable to live up to these expectations and effectively manage their emotional distress may be viewed as weak or deficient, which can lead to ostracism or rejection by the unit. Consistent with these cultural norms, pride and the perception that one is respected and valued by others are both associated with less severe suicidal ideation among military personnel (Bryan & Hernandez, in press; Bryan, Ray-Sannerud, Morrow, & Etienne, 2013b).

In contrast to the strengths-based perspective of the military culture, the culture of mental health is clinically oriented and typically conceptualizes problems from the perspective of illness and deficiency (e.g., *signs* and *symptoms* of *disorders*). Similarly, the typical approach to mental health care is to emphasize emotional vulnerability (e.g., "It's okay to talk about it and cry"), which conflicts with the military culture's valuation of strength and mental toughness. It is this "culture clash" between the military and mental health cultures that contributes to mental health stigma among military personnel (Bryan & Morrow, 2011). Unfortunately, most mental health outreach and antistigma efforts typically adopt an approach in which military personnel are explicitly encouraged to conform to the cultural norms of the mental health care system (e.g., "It's okay to get help") and implicitly ask the service member to abandon the cultural norms of the military. Outreach and antistigma efforts therefore conflict with service members' sense of identity and are generally ineffective. In contrast to this traditional approach to outreach, an alternative approach is to adopt a multicultural perspective by modifying or adapting mental health services to conform to the cultural norms of the military.

Military-Specific Modifications to BCBT to Prevent Suicide Attempts

In order to improve the acceptability of brief cognitive behavioral therapies (BCBT) to prevent suicide attempts among military personnel, several culturally relevant adaptations and modifications to the outpatient psychotherapy protocol described in Chapter 5 were accomplished to enhance the fit of this treatment within the military system, consistent with the recommendations of Bryan and Morrow (2011).

Incorporate Strengths-Based, Positive Psychology Conceptualizations

BCBT is presented to military personnel as a program for improving life satisfaction, job performance, and family life, and for solving or reducing problems. Instead of being conceptualized as a method to prevent suicide, the treatment process is conceptualized and described as learning how to live a life that is worth living. Specific interventions are introduced as "tools" or "techniques" designed to target specific problems or areas of concern in life, with the ultimate goal of helping patients to become better service members, spouses, parents, etc. To this end, the clinician functions as a sort of coach or personal trainer, working to help the service member improve his or her mental fitness and performance in life.

Present Concepts as Job Skills by Connecting Them to Preexisting, Military-Relevant Skills

New, military-relevant metaphors were developed to help explain concepts and skills. For example, crisis response planning (a.k.a., safety planning) is compared to a map and compass used to navigate across rugged, challenging, and unfamiliar terrain in order achieve an objective. In this metaphor, the rugged and challenging terrain features are like the challenges and obstacles we face in life, and the crisis response plan is like the map and compass that enables us to stay on course to achieve our objective despite the obstacles and challenges that get in the way.

Recognize the Potential for Personal Growth Associated With Adversity

Although military service is inherently stressful, it is also assumed that military personnel are inherently resilient. Adversity is reframed as an opportunity for growth, with stress being the "crucible" within which learning and development occur. Interventions designed to enhance emotion regulation skills and distress tolerance are presented as methods for refining mental toughness. Considerable responsibility for treatment progression and recovery is placed on the service member or veteran, with clinicians conveying considerable confidence in patients' ability to confront stress and successfully cope with it, even when it seems difficult or unbearable.

Overcome Traditional Assumptions Regarding the Format of Mental Health Care Delivery

The military is an action-oriented culture that emphasizes rapid, flexible problem solving. Military personnel therefore expect to "do something" when a problem is identified. Furthermore, the military's hierarchical structure and culture can contribute to an expectation by many military personnel that clinicians, as authority figures with greater knowledge, will tell them what to do. A skills-training emphasis was therefore seen as essential for successful implementation with military personnel. Consistent with the notion of being a "coach" to their patients, clinicians emphasize skills demonstration and practice in session, and the importance of reinforcing skills practice between sessions. This approach mirrors typical day-to-day military operations that similarly emphasize continual, repeated skills rehearsal (alternately referred to as training, drills, or exercises) in order to acquire automatic, overlearned behavioral responses (i.e., "muscle memory").

Sequencing BCBT for Suicidal Military Personnel

To facilitate the ease of treatment delivery on behalf of clinicians and treatment receipt on behalf of patients, BCBT was organized into three separate and sequential phases—emotion regulation, cognitive restructuring, and relapse prevention— with progression to each subsequent phase being contingent upon the patient's demonstrated mastery of skills and concepts from earlier phases (Bryan et al., 2012). Because BCBT does not have a prescribed session-by-session sequence of interventions, the phased treatment approach was introduced to provide clinicians with better structure and guidance regarding the prioritization and optimal sequencing of the treatment's interventions. As such, within each treatment phase is a "menu" of prescribed interventions from which the clinician can select, based upon the patient's specific needs. Selected interventions are practiced in-session and then assigned for between-session practice. These interventions are described in more detail below.

A second aspect of BCBT's phased model is that service members must show that they can effectively use basic emotion regulation skills in response to emotional distress and crises before cognitive restructuring is introduced; they must likewise show the ability to reliably identify and challenge maladaptive thoughts and suicidal beliefs before the relapse prevention task is introduced. The relapse prevention task serves as the final competency assessment, with termination of therapy occurring only after the service member successfully completes the relapse prevention task. In the majority of cases, the BCBT protocol is completed in an average of 12 sessions (five sessions for emotion regulation, five sessions for cognitive restructuring, and two sessions for relapse prevention), although the phased model enables clinicians to build-in sufficient flexibility for rapid responders who require less than 12 sessions and for slow responders who require more than 12 sessions.

A final modification developed for military personnel was the inclusion of a patient "smart book." Smart books are small, handheld notebooks approximately 3" × 5" in size (roughly the size of an index card) that are frequently carried by military personnel in a pocket for the purposes of taking notes or recording important information for use at a later time (e.g., mission-specific details, coordinates and physical description of unexploded ordnance). Treatment-specific smart books were added to BCBT so that suicidal military personnel could take notes and keep track of "lessons learned" in therapy. Critically, smart books are purchased by the clinical staff and given to patients; service members are not asked to go buy a notebook themselves. Giving the service member a smart book, as opposed to asking them to buy one on their own, is essential because patients are unlikely to buy a notebook on their own and because the act of giving the service member a notebook increases the emotional salience and personal meaningfulness of the object and conveys a sense of responsibility for maintaining the gift. This latter point was specifically designed to tap into the military culture's sense of honor and duty and to convey a sense of trust and confidence in the service member.

Phase I: Emotion Regulation Skills Training (Five Sessions)

The primary goal of the first phase of BCBT is to stabilize and reduce the service member's emotional distress through basic emotion regulation skills. This goal is accomplished through several primary tasks: describing the treatment, conducting a narrative review of the index suicidal episode, teaching the suicidal mode, developing a treatment plan and crisis response plan, and teaching emotion regulation skills. Several of these tasks are accomplished during the first session:

Narrative review of the index suicidal episode. During the narrative review of the index suicidal episode, the clinician asks the service member to "tell the story" of his or her most recent suicide attempt or suicidal episode in order to obtain information about the circumstances surrounding the suicidal crisis. These details include the location of the event, the thoughts and emotions experienced by the service member at the time of the crisis, and the sequence of events leading up to the suicide attempt.

Suicidal mode education. Immediately following the narrative review of the suicidal episode, the clinician provides the service member with a smart book and introduces the concept of the suicidal mode. Service members are asked to draw a picture of the suicidal mode in their smart book, and together the clinician and service member collaboratively conceptualize the case by "filling in" the suicidal mode with information acquired from the narrative review.

Crisis response plan. Before the end of the first session, the clinician assists the service member in developing a written list of steps to take during future emotional crises in order to reduce the likelihood of engaging in suicide attempts. (See Chapter 8 for detailed description of the crisis response plan, also known as a safety plan.)

During every follow-up session, clinicians ask service members if they have used their crisis response plan since the previous session. If yes, the clinician asks the service member to describe the circumstances that prompted use of the crisis response plan, how the plan was used successfully, and any aspects of the plan that should be changed or modified. If no, the clinician asks the service member to verbally review the steps detailed on the crisis response plan to facilitate mental rehearsal and learning. Clinicians should ask about the use of crisis response plans in every session to reinforce the intervention's importance, increase the service member's motivation to use the plan, facilitate learning, identify needed changes, and reinforce adherence and clinical improvement. Clinicians then introduce and teach emotion regulation skills over the course of subsequent Phase I sessions:

Sleep optimization. The clinician reviews basic guidelines for improving sleep quality and collaboratively identifies potential areas of change for the service member (e.g., limiting activities in bed to sleep and sex only; only getting in bed when sleepy) and then develops a plan with the service member to change agreed-upon sleep-related behaviors or habits.

Controlled breathing. The clinician teaches the service member to use breathing exercises to reduce autonomic arousal to ensure that he or she can successfully and effectively utilize the skill and then collaboratively establishes a plan for regular practice in between sessions.

Mindfulness exercises. The clinician teaches the service member to use brief mindfulness exercises to improve focus and reduce cognitive reactivity to stressful thoughts and emotions and then collaboratively establishes a plan for regular practice in between sessions.

Reasons for living list. The clinician assists the service member in identifying his or her personal reasons for living or reasons for not killing him- or herself and directs the service member to imagine these reasons for living in detail and to write them down on an index card. The clinician and service member then collaboratively establish a plan for regular practice in between sessions.

Survival kit. The clinician asks the service member to obtain a container of some kind (e.g., envelope, shoebox, tackle box) and fill it with objects that elicit positive emotions and memories (e.g., trinkets from vacations, pictures of loved ones, inspirational quotes). Service members are asked to bring the survival kit into the next session to review the contents with the clinician and are subsequently encouraged to review the contents of the survival kit during times of emotional distress or crisis.

Because skills training is an essential element of treatments that work for reducing suicide attempts, it is important for clinicians to practice new emotion regulation skills with service members in-session as opposed to simply "talking about" the interventions or recommending implementation without any actual demonstration or practice. Clinicians review between-session skills practice at the beginning of each session to reinforce adherence, problem solve obstacles or barriers, and support positive change. At the conclusion of each session, clinicians also ask service members to identify the "lessons learned" from the appointment. Typical lessons learned during Phase I include new knowledge or skill acquisition (e.g., "Controlled breathing helps me to calm down"), or improved self-awareness (e.g., "I can handle my stress"). Lessons learned are recorded in the service member's smart book as a written record of positive improvement, personal growth, enhanced competency, and hope, all of which are critical elements for relapse prevention. As the service member gains mastery of emotion regulation skills across the first phase of treatment, his or her emotional distress and suicidal ideation will begin to decrease in severity, at which time the treatment transitions into the second phase, focused on cognitive restructuring of the suicidal belief system.

Phase II: Cognitive Restructuring of the Suicidal Belief System

The primary goal of the second phase of BCBT is to undermine the components of the service member's suicidal belief system that contribute to and sustain long-term vulnerabilities for suicide attempts. This goal is accomplished through the use of written exercises and worksheets designed to teach service members the essential elements of critically evaluating and reappraising their automatic thoughts, assumptions, and core beliefs about themselves, others, and the world. Clinicians and service members also schedule events and activities designed to increase the service member's sense of self-worth, meaning in life, and social connectedness.

ABC worksheets. The clinician teaches the service member to use ABC worksheets to understand how events, thoughts, and emotions are interconnected, and how to develop more balanced and accepting perspectives of themselves, others, and life events (see Table 7.1 for example). Clinicians and service members complete several worksheets together in-session that are focused on their

TABLE 7.1. Sample ABC Worksheet

A Antecedents (What happened?)	B Beliefs (What do I tell myself?)	C Consequences (What emotion do I feel?)
Argument with my father; he tells me I've always been a failure.	He's right. I screw everything up, and I've always been a failure.	Guilt Anger Sadness

Is the belief above in box "B" helpful?
No because it just makes me feel worse.

What is something else I can tell myself in the future when in a similar situation?
Although I do make mistakes, I do a lot of good things too. My father isn't right.

suicidal crises as well as recent incidents in their lives and then collaboratively establish a plan to complete additional worksheets between sessions.

Challenging Questions worksheets. The clinician teaches the service member to use Challenging Questions worksheets to acquire the ability to critically evaluate his or her automatic thoughts, assumptions, and core beliefs (see Table 7.2 for example). Clinicians and service members complete several worksheets together in-session that are focused on suicidal beliefs and other maladaptive thoughts that have emerged during treatment and then collaboratively establish a plan to complete additional worksheets between sessions.

Patterns of Problematic Thinking worksheets. The clinician teaches the service member to use Patterns of Problematic Thinking worksheets to acquire the ability to identify and label his or her problematic thinking (also commonly referred to as "thinking errors" or "cognitive distortions"; see Table 7.3 for example). Clinicians and service members complete several worksheets together in-session that are focused on labeling and categorizing their suicidal beliefs and other maladaptive thoughts and then collaboratively establish a plan to complete additional worksheets between sessions.

Activity scheduling/behavioral activation. The clinician and service member collaboratively develop specific plans to increase the patient's engagement in pleasurable or personally meaningful activities in order to elevate mood and increase his or her social support. These plans are then implemented by the service member between sessions.

Coping cards. The clinician teaches service members to use coping cards to reinforce cognitive and behavioral skills learned in session. Coping cards can be created using 3" × 5" index cards that can be carried in service members' pockets, purses, backpacks, or in another easily accessible location. On the front side of the coping card, the clinician and service member identify a suicidal or maladaptive

TABLE 7.2. Sample Challenging Questions Worksheet

Belief: I can't take this anymore.

1. What is the evidence for and against this idea?
   For: I feel overwhelmed, I cry all the time.
   Against: Breathing exercises help, I've been able to get by okay so far.

2. Is your belief a habit or based on facts?
   Habit—I'm so used to saying this that I think it's true.

3. Are your interpretations of the situation too far removed from reality to be accurate?
   Not very accurate—I've been dealing with it okay for a week now.

4. Are you thinking in all-or-none terms?
   Yes, I think I can't take it at all when really it's just hard to.

5. Are you using words or phrases that are extreme or exaggerated (i.e., always, forever, never, need, should, must, can't, and every time)?
   Yes—can't

6. Are you taking the situation out of context and only focusing on one aspect of the event?
   Yes, just focusing on my stress, not how I've been able to do this before

7. Is the source of information reliable?
   No, it was my dad who used to say I couldn't handle it, but he was never supportive.

8. Are you confusing a low probability with a high probability?
   Yes—chances are that I'll be able to handle it even though it's hard.

9. Are your judgments based on feelings rather than facts?
   Based mostly on stress

10. Are you focused on irrelevant factors?
    Yes, I'm focusing on what my dad used to say to me, but that has nothing to do with what's going on now.

---

belief (e.g., "I'm worthless"), and on the back side of the card, the service member writes a positive response to this belief (e.g., "It's okay to make mistakes; everyone does"). Coping cards tend to be most effective after service members learn how to complete ABC worksheets and Challenging Questions worksheets.

As in the first phase of treatment, when introducing new worksheets or interventions for cognitive restructuring, it is important for clinicians to complete worksheets with service members in-session to ensure they understand the task and are able to complete it appropriately and to review any between-session skills practice at the beginning of each follow-up session to reinforce adherence and learning. Consistent with the importance of skills training in effective treatments, clinical experience suggests that service members who physically write their responses on their worksheets improve much faster than service members who do

TABLE 7.3. Sample Patterns of Problematic Thinking Worksheet

Jumping to conclusions when the evidence is lacking or even contradictory
"I shouldn't even try because I screw everything up"—Assuming things won't go well even though I haven't even tried yet.

Exaggerating or minimizing a situation (blowing things way out of proportion or shrinking their importance inappropriately)
"It can't get any worse"—Making things seem worse than they actually are

Disregarding important aspects of a situation
"It's my fault"—Blaming myself for my friend's death even though no one injured that badly would be able to survive

Oversimplifying things as good/bad or right/wrong
"I'm a failure"—Saying I'm completely bad based on one mistake even though I also do things right

Overgeneralizing from a single incident (a negative event is seen as a never-ending pattern)
"I always screw everything up"—Blowing things out of proportion based on a single mistake, even though I also do things right

Mind reading (you assume people are thinking negatively of you when there is no definite evidence for this)
"My family would be better off without me"—Assuming this is true when they actually love me and would miss me

Emotional reasoning (you have a feeling and assume there must be a reason)
"I can't take this anymore"—Assuming I can't handle things just because I feel bad

---

not, and they also improve faster than service members who only respond verbally (without writing) to the worksheets. It is possible that the act of writing out one's responses translates the service member's thoughts and internal experiences into an observable behavior, thereby facilitating or augmenting learning and internalization of concepts. At the conclusion of each session, clinicians continue to ask service members to identify the lessons learned from the appointment and record it in their smart books. In this second phase of treatment, it is common for lessons learned to involve changes in the service member's sense of identity (e.g., "Maybe I'm not such a bad person after all, and I'm being too hard on myself"). Such changes in self-perception serve as indicators of skill mastery and often correspond with improvements in day-to-day functioning, which signal readiness to transition to the third and final phase of treatment: relapse prevention.

Phase III: Relapse Prevention

The primary goal of the third phase of BCBT is to ensure competence and skill mastery of emotion regulation and cognitive restructuring skills learned in treatment. In this final stage, the clinician aims to "test" the service member's capacity to flexibly solve problems and effectively implement coping strategies *while emotionally aroused*. Emotional arousal is an important feature of assessing patient competence and skill mastery because it is in such states that cognitive constriction occurs and problem-solving capacity declines, and it is therefore the state during which the service member will be most vulnerable to suicide attempts. The relapse prevention task is used to assess the service member's competence and skill mastery during periods of emotional arousal and acute distress, and it facilitates the integration of concepts and skills learned over the course of treatment.

Relapse prevention task. The clinician introduces the relapse prevention task and explains its rationale in detail, answering any questions the service member may have about the intervention. The clinician and service member collaboratively review the patient's smart book and highlight the various emotional regulation and cognitive restructuring skills the service member has learned during the course of treatment. The clinician directs the service member to recount the sequence of events that occurred during the index suicide attempt or suicidal episode (i.e., the same crisis discussed in the narrative review of the suicidal episode during the first session). During the course of their imaginal rehearsal of the index suicidal episode, the service member "changes the outcome" by imaging him- or herself using a coping strategy or skill to resolve the crisis. Following the successful resolution of the crisis, the clinician and service member process the experience with a particular emphasis on how the service member successfully accomplished the objective.

This imaginal rehearsal of the index suicidal episode is repeated several times, with the requirement that the service member generate a different solution with each iteration. Requiring a different solution each time reinforces cognitive flexibility and minimizes the likelihood of a service member investing in only a single strategy, since most coping strategies will not be practical or effective in every situation. To further enhance cognitive flexibility, the clinician also increases the difficulty of the task for the service member with each rehearsal by introducing potential barriers to skill utilization that must be navigated or problem solved. For example, if a service member suggests that he will go for a walk to cope with agitation or a stressful interpersonal encounter, the clinician might ask what he would do if it were raining in this situation, thus requiring the service member to think of an alternative solution. Intentionally escalating the task's difficulty is an important part of teaching service members how to "think on their feet" when confronted with unexpected challenges or barriers.

After the service member has successfully demonstrated the ability to problem solve his or her way out of the index suicidal episode, the service member and clinician collaboratively generate hypothetical future scenarios to successfully problem solve. For some service members, suicidal crises frequently occur following conflicts with spouses; for others, suicidal crises frequently occur within the context of traumatic memories. Developing hypothetical future scenarios should therefore be based on those situations or circumstances that are most relevant to the individual service member's suicidal mode. The relapse prevention task is then repeated with the patient imagining him- or herself successful resolving the future crisis.

The relapse prevention task serves as the final competency check for the service member. Although the relapse prevention task typically spans only two sessions, clinicians can add additional sessions in order to continue repeating the task until the patient "passes the final exam." Once the service member can successfully complete the relapse prevention task, BCBT can be discontinued. Some service members will continue with other forms of treatment following the conclusion of BCBT such as trauma-focused therapy, marital therapy, substance abuse treatment, or other problem-specific treatments. Other service members, however, will experience sufficient resolution of their psychiatric and behavioral problems that no further treatment will be prescribed for the near term. Regardless of ultimate disposition, service members are informed about the procedures for reinitiating care in the future, or to receive "booster sessions" as needed.

Common Challenges When Treating Military Personnel and Veterans

As discussed at the beginning of this chapter, the US military differs in many ways from the general population both in terms of demographics and in its culture values and *raison d'etre*. These differences can paradoxically serve as both protective factors and vulnerabilities to suicide and can interfere with successful outcomes if they are not recognized and integrated into the treatment process. Several issues of particular relevance to the treatment of suicidal military personnel and veterans include mental toughness, collectivist orientation, self-reliance, self-sacrifice, and fearlessness of death (Bryan, Jennings, Jobes, & Bradley, 2012).

Mental Toughness

The military culture values strength, resilience, and courage; perceived weakness is avoided at all cost. Military personnel are trained, both explicitly and implicitly, to "suck it up" when facing adversity and experiencing discomfort. Minimization of pain and distress is therefore normative (e.g., "It's not that big a deal" or "I can just take care of it later"). Consistent with this cultural norm, emotional suppression and experiential avoidance are commonly used as coping strategies. Suppression and avoidance are considered by many military personnel to be "life-saving" coping skills because they improve functioning in dangerous and high-risk situations such as combat (Bonanno, 2004) and reduce emotional distress in the short term (Beck, Gudmundsdottir, Palyo, Miller, & Grant, 2006; Shipherd & Beck, 1999). Unfortunately, over the long term, suppression contributes to increased emotional distress (Beck et al., 2006; Shipherd & Beck, 1999) and suicide attempts (Najmi, Wegner, & Nock, 2007). Clinicians should recognize both the adaptive and the maladaptive functions of emotional suppression when working with military personnel, as focusing exclusively on its maladaptive aspects may be experienced by these patients as invalidation or a lack of understanding of who they are.

Collectivist Identity

The military culture emphasizes close, in-group bonds fostered from shared experiences, often in austere conditions, and reinforces a self-concept that is defined in terms of group membership and placing the group's needs and goals ahead of one's own (McGurk, Cotting, Britt, & Adler, 2006). This can promote very high levels of group cohesion that can buffer against emotional distress and contribute to reduced risk for suicide attempts. At the same time, the collectivist orientation of the military stresses the importance of protecting the group's reputation, identity, and security. Leaving the group to obtain help from "outsiders" can be viewed with suspicion and distrust and as a threat to group safety (Chang & Subramaniam, 2008). Clinicians should therefore be mindful of the "double-edged sword" of military cohesion with such groups, and incorporate a systems-based perspective during case conceptualization and treatment planning.

Self-Reliance

The military culture expects its members to be capable of performing duties competently and to quickly navigate around obstacles to successful mission completion, often with very limited information, time, resources, or guidance. Service members with deficient problem solving under duress can be perceived by others and by themselves as substandard, but asking for help violates the expectation of self-reliance. Over time, continuing problems with self-management can undermine the service member's sense of elitism and strength. Clinicians should therefore recognize that many suicidal service members feel trapped between the desire to improve and the desire to "fix things" on their own, and should frame the treatment process as a means for achieving or recapturing their autonomy and self-reliance.

Self-Sacrifice

Within the military, protecting one's safety and well-being are not necessarily viewed as the highest good. Rather, selflessness and self-sacrifice in the service of a good greater than oneself (e.g., suffering injury or death to protect others) is among the most highly revered and respected values. Because this notion of self-sacrifice is so similar to the concept of perceived burdensomeness, suicidal service members often mistake the two. Differentiating between "giving" one's life versus "taking" one's life is an important distinction for both clinicians and distressed military personnel to understand.

Fearlessness About Death

Fear of death is a protective factor for suicide (Linehan, Goodstein, Nielsen, & Chiles, 1983; Osman et al., 1996). Not surprisingly, individuals who are afraid to die tend not to attempt suicide. Fear of death does not make for an effective military, however. Military personnel, especially those in the combat arms professions, are therefore explicitly trained to overcome their fear of death through extensive conditioning throughout the course of their training; this habituation to the fear of death is further solidified in combat. This heightened capability to make a suicide attempt speaks to the importance of means restriction counseling for military personnel (see Chapter 9 for a detailed description of means restriction counseling), especially for those who own or possess firearms. Clinicians should therefore integrate the notion of fearlessness into their case conceptualizations when working with military personnel.

Future Directions

The treatment approach described in this chapter was specifically developed to "fit" within the cultural constraints of the military system. Preliminary data collected to date from a randomized controlled trial conducted with active duty military personnel indicate that service members who receive BCBT are more than half as likely as service members who receive treatment as usual to make a suicide attempt within the 2 years following treatment, with significant effects being observed during the first 6 months after the start of treatment. In general, the underlying principles for "what works" with suicidal military personnel and veterans do not differ substantially from what works with nonmilitary individuals. However, cultural differences between military and nonmilitary settings can influence engagement and outcomes and should therefore be integrated into treatments with this population.

References

Beck, J. G., Gudmundsdottir, B., Palyo, S. A., Miller, L. M., & Grant, D. M. (2006). Rebound effects following deliberate thought suppression: Does PTSD make a difference? *Behavior Therapy, 37*, 170–180.

Bonanno, G. (2004). Loss, trauma, and human resilience: Have we underestimated the human capacity to thrive after extremely aversive events? *American Psychologist, 59*, 20–28.

Bossarte, R. M., Knox, K. L., Piegari, R., Altieri, J., Kemp, J., & Katz, I. R. (2012). Prevalence and characteristics of suicide ideation and attempts among active military and veteran participants in a national health survey. *American Journal of Public Health, 102*(S1), S38–S40.

Bryan, C. J. (2011). The clinical utility of a brief measure of perceived burdensomeness and thwarted belongingness for the detection of suicidal military personnel. *Journal of Clinical Psychology, 67*, 981–992.

Bryan, C. J., & Bryan, A. O. (in press). Nonsuicidal self-injury among a sample of United States military personnel and veterans enrolled in college classes. *Journal of Clinical Psychology*.

Bryan, C. J., Bryan, A. O., Ray-Sannerud, B. N., Etienne, N., & Morrow, C. E. (in press). Suicide attempts before joining the military increase risk for suicide attempts and severity of suicidal ideation among military personnel and veterans. *Comprehensive Psychiatry*.

Bryan, C. J., & Clemans, T. A. (2013). Repetitive traumatic brain injury, psychological symptoms, and suicide risk in a clinical sample of deployed military personnel. *JAMA Psychiatry, 70*, 686–691.

Bryan, C. J., & Hernandez, A. M. (in press). The functions of social support as protective factors for suicidal ideation in a sample of Air Force personnel. *Suicide and Life-Threatening Behavior*.

Bryan, C. J., & Morrow, C. E. (2011). Circumventing mental health stigma by embracing the warrior culture: Feasibility and acceptability of the Defender's Edge Program. *Professional Psychology: Research and Practice, 42*, 16–23.

Bryan, C. J., & Rudd, M. D. (2012). Life stressors, emotional distress, and trauma-related thoughts occurring within 24 h of suicide attempts among active duty U.S. soldiers. *Journal of Psychiatric Research, 46*, 843–848.

Bryan, C. J., Clemans, T. A., & Hernandez, A. M. (2012). Perceived burdensomeness, fearlessness of death, and suicidality among deployed military personnel. *Personality and Individual Differences, 52*, 374–379.

Bryan, C. J., Clemans, T. A., Hernandez, A. M., & Rudd, M. D. (2013). Loss of consciousness, depression, posttraumatic stress disorder, and suicide risk among deployed military personnel with mild traumatic brain injury (mTBI). *Journal of Head Trauma Rehabilitation, 28*, 13–20.

Bryan, C. J., Griffith, J., Clemans, T. A., & Montieth, L. (2014, April). Combat and suicidality: Are we asking the right questions? Research symposium presented at the annual conference of the American Association of Suicidology, Los Angeles, CA.

Bryan, C. J., Hernandez, A. M., Allison, S., & Clemans, T. (2013). Combat exposure and suicidality in two samples of military personnel. *Journal of Clinical Psychology, 69*, 64–77.

Bryan, C. J., Jennings, K. W., Jobes, D. A., & Bradley, J. C. (2012). Understanding and preventing military suicide. *Archives of Suicide Research, 16*, 95–110.

Bryan, C. J., McNaughton-Cassill, M., & Osman, A. (2013). Age and belongingness moderate the effects of combat exposure on suicidal ideation among active duty military personnel. *Journal of Affective Disorders, 150*, 1226–1229.

Bryan, C. J., McNaughton-Cassill, M., Osman, A., & Hernandez, A. M. (2013). The association of physical and sexual assault with suicide risk in nonclinical military and undergraduate samples. *Suicide and Life-Threatening Behavior, 43*, 223–234.

Bryan, C. J., Morrow, C. E., Anestis, M. D., & Joiner, T. E. (2010). A preliminary test of the interpersonal-psychological theory of suicidal behavior in a military sample. *Personality and Individual Differences, 48*, 347–350.

Bryan, C. J., Morrow, C. E., Etienne, N., & Ray-Sannerud, B. (2013). Guilt, shame, and suicidal ideation in a military outpatient clinical sample. *Depression and Anxiety, 30*, 55–60.

Bryan, C. J., Ray-Sannerud, B. N., Morrow, C. E., & Etienne, N. (2013a). Optimism reduces suicidal ideation and weakens the effect of hopelessness among military personnel. *Cognitive Therapy and Research, 37*, 996–1003.

Bryan, C. J., Ray-Sannerud, B. N., Morrow, C. E., & Etienne, N. (2013b). Shame, pride, and suicidal ideation in a military clinical sample. *Journal of Affective Disorders, 147*, 212–216.

Centers for Disease Control (2013). *Fatal injury reports, national and regional, 1999–2010*. Atlanta, GA: Centers for Disease Control. Retrieved from http://webappa.cdc.gov/sasweb/ncipc/mortrate10_us.html

Chang, T., & Subramaniam, P. R. (2008). Asian and Pacific Islander American men's help-seeking: Understanding the role of cultural values and beliefs, gender roles, and racial stereotypes. *International Journal of Men's Health, 7*, 121–136.

Department of Defense (2011). *DODSER: Department of Defense Suicide Event Report: Calendar year 2010 Annual Report*. Washington, DC: Department of Defense.

Fontana, A., Rosenheck, R., & Brett, E. (1992). War zone traumas and posttraumatic stress disorder symptomatology. *Journal of Nervous and Mental Disease, 180*, 748–755.

Griffith, J. E., & Vaitkus, M. (2013). Perspectives on suicide in the Army National Guard. Armed Forces & Society. Retrieved from http://afs.sagepub.com/content/early/2013/01/29/0095327X12471333.full.pdf+html

Kline, A., Ciccone, D. S., Falca-Dodson, M., Black, C. M., & Losonczy, M. (2011). Suicidal ideation among National Guard troops deployed to Iraq: The association with postdeployment readjustment problems. *Journal of Nervous and Mental Disease, 199*, 914–920.

LeardMann, C. A., Powell, T. M., Smith, T. C., Bell, M. R., Smith, B., Boyko, E. J., . . . , & Hoge, C. W. (2013). Risk factors associated with suicide in current and former US military personnel. *JAMA, 310*, 496–506.

Linehan, M. M., Goodstein, J. L., Nielsen, S. L., & Chiles, J. A. (1983). Reasons for staying alive when you are thinking of killing yourself: The Reasons for Living Inventory. *Journal of Consulting and Clinical Psychology, 51*, 276–286.

Logan, J., Skopp, N. A., Karch, D., Reger, M. A., & Gahm, G. A. (2012). Characteristics of suicides among US Army active duty personnel in 17 US states from 2005 to 2007. *American Journal of Public Health, 102*(S1), S40–S44.

Luxton, D. D., Greenburg, D., Ryan, J., Niven, A., Wheeler, G., & Mysliwiec, V. (2011). Prevalence and impact of short sleep duration in redeployed OIF Soldiers. *SLEEP, 34*, 1189–1195.

Maguen, S., Metzler, T. J., Bosch, J., Marmar, C. R., Knight, S. J., & Neylan, T. C. (2012). Killing in combat may be independently associated with suicidal ideation. *Depression and Anxiety, 29*, 918–923.

McGurk, D., Cotting, D., Britt, T., & Adler, A. (2006). Joining the ranks: The role of indoctrination in transforming civilians to service members. In T.W. Britt, A.B. Adler, & C.A. Castro (Eds.), *Military life: The psychology of service in peace and combat (Vol. 2: Operational stress*, pp. 13–31). Westport, CT: Praeger Publishers.

Najmi, S., Wegner, D. M., & Nock, M. K. (2007). Thought suppression and self-injurious thoughts and behaviors. *Behaviour Research and Therapy, 45*, 1957–1965.

Osman, A., Kopper, B. A., Barrios, F. X., Osman, J. R., Besett, T., & Linehan, M. M. (1996). The Brief Reasons for Living Inventory for Adolescents (BRFL-A). *Journal of Abnormal Child Psychology, 24*, 433–443.

Ramchand, R., Acosta, J., Burns, R. M., Jaycox, L. H., & Pernin, C. G. (2011). *The war within: Preventing suicide in the U.S. military*. Santa Monica, CA: The RAND Corporation.

Ribiero, J. D., Pease, J. L., Gutierrez, P. M., Silva, C., Bernert, R. A., Rudd, M. D., & Joiner, T. E. (2012). Sleep problems outperform depression and hopelessness as cross-sectional longitudinal predictors of suicidal ideation and behavior in young adults in the military. *Journal of Affective Disorders, 136*, 743–750.

Rudd, M. D. (in press). Severity of combat exposure, psychological symptoms, social support, and suicide risk in OEF/OIF veterans. *Journal of Consulting and Clinical Psychology*.

Rudd, M. D., Goulding, J., & Bryan, C. J. (2011). Student veterans: A national survey exploring psychological symptoms and suicide risk. *Professional Psychology: Research and Practice, 42*, 354–360.

Sareen, J., Cox, B. J., Afifi, T. O., Stein, M. B., Belik, S., Meadows, G., & Asmundson, G. J. G. (2007). Combat and peacekeeping operations in relation to prevalence of mental disorders and perceived need for mental health care. *Archives of General Psychiatry, 64*, 843–852.

Shipherd, J. C., & Beck, J. G. (1999). The effects of suppressing trauma-related thoughts on women with rape-related posttraumatic stress disorder. *Behaviour Research and Therapy, 37*, 99–112.

Thoresen, S., & Mehlum, L. (2008). Traumatic stress and suicidal ideation in Norwegian male peacekeepers. *Journal of Nervous and Mental Disease, 196*, 814–821.

eight
Treating Suicide Risk in Emergency Departments

Emily Biggs, Cemile Ceren Sonmez, and Barbara Stanley

COLUMBIA UNIVERSITY AND NEW YORK STATE
PSYCHIATRIC INSTITUTE

The hospital emergency department (ED) is arguably one of the most utilized treatment settings for acutely suicidal individuals in the general population. Unfortunately, because admission to inpatient facilities is increasingly unlikely and follow-up with outpatient mental health treatment is sporadic for many suicidal individuals, the care they receive in the ED may be their only intervention. Therefore, increased attention has been given to brief, single-session interventions that can be easily administered in emergency settings. This chapter will provide a description and overview of safety planning, a brief intervention derived from longer-term, effective cognitive behavioral treatments for suicide risk.

Suicide is a leading cause of death. In the United States more than 38,000 people die by suicide each year, and approximately 105 Americans take their own lives each day (National Center for Injury Prevention and Control, 2012b). Among young people, suicide is the third leading cause of death (National Center for Injury Prevention and Control, 2012b). Although these figures seem high, they may actually be an underestimate. At times it is difficult to determine if a death is a suicide, such as a single-occupant automobile accident. Moreover, suicide attempts in the United States occur at rates up to 25 times higher than completed suicides (Goldsmith, Pellmar, Kleinman, & Bunney, 2002), which may also be an underestimation, since many attempts are not reported and do not come to the attention of mental health professionals or physicians. Given the incidence and prevalence rates of suicide and suicide attempts, it is imperative to identify interventions to prevent suicide and suicide attempts in at-risk individuals.

There have been heightened prevention efforts, greater public awareness, and increased efficacy of treatment interventions in the United States and worldwide in recent years; however, the number of suicides and suicide attempts remain stable or increase each year. It is concerning that success in reducing suicide attempts and suicide has met with limited success (Lizardi & Stanley, 2010). There may be several factors related to why the suicide rate has not decreased, including a failure in identifying acutely suicidal patients, lack of treatment engagement, and assurance of continuity of care. Since the first contact with these high-risk patients often occurs in acute care settings, assessment and intervention techniques employed in the ED play a crucial role in decreasing risk.

Oftentimes the ED is the most frequent and possibly the only point of contact suicidal individuals have with the mental health system. It is in this emergency setting that clinicians assess imminent danger and decide whether to admit the individual or discharge and refer for outpatient treatment (Allen, Forster, Zealberg, & Currier, 2002). Typically, when inpatient admission is not clinically indicated, a referral for outpatient mental health treatment is provided but no other clinical tools are employed to help the patient immediately. This approach stands in contrast to other acute problems seen in the ED. For instance, fractures not requiring surgery are set prior to the patient being discharged and are followed up in outpatient care.

The current practice of conducting risk assessments and referring patients to outpatient care is often disconcerting to patients and their families, as well as the clinicians making the disposition plans. There is concern about patient safety as well as anxiety and distress associated with potentially not hospitalizing patients who may actually need it. Among acutely suicidal patients who are seeking emergency treatment, many remain undetected for various reasons (Claassen and Larkin, 2005). For instance, patients who are contemplating suicide may not always disclose this information to their health care professional (Isometsa et al., 1995), or a mental health professional may not be readily available in the emergency settings.

Adding to the apprehension of discharging patients who are experiencing some degree of suicidal feelings is the unfortunate probability that many suicidal individuals do not attend recommended outpatient treatment post-discharge from the ED (Rudd, 2006). According to a survey of trends in suicidal ideation, plans, gestures, and attempts in the United States, between 11% and 50% of suicidal individuals refuse outpatient treatment or drop out quickly (Kessler, Berglund, Borges, Nock, & Wang, 2005; Kurz & Moller, 1984). Furthermore, up to 60% of attempters attend only 1 week of outpatient treatment following an ED visit (Granboulan et al., 2001; Piacentini et al., 1995). Among those suicide attempters who attend treatment, 38% terminate within 3 months (Monti, Cedereke, & Ojehagen, 2003), a statistic that is particularly concerning because individuals are at the highest risk of making another suicide attempt during the first 3 months following a first attempt (Monti, Cedereke, & Ojehagen, 2003).

Given that attempters who are seen in acute care settings do not consistently follow up with recommended outpatient treatment, brief interventions, such as completing a safety plan, could be especially helpful with suicide risk reduction. Stanley and Brown (2012) developed the safety planning intervention as a brief intervention that may be administered in the EDs as well as other settings (e.g. primary care, inpatient units, outpatient clinics) in order to decrease patients' imminent risk of suicide until there is an outpatient treatment in place. For those who refuse outpatient treatment, the safety plan may also be used in ongoing care.

No-Suicide Contract vs. Safety Plan

A "no-suicide" contract (also known as a "contract for safety") is a brief intervention that has been used extensively in the past with suicidal patients. This is not a safety plan intervention. No-suicide contracts are typically written or verbal agreements between the clinician and patient requesting that the patient stay alive and abstain from attempting suicide. Unlike the safety plan, the no-suicide contract intervention does not provide detailed information about what individuals should do if they become suicidal. In no-suicide contracts, clinicians request that patients promise to refrain from attempting suicide and to contact professionals during times of crisis. The patient then signs the contract memorializing this agreement (Jobes, 2006). There are some downfalls regarding no-suicide contracts, as they may provide a false sense of assurance to the clinician and institution that patients are safe once they leave the clinician's office. Furthermore, there is no empirical evidence supporting the effectiveness of no-suicide contracts for the prevention of suicide and suicide attempts (Kelly & Knudson, 2000; Reid, 1998; Shaffer & Pfeffer, 2001; Standford, Goetz, Bloom, 1994). It is also suggested that when no-suicide contracts are used to have patients commit to not killing themselves, the patient's actual risk for suicide might be obscured (Rudd et al., 2006; Shaffer & Pfeffer, 2001). For instance, patients may withhold information about recent behaviors or desire to hurt themselves for fear that they will let down their clinician by violating the contract. The safety plan intervention, on the other hand, is presented as an approach to help illustrate how to prevent a future attempt and identifies warning signs, coping skills, and help-seeking strategies for use during times of crisis.

Assessing and Mitigating Suicide Risk

A thorough evaluation is typically conducted in order to set up a treatment and disposition plan for patients with psychiatric disorders presenting in the ED. Assessing for suicide risk constitutes a crucial component of the evaluation, and there exists clinical practice guidelines intending to assess suicide risk in emergency settings (American Psychiatric Association, 2003). However, those assessments do not usually incorporate psychosocial interventions aiming to reduce suicide risk for patients in acute care settings (Allen, Forster, Zealberg, & Currier, 2002).

As mentioned earlier, when patients are seen in the ED or acute care settings, they are either hospitalized or referred out to an outpatient mental health care setting. Patients who get discharged or referred to an outpatient treatment may not receive follow up on a consistent basis (Claassen & Larkin, 2005). Therefore, adequate outpatient mental health care during the high-risk period is not always guaranteed. A safety plan can be used as a tool at this point in order to provide insight to patients about the internal and external triggers to a suicidal crisis and effective coping skills and help-seeking behaviors.

The ED as a Site for Brief Psychosocial Interventions

The ED is a site where brief psychosocial interventions for indications other than reducing suicide risk are administered (Larkin & Beautrais, 2010). One of these interventions successfully employed in EDs is used with substance abusers: the Screening, Brief Intervention, and Referral to Treatment (SBIRT). This 10- to 15-minute intervention aims to reduce substance use and related negative consequences while increasing adherence to follow-up treatment recommendations (Babor et al., 2007; Longabaugh et al., 2001, Monti et al., 1999; Crawford et al., 2004; Hungerford et al., 2000). The SBIRT has a screening component serving to identify the existence and severity of substance use, followed by a brief intervention fostering awareness about the problem and motivation regarding behavioral change. SBIRT also provides referral for those who need more extensive treatment. Self-reported data indicate that this intervention can lead to a significant improvement for illicit drug and heavy alcohol use at 6 months compared to baseline across settings (Babor et al., 2007; Madras et al., 2009).

Other brief interventions employed in the ED that have proven to be effective include the use of a 30- or 40-minute brief motivational interview for patients who are admitted with acute alcohol intoxication prior to discharge (Longabaugh et al. 2001; Monti et al., 1999) and, for suicidal teens who visit the ED, King and colleagues (2006) have developed a novel intervention instructing adolescents to identify adults in their lives who could offer ongoing support. In this latter study, female subjects in the study intervention group reported greater decreases in suicidal ideation when compared to female subjects in the control group.

Suicidal Crisis Response Plans in Ongoing Treatment

Crisis interventions targeting acute suicidal crises have been developed; however, these are predominantly used in the context of an ongoing treatment, rather than stand-alone interventions. As part of a cognitive behavioral therapy intervention, for instance, Rudd and colleagues developed a crisis response plan aiming to reduce suicide risk (Rudd, Joiner, & Rajab, 2001). The plan involves identification of the triggers, utilization of skills to tolerate distress or regulate emotions, and access to emergency care when the crisis is not resolved. The therapeutic interventions that are covered in the response plan ensure safety by removing access to lethal means; facilitating self-monitoring of the suicidal thoughts, feelings, and behaviors; and targeting hopelessness, sense of isolation, and other symptoms that could damage daily functioning. It also encourages treatment commitment and fosters therapeutic relationships.

Similarly, in the context of a psychotherapeutic approach called Collaborative Assessment and Management of Suicidality (CAMS), Jobes (2006) employed another safety plan. The CAMS safety plan also focuses on preventing access to means to make a suicide attempt, but in addition, it helps the patient to determine whom to call whenever there is a suicidal crisis. As a result of a collaborative effort, the patient's subjective experience of negative emotions, his or her reasons for living versus reasons for dying, his or her estimation of an eventual death by suicide, and the "one thing" that would remove the patient from a suicidal state are assessed by the clinician and the patient. Psychological pain, stress, agitation, hopelessness, and self-hate are rated on a scale from 1–5, and these ratings are used as a major focus for individual therapy sessions for the identification of triggers and coping responses (Ellis, Allen, Woodson, Frueh, & Jobes, 2009).

The Safety Planning Intervention

Stanley & Brown (2012) developed an innovative and brief treatment, the Safety Planning Intervention (SPI), for suicidal patients evaluated in EDs, trauma centers, crisis hotlines, psychiatric inpatient units, and other acute care settings (Stanley & Brown, 2008). This intervention has its roots in a form of cognitive behavior therapy (CBT) intervention shown to reduce the rate of repetition for suicide attempts over an 18-month interval (Brown et al., 2005, described in Chapter 5). The central feature of this CBT is the identification of thoughts, images, and core beliefs that were activated prior to the suicide attempt; then cognitive and behavioral strategies are applied to develop adaptive coping skills and address identified proximal stressors. The SPI is also used in a treatment for suicidal adolescents called Cognitive Behavioral Therapy for Suicide Prevention (CBT-SP), a manual-based approach to prevent repeat suicide attempts. The SPI is used as a risk reduction and relapse prevention approach within CBT-SP (Stanley et al., 2009).

There were three theoretical perspectives considered upon development of the safety planning intervention: 1) suicide risk fluctuates over time, and it is not only determined by a psychiatric illness but also other genetic or situational factors (e.g., diathesis-stress model of suicidal behavior; Mann, Waternaux, Haas & Malone, 1999); 2) problem-solving capacity diminishes during crises, including suicidal crises (Salkovskis, Atha, and Storer, 1990), and having a specific set of instructions to follow during a crisis enhances coping; 3) cognitive behavioral approaches that have previously shown to be effective incorporate the identification of warning signs and stressors precipitating suicide attempts and determining cognitive behavioral strategies the patient can use to manage suicidal crises (Stanley et al., 2009).

Furthermore, the SPI draws on empirical literature that has identified effective suicide prevention techniques and, thus, is a compilation of evidence-based strategies. These strategies include emotion regulation (primarily through distraction), social support, and restriction of access to potentially lethal means to prevent acting on suicidal ideation. The SPI is developed using a stepwise increase in the level of intervention from internal (within the self) strategies to external (outside the self) strategies. It is developed this way to strengthen self-efficacy and to teach the individual how he or she can help cope on his or her own (e.g., distraction) to decrease suicidal ideation and urges prior to seeking help from others (Stanley et al., 2009). In terms of social support, there are several studies demonstrating the importance of social support in reducing suicide risk. For instance, improved peer and family connectedness are shown to be associated with decreased suicidal ideation and suicide attempts among inpatient adolescents within 12 months of discharge from the hospital (Czyz, Liu, & King, 2012). Moreover, a social network intervention found that peer support decreased suicidal ideation in a group of adolescents in comparison to a treatment-as-usual group (King et al., 2006). Social support has proven to be a protective factor against suicide attempts and an important aspect to consider as part of suicide prevention (Kleinman & Liu, 2013). Finally, means restriction is strongly supported by empirical studies (Yip et al., 2012). Thus, the SPI includes a discussion with patients and their family members, if appropriate, regarding the elimination of any potential lethal means in the patients' environments. Empirical support for means restriction and a general approach to means restriction counseling are discussed in greater detail in Chapter 9.

Implementation of the SPI

The SPI consists of developing a safety plan in a *collaborative* manner between a mental health clinician and the person at risk for increased suicidal ideation and suicide attempts. The basic components of the safety plan include: 1) recognizing warning signs of imminent suicidal crisis; 2) employing internal coping strategies; 3) utilizing social contacts and social settings as a means of distraction; 4) asking family members or friends to help resolve the crisis; 5) contacting mental health professionals or agencies; and 6) restricting access to lethal means (Stanley & Brown, 2012).

Completing the safety plan with the patient takes very little time, approximately 20 to 45 minutes. It is important to note that the safety plan is generated together by the clinician and patient, and the patient's own words are used in the written document. The collaborative nature of the safety plan is essential to developing an effective plan that will be useful in times of elevated crisis. A clinician-generated list of coping strategies is unlikely to be useful to a patient in the absence of knowing what strategies are the most compelling and effective for the individual. Similarly, "common" triggers to suicidal feelings in the general population are not useful if they do not have personal relevance. For instance, taking a hot shower may reduce suicidal urges for one person but may not be helpful for another. In addition, the patient is not left alone to struggle and figure out his or her triggers and best means of coping. Instead, clinicians can offer suggestions in a supportive manner to help the patient complete the safety plan.

Patients leave the SPI with a written safety plan that consists of personalized warning signs, a prioritized and specific list of coping strategies, and sources of support that can be used should suicidal thoughts reemerge or increase. It also includes a plan to restrict access to means that patients might use or have used in the past. It is suggested that the intervention be followed in a stepwise manner, going through each section of the safety plan in sequential order. It is important to note that if a patient feels at imminent suicide risk at any point and feels unable to stay safe even for a brief time, the safety plan should direct the patient to immediately go to an emergency setting. In some situations, patients may feel they do not wish to use one of the steps in the safety plan. These patients should not feel obligated or coerced to continue developing the plan, as the intent of the safety plan is to be helpful, not to cause additional stress or burden (Stanley & Brown, 2012). Instead, it is important for the clinician to discuss barriers to completing the safety plan.

During the initial evaluation and risk assessment, the clinician typically obtains an accurate account of the events that transpired before, during, and after the recent suicidal event. This review of the crisis facilitates the identification of warning signs to be included in the safety plan and helps to build rapport. The first step in developing the SPI involves the identification of the signs that immediately precede a suicidal crisis so the patient will know when to use their safety plans. These warning signs might include personal situations, thoughts, images, moods, or behaviors that signal a crisis. One of the most effective ways for averting a suicidal crisis is to be aware of the problem and address it before it fully emerges. Examples of warning signs include feeling depressed, hopeless, or irritable; having thoughts such as, "Nothing will ever get better in my life"; or behavioral indicators such as significant change in sleeping habits or increased alcohol consumption. It is important to note that specific warning signs rather than vaguely described warning signs will better cue the patient to use the SPI (Stanley & Brown, 2012).

As a therapeutic strategy, it is helpful to have patients attempt to cope with their suicidal thoughts on their own, even if it is just for a brief time. When constructing the safety plan, the second step encourages patients to identify what they can do without the assistance of another person. Prioritizing internal coping strategies enhances patients' self-efficacy and can help to induce a sense that suicidal urges can be mastered. This, in turn, may help them feel less vulnerable and at the mercy of their suicidal thoughts. Once the list of coping strategies has been generated, the clinician may use a collaborative, problem-solving approach to address potential roadblocks to using these strategies and/or identify alternative coping strategies (Stanley & Brown, 2012). Examples of internal strategies include watching television programs that are calming and distracting, listening to comforting music, and exercising.

If internal coping strategies are ineffective and do not reduce suicidal ideation, patients can utilize two types of socialization strategies that serve as distractions: socializing with others (e.g. family, friends) in healthy social environments or visiting healthy social settings (e.g. coffee shops, places of worship, shopping malls, bookstores; Stanley & Brown, 2012). This strategy is not intended for patients to seek specific help for a suicidal crisis but rather to distract themselves from suicidal thoughts and gain a sense of belongingness and connectedness with others.

At this point, if individuals do not feel that the previous two steps alleviated the suicidal crisis, the next step involves turning to family members or friends for support. In this step, patients openly reveal to others that they are in crisis and need support and assistance. The clinician and patient should work collaboratively to include names of individuals with whom the person will feel comfortable contacting and disclosing suicidal thoughts (Stanley & Brown, 2012). It is helpful for patients to inform these people in advance that their name and contact information are on the safety plan. It is important to keep in mind that the application of the SPI will vary depending on the population. For instance, when creating safety plans with younger populations, such as adolescents, it is important to identify key adults who may become part of the plan. As part of the collaborative manner of the SPI, it is essential to help adolescents determine which family member or another responsible adult is more likely to have a calming and positive influence, as some family members, particularly those with whom the adolescents have had frequent conflicts, may not be good candidates. Family members can also be coached to help adolescents use the safety plan and to help with identifying the appropriate moments to utilize the plan.

If the previous strategies are not effective for resolving the crisis, patients are instructed to contact an appropriate professional or helping agency. The clinicians' or agencies' names and the corresponding telephone numbers and/or locations are listed on the plan and may be prioritized. For instance, the patient may feel more comfortable contacting their treating clinician before calling a national hotline. In the event that their provider is not available, the safety plan should also include on-call contacts or information for alternative providers, as well as a local 24-hour emergency treatment facility and national support services that handle emergency calls, such as the national Suicide Prevention Lifeline: 1-800-273-8255 (TALK). Patients may be reluctant, at times, to contact professionals and disclose their suicide ideation for fear of being hospitalized or being intruded upon by emergency crisis personnel. As with other components of the plan, the clinician should discuss any concerns or other obstacles that may hinder patients from contacting a professional or agency. Only those professionals patients are willing to contact should be included on the safety plan (Stanley & Brown, 2012).

In developing a safety plan, means restriction is addressed after patients have identified ways of coping with suicidal feelings. Ideally, if patients feel there are other options to acting on their suicidal urges than making a suicide attempt, they may be more likely to engage in a discussion about removing or restricting access to lethal means. The risk for suicide is amplified when patients report a specific plan to kill themselves that involves a readily available lethal method (Joiner et al., 2003). Therefore, it is important for clinicians to ask what methods patients would consider using during a suicidal crisis and collaboratively identify ways to eliminate or secure access to these means. Means restriction may include safely storing and dispensing of medication, restricting access to knives or other lethal means, or implementing firearm safety procedures.

Clinicians should routinely ask whether patients have access to firearms, regardless of whether it is considered a "method of choice," and make arrangements for securing them. The specific behaviors necessary to make the patients' environment safer should be noted on the safety plan as well as the length of time (e.g., 1 week, 2 months) that this restriction should be in place. The patients' risk for suicide will increase further due to direct contact with the highly lethal method; therefore, an optimal plan would be for a designated and responsible person (e.g., friend, family member) to restrict the patients' access to the lethal means and store it in a safe environment (Simon, 2007). Patients may become anxious at the thought of removing all methods from their possession, as they may consider possessing such means as a safety factor. The removal of lethal means should be presented to the patient as an opportunity to provide more time to process their suicidal feelings during a crisis (Linehan, 1993).

It is important to note that restricting access to a lethal means does not guarantee patients' safety, as they may choose another method; however, studies have shown that suicidal patients typically have a preferred method for making a suicide attempt and, if that means is restricted, it is unlikely that they will substitute for another method. Furthermore, suicidal crises are often short lived (fueled by ambivalence or impulsiveness), and if their fatal outcome is prevented, help will more likely be made available after the crisis (Daigle, 2005).

As each step is completed, patients should be asked to identify obstacles to its use and to problem solve ways to remove obstacles. After the safety plan is completed, clinicians should assess patients' reactions to it and the likelihood of use. One strategy for increasing patient motivation to use the safety plan is to ask the patient to identify the most helpful aspects. If the patient reports or the clinician determines that there is reluctance or ambivalence to use the plan, then the clinician should collaborate with the patient to identify and problem solve potential difficulties to using the safety plan. In order to increase the likelihood that the safety plan would be used, the clinician may consider conducting a role-play during which patients would describe a suicidal crisis and then would provide a detailed description of locating the safety plan and following each step. Once patients indicate their willingness to use the safety plan during a crisis, and then the original document is given to them so they can take it with them. A copy is also kept in the medical record.

As mentioned earlier, a safety plan should be developed in a collaborative manner with patients using a problem-solving approach. In order to increase effectiveness, patients should use their own words when creating and writing the safety plan. Doing this will allow for patients to remember the strategies and will increase the likelihood of utilization. It is important that the safety plan is readily accessible to patients during crises. It is recommended that the clinician discuss where the safety plan will be stored and how it will be retrieved during a crisis. This may include making multiple copies of the plan to keep in various locations or changing the size or format of the plan so it could be stored in a wallet or electronic device that is easily accessible (e.g., a smartphone; Stanley & Brown, 2012).

Summary

In this chapter, we discussed the development of the SPI, outlining its roots in cognitive behavioral treatments and describing how to effectively use the brief intervention when evaluating and treating patients at risk of suicide in emergency care settings. For many suicidal individuals, the care they receive at the ED may be their only contact with mental health treatment. Admission to inpatient facilities is not always indicated, but consistent follow-up with outpatient mental health providers often does not occur. Thus, the ED is an important setting for developing safety plans. Not only will individuals at suicide risk leave the ED with an effective tool, the safety plan has other advantages: 1) it is both easy to learn and utilize; and 2) staff can be trained readily. Finally, it is important to keep in mind when implementing the SPI that it should ideally be only one aspect of suicide prevention. Also, the safety plan is not indicated when an individual is in imminent risk and requires immediate rescue. In such cases, a higher level of care should be sought immediately, as the purpose and steps of the plan may not be processed appropriately and effectively. In summary, the SPI can be an effective intervention utilized in the ED to help mitigate suicide risk. Ideally, it will provide individuals with a tool that will instill hope and self-efficacy that when they leave, they can cope better with suicidal feelings and maintain their safety.

References

Allen, M.H., Forster, P., Zealberg, J., & Currier, G. (2002). *Report and recommendations regarding psychiatric emergency and crisis services: A review and model program descriptions.* Washington, DC: American Psychiatric Association Task Force on Psychiatric Emergency Services.

American Psychiatric Association (2003). *Practice guideline for the assessment and treatment of patients with suicidal behaviors.* Washington, DC: American Psychiatric Pub.

Babor, T.F., McRee, B.G., Kassebaum, P.A., Grimaldi, P.L., Ahmed, K., & Bray, J. (2007). Screening, Brief Intervention, and Referral to Treatment (SBIRT) toward a public health approach to the management of substance abuse. *Substance Abuse, 28*(3), 7–30.

Brown, G.K., Ten Have, T., Henriques, G.R., Xie, S.X., Hollander, J.E., & Beck, A.T. (2005). Cognitive therapy for the prevention of suicide attempts: A randomized controlled trial. *JAMA, 294*(5), 563–570.

Claassen, C.A., & Larkin, G.L. (2005). Occult suicidality in an emergency department population. *The British Journal of Psychiatry, 186*(4), 352–353.

Crawford, M.J., Patton, R., Touquet, R., Drummond, C., Byford, S., Barrett, B., ... & Henry, J.A. (2004). Screening and referral for brief intervention of alcohol-misusing patients in an emergency department: A pragmatic randomised controlled trial. *The Lancet, 364*(9442), 1334–1339.

Czyz, E.K., Liu, Z., & King, C.A. (2012). Social connectedness and one-year trajectories among suicidal adolescents following psychiatric hospitalization. *Journal of Clinical Child & Adolescent Psychiatry, 42*(2), 214–226.

Daigle, M.S. (2005). Suicide prevention through means restriction: Assessing the risk of substitution. A critical review and synthesis. *Accident Analysis and Prevention, 37*, 625–632.

Ellis, T.E., Allen, J.G., Woodson, H., Frueh, B.C., & Jobes, D.A. (2009). Implementing an evidence-based approach to working with suicidal inpatients. *Bulletin of the Menninger Clinic, 73*, 339–354.

Goldsmith, S.K., Pellmar, T.C., Kleinman, A. M., & Bunney, W.E. (Eds.). (2002). *Reducing suicide: A national imperative*. Washington, DC: National Academies Press.

Granboulan, V., Roudot-Thoraval, F., Lemerle, S., & Alvin, P. (2001). Predictive factors of post-discharge follow-up care among adolescent suicide attempters. *Acta Psychiatrica Scandinavica, 104*(1), 31–36.

Hungerford, D.W., Pollock, D.A., & Todd, K.H. (2000). Acceptability of emergency department-based screening and brief intervention for alcohol problems. *Academic Emergency Medicine, 7*(12), 1383–1392.

Isometsa, E.T., Heikkinen, M.E., Marttunen, M.J., Henriksson, M.M., Aro, H.M., & Lonnqvist, J.K. (1995). The last appointment before suicide: Is suicide intent communicated? *American Journal of Psychiatry, 152*(6), 919–922.

Jobes, D.A. (2006) *Managing suicidal risk: A collaborative approach*. New York: The Guilford Press.

Joiner, Jr., T.E., Steer, R.A., Brown, G., Beck, A.T., Pettit, J.W., & Rudd, M.D. (2003). Worst-point suicidal plans: A dimension of suicidality predictive of past suicide attempts and eventual death by suicide. *Behaviour Research and Therapy, 41*(12), 1469–1480.

Kelly, K.T., & Knudson, M.P. (2000). Are no-suicide contracts effective in preventing suicide in suicidal patients seen by primary care physicians? *Archives of Family Medicine, 9*, 1119–1121.

Kessler, R.C., Berglund, P., Borges, G., Nock, M., & Wang, P.S. (2005). Trends in suicide ideation, plans, gestures, and attempts in the United States, 1990–1992 to 2001–2003. *Journal of the American Medical Association, 293*, 2487–2495.

King, C.A., Kramer, A., Preuss, L., Kerr, D.C., Weisse, L., & Venkataraman, S. (2006). Youth-Nominated Support Team for suicidal adolescents (Version 1): A randomized controlled trial. *Journal of consulting and clinical psychology, 74*(1), 199.

Kleinman, E.M., & Liu, R.T. (2013). Social support as a protective factor in suicide: Findings from two nationally representative samples. *Journal of Affective Disorders, 150*(2), 540–545.

Kurz, A., & Moller, H.J. (1984). Help-seeking behavior and compliance of suicidal patients. *Psychiatrische Praxis, 11*, 6–13.

Larkin, G.L., & Beautrais, A.L. (2010). Emergency departments are underutilized sites for suicide prevention. *Crisis: The Journal of Crisis Intervention and Suicide Prevention, 31*(1), 1–6.

Linehan, M. (1993) *Cognitive behavior therapy for borderline personality disorder*. New York: Guilford.

Lizardi, D., & Stanley, B. (2010). Treatment engagement: A neglected aspect in the psychiatric care of suicidal patients. *Psychiatric Services, 61*(12), 1183–1191.

Longabaugh, R., Woolard, R.F., Nirenberg, T.D., Minugh, A.P., Becker, B., Clifford, P.R., . . . & Gogineni, A. (2001). Evaluating the effects of a brief motivational intervention for injured drinkers in the emergency department. *Journal of Studies on Alcohol and Drugs, 62*(6), 806.

Madras, B. K., Compton, W. M., Avula, D., Stegbauer, T., Stein, J. B., & Clark, H. W. (2009). Screening, brief interventions, referral to treatment (SBIRT) for illicit drug and alcohol use at multiple healthcare sites: comparison at intake and 6 months later. *Drug and Alcohol Dependence, 99*(1), 280–295.

Mann, J. J., Waternaux, C., Haas, G. L., & Malone, K. M. (1999). Toward a clinical model of suicidal behavior in psychiatric patients. *American Journal of Psychiatry, 156*(2), 181–189.

Monti, K., Cedereke, M., & Öjehagen, A. (2003). Treatment attendance and suicidal behavior 1 month and 3 months after a suicide attempt: A comparison between two samples. *Archives of Suicide Research, 7*(2), 167–174.

Monti, P. M., Colby, S. M., Barnett, N. P., Spirito, A., Rohsenow, D. J., Myers, M., . . . & Lewander, W. (1999). Brief intervention for harm reduction with alcohol-positive older adolescents in a hospital emergency department. *Journal of Consulting and Clinical Psychology, 67*(6), 989.

National Center for Injury Prevention and Control (2012a). *Suicide: Facts at a glance.* Retrieved from www.cdc.gov/violenceprevention/pdf/Suicide-DataSheet-a.pdf

National Center for Injury Prevention and Control (2012b). *Suicide prevention: Youth suicide.* Retrieved from www.cdc.gov/violenceprevention/pub/youth_suicide.html

Piacentini, J., Rotheram-Borus, M. J., Gillis, J. R., Graae, F., Trautman, P., Cantwell, C., . . . & Shaffer, D. (1995). Demographic predictors of treatment attendance among adolescent suicide attempters. *Journal of Consulting and Clinical Psychology, 63*(3), 469.

Reid, W. H. (1998) Promises, promises: Don't rely on patients' non-suicide, no-violence 'contracts'. *Journal of Practice Psychiatry and Behavioral Health, 4*, 316–318.

Rudd, M. D. (2006). *The assessment and management of suicidality.* Sarasota, FL: Professional Resource Press.

Rudd, M. D., Berman, A. L., Joiner, T. E., Nock, M. K., Silverman, M. M., Mandrusiak, M., . . . & Witte, T. (2006). Warning signs for suicide: Theory, research, and clinical applications. *Suicide and Life-Threatening Behavior, 36*(3), 255–262.

Rudd, M. D., Joiner, T., & Rajab, M. H. (2001). *Treating suicidal behavior: An effective, time-limited approach.* New York: Guilford.

Salkovskis, P. M., Atha, C., & Storer, D. (1990). Cognitive-behavioural problem solving in the treatment of patients who repeatedly attempt suicide. A controlled trial. *The British Journal of Psychiatry, 157*(6), 871–876.

Simon, R. I. (2007). Gun safety management with patients at risk for suicide. *Suicide and Life-Threatening Behavior, 37*, 518–526

Shaffer, D., & Pfeffer, C. (2001). Practice parameter for the assessment and treatment of children and adolescents with suicidal behavior. *Journal of the American Academy of Child and Adolescent Psychiatry, 40*, 24S–51S.

Stanford, E. J., Goetz, R. R., & Bloom, J. D. (1994). The no-harm contract in the emergency assessment of suicidal risk. *The Journal of Clinical Psychiatry, 55*, 344–348.

Stanley, B., & Brown, G. K. (2012). Safety planning intervention: A brief intervention to mitigate suicide risk. *Cognitive and Behavioral Practice, 19*, 256–264.

Stanley, B., & Brown, G. K. (with Karlin, B., Kemp, J., & Von Bergen, H.) (2008). *Safety Plan Treatment Manual to Reduce Suicide Risk: Veteran version.* Washington, DC: United States Department of Veterans Affairs.

Stanley, B., Brown, G., Brent, D. A., Wells, K., Poling, K., Curry, J., . . . & Hughes, J. (2009). Cognitive-behavioral therapy for suicide prevention (CBT-SP): Treatment model, feasibility, and acceptability. *Journal of the American Academy of Child & Adolescent Psychiatry, 48*(10), 1005–1013.

Yip, P. S., Caine, E., Yousuf, S., Chang, S. S., Wu, K. C. C., & Chen, Y. Y. (2012). Means restriction for suicide prevention. *The Lancet, 379*(9834), 2393–2399.

nine
Treating Self-Directed Violence in Primary Care Settings

Craig J. Bryan

NATIONAL CENTER FOR VETERANS STUDIES AND
THE UNIVERSITY OF UTAH

Peter C. Britton

VA CENTER OF EXCELLENCE FOR SUICIDE PREVENTION

Across studies of primary care settings, prevalence rates for suicidal ideation and suicide attempts typically range from 2% to 5% of patients, with higher rates observed among higher-risk subgroups (e.g., patients with depression). In the Epidemiological Catchment Area study, for instance, an estimated 2.2% of patients accessing services from a general medical setting reported suicidal ideation during the past year (Cooper-Patrick, Crum, & Ford, 1994). When considering only the past month, Olfson and colleagues (1996) similarly found a 2.4% prevalence rate among adult primary care patients. Slightly higher rates have been reported among older adults over the age of 60 (5.8%; Pfaff & Almeida, 2005) and in urban general medical settings, the latter of which has been found to range from 3.3% to 7.1% (Olfson et al., 2000; Zimmerman et al., 1995). Given that a considerable majority of the general population visits a primary care provider at least once per year (Centers for Disease Control, 2010; Regier et al., 1993), it is not surprising that the estimated prevalence of suicidal ideation among primary care patients is similar to the estimated prevalence of the general US population at large (3.3%; Kessler, Berglund, Borges, Nock, & Wang, 2005). Among primary care patients with identified mental health symptoms and problems, however, the prevalence of suicidal ideation rises. Twelve percent of patients referred to an embedded mental health specialist by a primary care provider (PCP) for an identified behavioral or psychosocial health issue report suicidal ideation (Bryan et al., 2008), as do 22% of patients who are prescribed psychotropic medications for mood or anxiety disorders (Verger et al, 2007). Similarly, up to 30% of patients with depressive disorders report suicidal ideation (Bruce et al., 2004).

In the United States's health care system, the PCP is typically the first point of contact for accessing medical services, whether it is for basic health, mental health, or substance abuse treatment. When experiencing any health-related problems or concerns about well-being or life problems, it is "my doctor" to whom patients are most likely to visit. As a result, the PCP is frequently the first medical professional with whom a patient discusses mental health problems or behavioral difficulties, which can include suicidal and non-suicidal self-directed violence. Tragically, the PCP is also frequently the *last* medical professional with whom an individual visits before dying by suicide. Almost half of individuals who die by suicide visit a PCP during the month immediately preceding their deaths (Luoma, Martin, & Pearson, 2002), and up to 20% visit a PCP *within 1 day* of their deaths (Pirkis & Burgess, 1998). Among elderly patients, rates are even higher: 73% of elderly suicide decedents visit a PCP in the month preceding their deaths, and almost half visit within the preceding week (Juurlink et al., 2004). By comparison, only 15% of suicide decedents visit a mental health specialist in the month prior to their deaths (Luoma et al., 2002). More recent data from the military mirror this pattern: service members who died by suicide visited a primary care clinic four times more often in the month preceding their deaths than a mental health clinic (Trofimovich, Skopp, Luxton, & Reger, 2012).

Suicidal individuals also tend to make multiple, repeated visits to primary care in the time immediately preceding their deaths. Juurlink and colleagues (2004) observed that the number of primary care visits increased from one or two visits per year to an average of three visits *per month* immediately preceding patients' deaths by suicide. Trofimovich and colleagues (2012) similarly reported "excess visits" to primary care clinics in the month preceding service members' deaths by suicide. Although excess visits were also observed in other clinic types (e.g., emergency departments), primary care clinics experienced the greatest magnitude increase relative to all other clinic types. It is not yet entirely clear why suicidal individuals visit primary care clinics in particular during the month immediately preceding their deaths by suicide, but one possibility is that suicidal individuals experience increased health problems as they become more emotionally distressed. As compared to non-suicidal individuals, for instance, suicidal individuals report more bodily pain, fatigue, and physical limitations (Goldney, Fisher, Wilson, & Cheok, 2001) and are diagnosed with a greater number of illnesses (Druss & Pincus, 2000; Juurlink et al., 2004). Many of these are somatic problems (e.g., headaches, diffuse pain, gastrointestinal complaints) influenced by emotional distress, especially depression.

In light of these findings, many have come to view primary care as an essential component of effective and comprehensive suicide prevention. The role of primary care in suicide prevention was noted in the 1999 Surgeon General's Call to Action to Prevent Suicide (US Public Health Service, 1999), but specific strategies and recommendations for primary care settings were not clearly articulated until the past year as part of the National Strategy for Suicide Prevention (US Department of Health and Human Services, 2012). Specifically, Strategic Direction #2 of the National Strategy for Suicide Prevention notes that "suicide assessment and preventive screening by primary care and other health care providers are crucial to assessing suicide risk and connecting individuals at risk for suicide to available clinical services and other sources of care" (p. 40) and that "assessment of suicide risk should be an integral part of primary care" (p. 58). Widespread implementation of these recommendations has been slow in coming, however, due in large part to the lack of evidence supporting the ability of any particular screening method to sufficiently predict and contribute to reductions in future suicide attempts when implemented in primary care clinics (Gaynes et al., 2004; O'Connor, Gaynes, Burda, Soh, & Whitlock, 2013). Despite the current lack of evidence, however, the US Preventive Services Task Force (USPSTF) nonetheless notes that PCPs can play an important role in the management of suicidal patients through regular monitoring, providing follow-up services, and coordinating care with other service providers such as mental health specialists.

Adapting the Brief Cognitive Behavioral Model to Primary Care Settings

Traditional mental health care settings tend to be characterized by high-intensity interventions or treatments delivered to a relatively small segment of the overall population. For example, most psychotherapists provide services to a relatively small number of patients, with the traditional format of psychotherapy occurring in 50-minute sessions approximately once or twice per week. Even for therapists utilizing briefer models of psychotherapy, such as those described in previous chapters, an entire course of treatment could span several months or more. In contrast to the traditional psychotherapy setting, the primary care medical setting takes a more population-based approach to health care that seeks to prevent the onset of acute illness and/or maintain the health of a very large segment of the population through high-volume, low-intensity interventions. For instance, a typical primary care provider (e.g., family physician, internist, physician assistant, nurse practitioner) may see up to 20 or 30 patients per day, often during appointments that last only 10 to 15 minutes (or less) in duration. This high-volume, low-intensity approach has increasingly been adopted by primary care behavioral health providers, many of whom meet with patients in 15- to 30-minute appointments to better match the population health philosophy of primary care. In light of these contextual differences, traditional psychotherapies are generally not feasible in primary care. Individual interventions must therefore be pulled from these effective psychotherapies and adapted to fit within the contextual parameters of a primary care clinic.

When considering all of the possible interventions that one can pull from effective psychotherapies and adapt for use in a primary care clinic, clinicians actually have a reasonable range of options, as can be seen in Table 9.1. These interventions

TABLE 9.1. Core interventions of brief cognitive behavioral therapy for suicide risk that can be adapted to primary care settings

---

Behavioral activation/activity scheduling
Cognitive restructuring
- Thought record
- ABC worksheets
- Challenging Beliefs worksheets
- Patterns of Problematic Beliefs worksheets
Crisis response plan/safety plan
Hope box/survival kit
Means restriction counseling
Mindfulness skills training
Reasons for living list
Relaxation skills training
Stimulus control for insomnia

---

are common "ingredients" of effective psychotherapies to reduce suicide attempts and can be easily adapted to the contextual demands of primary care. Because of the time-limited nature of assessment and intervention in primary care, however, clinicians should select those interventions that flow directly and naturally from the suicide risk assessment interview and that are matched to each individual patient's unique clinical presentation. As noted previously by Bryan and Rudd (2010), it is much better to do a single, empirically supported intervention very well than to implement multiple interventions with lesser quality.

In many cases, the PCP will be the first and only medical professional to whom the suicidal patient has talked about suicide-related thoughts and urges. Consequently, the first opportunity for intervention will often occur within the primary care setting, during a time when the suicidal patient's level of intent and desire may be especially elevated. Interventions that maximize safety should therefore be prioritized until the patient can be connected to a higher level of care (e.g., outpatient psychotherapy) and other interventions can be successfully implemented. One intervention in particular that has garnered considerable attention and discussion for use within primary care settings is the *safety plan* (Stanley & Brown, 2012), also known as the *crisis response plan* (Bryan, Corso, Neal-Walden, & Rudd, 2009; Bryan & Rudd, 2010). The safety plan is an intervention that can easily be implemented into the constraints of primary care settings to help patients make effective decisions and manage their emotional distress during periods of crises, and it is described and discussed in great detail in Chapter 8; it is therefore not repeated here. Although discussed as an intervention for emergency department settings, it should be noted that PCPs can use this very same intervention and clinical approach with suicidal patients. A second intervention designed to maximize short-term patient safety is *means restriction counseling.*

Means Restriction Counseling

Restriction of access to potentially lethal means for suicide (a.k.a., *means restriction*) is widely considered to be an important element of effective risk management with actively suicidal individuals and is routinely recommended as an intervention in treatment texts and practice guidelines (e.g., American Psychiatric Association, 2003; Berman, 2006; Bryan & Rudd, 2010; Rudd, Joiner, & Rajab, 2001; Wenzel, Brown, & Beck, 2009). The collaborative process by which clinicians and suicidal patients work together to accomplish means restriction is referred to as *means restriction counseling*. As an intervention for suicide prevention, means restriction is based on two core premises: first, that an individual's preferred method for suicide is most strongly related to convenient access to the method, and second, that acute suicidal episodes are often brief and fleeting. When these two factors co-occur (i.e., convenient access to potentially lethal means during an acute crisis), especially when the easily available method for suicide is potentially highly lethal (e.g., firearms), the likelihood of death by suicide increases dramatically. By restricting access to lethal means during acute suicidal episodes, an individual is much more likely to survive relatively transient periods of intense emotional distress.

Unfortunately, very few clinicians actually utilize means restriction counseling in their clinical practice. For instance, an estimated 80% of emergency department nurses indicated that they provided direct care for a patient who had made a suicide attempt during the preceding 6 months, but only 28% actually talked with the patient and/or the patient's parents about restricting access to lethal means (Grossman, Dontes, Kruesi, Pennington, & Fendrich, 2003). Mental health providers do not fare much better: only 3% of pediatric patients assessed in psychiatric emergency department were assessed for firearm access by the psychiatric residents who evaluated them (Giggie, Olvera, & Joshi, 2007), and less than one-quarter of psychologists report that they should even discuss access to lethal means with patients (Sullivan, 2004). Even less encouraging is evidence suggesting these numbers might actually be overestimates. McManus and colleagues (1997), for instance, interviewed parents several months after their children had received treatment at an emergency department for a suicide attempt and found that only 14% of parents reported receiving means restriction counseling from the medical staff. It is possible that the discrepancy between clinician and parent report of means restriction counseling is due to clinician overreporting of the frequency with which they are actually providing means restriction counseling. Alternatively, it is possible that what clinicians consider to be means restriction counseling is different from what patients (or their caregivers) consider to be means restriction counseling.

Means restriction counseling is especially relevant to primary care settings for a number of reasons. First, means restriction counseling is not very time consuming and can usually be accomplished in less than 10 or 15 minutes. It therefore fits easily within the fast pace of primary care medical settings. Second, means restriction counseling can be effectively accomplished by a wide range of individuals with varying levels of professional training (e.g., physician, nurse, psychologist, social worker), so it can be accomplished flexibly within primary care settings. Patient education, for instance, is often completed by nurses and medical technicians in primary care; means restriction counseling, as one particular form of patient education, can be similarly approached from this perspective. Because of these reasons, means restriction counseling is a relatively "low-intensity" intervention than can be easily administered to a wide spectrum of the population; it is therefore consistent with the prevention and health promotion philosophy of primary care.

When approached about the possibility of restricting access to potentially lethal means, many patients will be willing to engage in such activities, at least temporarily (Kruesi et al., 1999). However, as many primary care providers know, patients do not always easily change their behaviors, even when they realize that change may be in their best interest. This ambivalence, or conflict between two competing interests (e.g., change versus no change) is common for many patients and can influence their subsequent actions and decisions. Ambivalence is a central feature of the suicidal state: most patients who desire to die also desire to continue living (Jobes, 2006). Jobes and Mann (1999), for instance, reported that suicidal patients are able to list both reasons for dying *and* reasons for living. PCPs should therefore assume that suicidal patients desire to live to some extent, since a suicidal patient with absolutely no desire to live probably would not be alive and talking to a health care provider. Indeed, research suggests that suicidal intent is lower among suicidal patients who are ambivalent as compared to suicidal patients who are less ambivalent (i.e., high desire to die, low desire to live; Kovacs & Beck, 1977), and greater ambivalence about living and dying is associated with decreased likelihood of subsequent death by suicide (Brown et al., 2005).

For many suicidal patients, ambivalence about life and death extends to their willingness to pursue treatment in general, and their willingness to consider means restriction as an intervention in particular: on the one hand, suicidal patients want to live, and on the other hand, they do not want to relinquish their autonomy by removing a coping strategy or "solution" to their problem. Clinical experience suggests that ambivalence about means restriction is especially heightened for patients who own or possess firearms, as these patients may also have strong beliefs about gun ownership. When viewed through the lens of ambivalence and motivation for behavior change, the primary challenge for clinicians is recognizing that pushing too hard for means restriction can paradoxically decrease the patient's desire to accept the intervention. When clinicians emphasize only one side of issue, the suicidal patient views the intervention as threatening and tends to defends their freedom and autonomy (i.e., becomes "resistant") even though the patient may also recognize that possession of lethal means could be potentially harmful or unsafe. An approach to means restriction counseling that is informed by motivational interviewing (MI) can therefore be a useful and practical strategy for PCPs.

MI is a therapeutic approach designed specifically to increase the ambivalent patient's motivation for change (Miller & Rollnick, 2012). Originally developed as an intervention strategy for substance abuse, MI has subsequently been applied to a wide range of health-related behaviors such as diet, exercise, and medication adherence (Hettema, Steele, & Miller, 2005). More recently, MI has been extended to clinical interventions with patients at risk for suicide (Britton, Williams, & Conner, 2008; Britton, Conner, & Maisto, 2012), with results of pilot studies suggesting that patients find the approach acceptable and experience large, rapid reductions in suicidal ideation (Britton et al., 2012). As applied to means restriction counseling, MI takes into consideration both the patient's reasons for changing (e.g., maintaining safety, living) and reasons for *not* changing (e.g., maintaining autonomy and freedom, protecting their right to bear arms). Specifically, if the clinician only seems interested in securing or restricting the patient's access to lethal means without considering their reasons for wanting to maintain access to the means, the patient is more likely to argue against safety and for death.

Although a full course of MI may be beyond the scope of a primary care setting, select principles of MI may improve clinicians' ability to have an impact with ambivalent patients in the short period of time allotted to means restriction. These select principles can be described as adopting a guiding style rather than a directive style (Rollnick et al., 2005). When taking a directive style, clinicians tell clients what they should be doing and why they should do it. When taking a guiding style, clinicians ask clients to explore their thoughts and feelings about a behavior change and how they can best go about making that change. Adopting an approach based on three elements can enhance a guiding style. The first element is *evocation*, which is based on the belief that the reasons and means for change are within the individual and it is the clinician's job to access them. Second is *collaboration*, which takes the view that patients are the experts and that clinicians can provide additional expertise to help them solve their problems. Third is *autonomy support*, which assumes that patients must provide the reasons to change and means to do so. Ultimately, patients leave the primary care office and have to follow through with any means restriction plan that is agreed upon. It is therefore critical that they feel responsible for and are committed to following through with the plan.

In the context of a guiding spirit, MI clinicians guide patients toward change through the strategic use of specific techniques. Clinicians ask *open-ended questions* to evoke patients' reasons for and against a behavior and the best way of accomplishing it. They use *reflective listening* by sharing their understanding of their patients' perspectives to ensure that patients feel their reasons for and against restricting access are understood and respected. When progress toward restriction is made, clinicians use *affirmations* to reinforce movement. Although clinicians who are taking a guiding approach can provide information or make recommendations, they use the *elicit-provide-elicit* technique. The clinician shows that he or she respects the patient's autonomy by asking permission to provide information before providing the information and then asks the patient about his or her thoughts concerning the information given. This process ensures collaboration between patient and clinician, thereby increasing the likelihood of success.

Bryan, Stone, and Rudd (2011) recently delineated several steps involved in structuring the content of means restriction counseling (see Figure 9.1), thereby

Raise the issue

1. Suicidal desire can change in intensity very quickly.
   - Can you describe to me how your suicidal thoughts emerge over time?
   - What's it like for you to "become suicidal"?
   - It's common for people to feel suicidal very quickly, without much warning, sort of like they are suddenly overwhelmed and just can't take it anymore.
   - Just because you're feeling okay now doesn't mean you won't be feeling worse when facing an unexpected problem or crisis.
   - It's best to play it safe by limiting access to potentially lethal means for suicide.

2. When emotionally upset, solving problems can be very difficult.
   - When you're upset and thinking about killing yourself, is it easy to think of options to solve your problems or figure out what to do?
   - Most people think about suicide as a way to manage emotional pain or suffering.
   - Having access to lethal means for suicide can be dangerous when in this state of mind.
   - If you don't have access to [method], it increases the likelihood that you'll find another strategy or option that doesn't result in physical harm or death.

3. Restricting access to lethal means can reduce the likelihood of a bad outcome during a crisis.
   - Developing a plan for temporarily limiting your access to [method] is a simple way to reduce the likelihood that you will die before you can receive the help you need to reduce your suffering or solve your problems.
   - I'm wondering if we could talk a bit about how we can work together to come up with a plan to keep you safe during crises.
   - Would you be willing to talk with me about safety?

Conduct means restriction counseling

4. Because you are currently at higher risk for making a suicide attempt than usual, having access to [method] increases the likelihood that a suicide attempt will be fatal.
   - What are your reasons for living? What keeps you from making a suicide attempt despite some desire to do so?
   - What benefit might there by to temporarily limiting your access to [method]?

5. Identify a menu of options for restricting access to means.
   - What are some ways we could reduce the likelihood of your using [method] when emotionally upset?
   - If we wanted to prevent your children from using [method], what are some options we might consider?

6. Encourage options other than hiding potentially lethal means.
   - Hiding [method] is one idea. What are some other options we might consider as well?
   - My concern is that hidden objects can be easily found. So I'm wondering if there might be another good option for us to consider instead; what do you think?
   - Now that we've identified several options, what are the pros and cons of each?

7. Develop a written plan.
   - It sounds like you've come to a decision. What do you think about writing this down so we can make sure we are both clear on what the plan is?
   - Is there anyone in your life who might be able to help us with this plan?
   - Is there someone you trust and who would be supportive of this plan?

Enlist the support of a significant other

8. Add supportive other to means restriction receipt.
   - *For patients unable to identify a significant other*: That may be an area to work on in the future. We should keep that in mind as we develop your treatment plan and recommendations.

FIGURE 9.1. Suggested approach for means restriction counseling

providing a template of "what to do" in means restriction counseling: 1) raise the issue; 2) conduct means restriction counseling; and 3) enlist the support of a significant other. The integration of the MI-based guiding approach into this general framework for means restriction counseling provides clinicians a framework for "how" to conduct means restriction counseling, particularly with ambivalent patients who are reluctant about engaging in such behavior. From an MI perspective, it is critical that clinicians are flexible and realize that the three phases of means restriction counseling may not necessarily unfold linearly but rather can be recursive in nature. Consistent with this nonlinear approach, means restriction counseling may need to be repeatedly addressed and/or revisited over the course of several primary care appointments. For instance, some patients will not agree to remove or restrict their access to firearms when means restriction counseling is first conducted, but over the course of follow-up appointments, a patient may subsequently change his or her mind about the matter. Means restriction counseling should therefore be approached consistently with a chronic disease management model, which entails periodic "check-ups" designed to maintain health over time, with more intensive or aggressive intervention during periods of acute exacerbation.

Raising the Issue

To maximize the success of means restriction counseling, clinicians must be able to establish a collaborative working relationship with the patient. A great deal has been written about the importance of the *therapeutic alliance* (alternately referred to as *rapport, therapeutic relationship*, or *bedside manner*) on treatment adherence and outcomes, with a considerable line of research supporting the notion that strong therapeutic alliance is associated with clinical improvement in mental health care (Martin, Garske, & Davis, 2000). In primary care clinics, the fast pace and high volume of patient care, which can be marked by frequent interruptions and delays in service delivery, lends itself to very directive clinical styles in which the clinician plays a very active role, while the patient plays a very passive role during appointments. This relative imbalance in participation can potentially interfere with clinicians' ability to effectively discuss suicide ideation, suicide attempts, and means restriction. Communicating a desire to align with the patient against the problem of emotional distress and suicidal desire, as opposed to merely telling the patient what to do, increases the likelihood that the patient will take steps to remove or restrict access to potentially lethal means. When raising the issue of means restriction, clinicians should therefore first provide a rationale for introducing the topic and emphasize their willingness to hear and consider the patient's perspective. In this first phase of means restriction counseling, the clinician seeks to *engage* with the patient and should emphasize several key points:

1. *Suicidal desire can change in intensity very quickly.* Just because a patient is feeling okay now does not mean that this will not change when they are confronted

with an unexpected problem or crisis. Along these same lines, because suicidal desire and intent can change so quickly, it is best to "play it safe" by limiting the patient's access to potentially lethal methods of suicide. Clinicians can personalize this point by asking open-ended questions about how the patient has typically experienced the onset of suicidal desire in his or her life. For example, "Can you describe to me how your suicidal thoughts emerge over time? What is it like for you?" Many patients will describe the onset of suicidal intent as sudden or rapid, or will indicate that their decision to make a suicide attempt occurred "impulsively" or without any forethought, as if their suicidal thoughts and urges emerged out of the blue. Although growing scientific evidence appears to speak against the notion of "impulsive" suicide attempts, this does not change the patient's *subjective experience* of how suicidal desire emerges within his or her own life. Given that most suicidal patients experience the onset of suicidal desire and intent as very sudden and rapid, clinicians can raise the issue of means restriction by directly tying the intervention's rationale to the patient's own experience.

2. *When emotionally upset, solving problems is very difficult.* Because most people think about suicide or make a suicide attempt as a coping strategy to alleviate emotional pain and suffering, having access to lethal means for suicide can be very dangerous when in a crisis. Means restriction can "buy time" for the patient during such a crisis by increasing the likelihood that he or she will identify an alternative coping strategy that does not result in physical harm or death. Open-ended questions and reflections can personalize this point for patients: "It sounds like when you're really upset and you're thinking about killing yourself, it's not easy to think of options or figure out what to do. Is that right?" Because feeling trapped or backed into a corner is a common experience of suicidal individuals, many suicidal patients will agree that generating options or alternatives is difficult or even "impossible."

3. *Restricting access to lethal means can reduce the likelihood of a bad outcome during a crisis.* Developing a plan for *temporarily* restricting access to potentially lethal means for suicide, especially firearms, is a simple way to make sure the patient does not die by suicide before he or she completes treatment that is designed to reduce emotional pain. Emphasizing the temporary nature of means restriction can make a big difference for patients who are concerned about restriction of their autonomy, especially those who own firearms. At this point in the intervention, it can be very useful to ask the patient for his or her permission to discuss means restriction further: "Because of all of these issues, I'm wondering if we could talk a little bit about how we can work together to come up with a plan to keep you safe during crises. Would you be willing to talk with me about safety?" Asking for permission to discuss means restriction further, as opposed to merely moving forward with such a conversation, respects the patient's autonomy and establishes a collaborative process in which the patient is an active participant in the intervention and treatment process. In the event that a patient declines the invitation, clinicians should ask

open-ended questions to identify potential sources of anxiety or hesitation: "Is there something about this topic that makes you uncomfortable? What do you think will happen when we talk about this more?" In many cases, patients are afraid that their freedoms will be restricted or they will not be listened to. Directly addressing these concerns and reinforcing the importance of a collaborative effort is often sufficient to reduce the patient's reluctance and to move forward with means restriction counseling.

Discuss Restriction of Access to Lethal Means

Once the clinician has introduced the issue of means restriction and obtained initial buy-in from the patient, the clinician should next focus on the primary components and elements of means restriction counseling. Focusing on suicide prevention and means restriction is easier with patients who have voluntarily reported suicidal thoughts or suicide attempts, but in primary care settings it is more common for suicidal patients to visit the clinic for reasons other than these. For instance, many suicidal patients present to primary care clinics with somatic or physical complaints such as headaches, insomnia, fatigue, or generalized pain. Clinicians should therefore balance their approach between a *directive* approach in which the clinician takes the lead, and a *following* approach in which the patient takes the lead. The former could interfere with collaboration and reduce patient engagement, while the latter could result in a loss of focus on the topic at hand. In between a directive approach and a following approach is a *guiding* approach, in which the clinician remains focused on the topic of means restriction but with sufficient flexibility to keep patients engaged. In most cases, patients will be more willing to discuss means restriction when they feel that their priorities and needs are being sufficiently acknowledged and addressed. In this phase of means restriction counseling, clinicians should emphasize the following key points:

1. *Because the patient is currently at higher risk for making a suicide attempt than usual, having easy access to potentially lethal means for suicide increases the likelihood that a suicide attempt will be fatal.* This is especially relevant for firearm owners. Guiding the patient to discuss his or her personal reasons for living is an effective and useful way for clinicians to help suicidal patients understand how access to lethal means could potentially work against them. In short, clinicians work to build discrepancy between a particular action (i.e., possessing lethal means) and the desired change (i.e., living) by asking patients to elicit their reasons for restricting access. This is based on the assumption that individuals can talk themselves into a behavior change. Clinicians can evoke change talk by asking questions such as, "What are some of your reasons for living? What benefit might there be to temporarily limiting your access to this method?" However, it is important for clinicians to remember to also acknowledge the patient's reasons *against* means restriction (referred to in MI as *sustain talk*), since dismissing these reasons or attempting to talk a patient

out of possessing lethal means could actually reduce the patient's motivation to make the desired change. The primary goal of this stage is to obtain an agreement from the patient that means restriction may be an acceptable method for maximizing safety and achieving their desired goal of living.

2. *Identify a menu of options for restricting access to lethal means.* Although complete removal of potentially lethal means is preferable, especially in the case of firearms, this option is not always feasible or acceptable to the patient. Clinicians should therefore be prepared to help guide the patient in generating a menu of options that can each be evaluated and considered, so that the patient can select an option that will work best for him or her. For instance, in the case of firearms, some options include temporarily allowing a friend or family member to secure the weapon in a safe location, locking the firearm in a gun safe and asking a friend or spouse to change the combination, placing a trigger lock on the firearm, storing ammunition separate from the weapon, and/or dismantling the weapon. A clinician can initiate this menu-building process by asking questions such as, "What are some ways we could reduce the likelihood of you using [method] when emotionally upset? If we wanted to prevent your children from using [method], what are some options we might consider?"

3. *Encourage options other than "hiding" potentially lethal means.* In some cases, patients will suggest hiding the lethal means as a method of means restriction (e.g., "I'll just have my wife hide my gun somewhere in the house"). Hiding lethal means is generally not considered to be sufficient, however, since hidden objects can be discovered fairly easily. Clinicians should be careful not to aggressively dismiss or discourage hiding as a solution, though, as this could disengage the patient from the task at hand or motivate him or her to defend the option. Instead, clinicians should guide patients to consider other options in addition to hiding lethal means. For example, a clinician might say, "That's one idea. What are some other options we might consider as well?" Clinicians can then encourage patients to weigh the pros and cons of each option identified, and guide patients to talk about how hiding might not be as effective as other options.

4. *Develop a written plan.* Once the patient has identified an acceptable plan for means restriction, clinicians should invite the patient to formalize this plan in writing: "It sounds like you've come to a decision. What do you think about writing this down so we make sure we both are clear about what the plan is?" Writing down the means restriction plan not only ensures that the clinician and patient agree upon the details of the plan, but it can also reinforce the patient's commitment, since it is "in writing." Written plans can also facilitate the enlistment of aid from others (e.g., spouses, parents) who can provide considerable support for means restriction. A *means receipt* is displayed in Figure 9.2 and was developed as a template for written means restriction plans (Bryan, Stone, & Rudd, 2011). The means receipt details how lethal means will be specifically restricted (e.g., complete removal, use of trigger locks, etc.),

Means Restriction Receipt

Questions? Contact your provider: _____
Emergencies call: 911

    Patient Name: _____

    Support's Name: _____

    Type of means: _____

    Safety Plan: _____

    _____

    _____

    Release Terms: _____

    **Support's
signature:** _____

(To be signed upon completion of means restriction)

FIGURE 9.2. Means restriction receipt

who will implement the plan, who will support the plan, and under what conditions the means restriction plan is terminated. This latter point is an especially helpful component of means restriction counseling, as it reinforces the temporary nature of acute crises and facilitates hope through the implication that the patient's life will eventually get better. The means restriction receipt can also be used to verify that a means restriction plan has been implemented by a supportive person in the patient's life.

Enlist the Aid and Support of Others

Patients may be more likely to implement means restriction if significant others can assist or otherwise support the intervention. Including significant others in means restriction planning can also facilitate social support, a well-established protective factor for suicide attempts. As such, clinicians should invite patients to enlist the aid and support of family members, friends, and/or other supportive individuals in their lives. For example, clinicians might ask patients, "Is there anyone in your life who might be able to help us with this plan? Someone you trust and who would be supportive?" Identified supportive others should be included on the patient's written means restriction plan, with a clear delineation of how this supportive other will contribute to the plan (e.g., removing a firearm from the home and securing it elsewhere, verifying that gun safes are properly locked). In primary care settings, it is common for patients to be accompanied to a medical appointment by a family member or other supportive person. If a patient indicates that a supportive other has accompanied him or her to the medical appointment, clinicians may consider asking the patient for permission to have this significant other join them in the office to review the means restriction plan. For patients who decline to include any supportive others in their means restriction plan (i.e., "I can do it by myself"), clinicians should accept this decision and not push the patient to include a supportive other, consistent with the philosophy of MI, since pushing too hard for one side of the issue will typically result in the patient arguing for the other side. Sometimes patients will indicate that they do not have any supportive individuals who can assist (e.g., "I don't have any friends or family who can help"). In these cases, clinicians should suggest this as a potential target for future treatment (e.g., "That may be an area to work on in the future"), which is typically accomplished in psychotherapy with a mental health specialist.

Common Barriers and Future Directions

Perhaps one of the most pressing barriers for means restriction counseling is clinician perceptions that patients will not cooperate with them and will refuse to secure or remove potentially lethal means for suicide. This concern is often magnified and especially salient among patients who own or possess firearms. For instance, clinicians estimate that less than half of gun-owning patients would take steps to store their firearms unloaded in a secured location and less than one in four would completely remove the firearm from their homes if recommended to do so by the clinician (Price, Kinnison, Dake, Thompson, & Price, 2007). Not surprisingly, clinicians who do not believe means restriction counseling will be effective are five times less likely to talk about it with their patients (Price et al., 2007). Another common barrier that interferes with the use of means restriction counseling is the assumption of *means substitution*. Means substitution assumes that if one potentially lethal method is removed, suicidal patients will simply select an alternative method. As a result, means restriction counseling is assumed to have very limited (or no) effectiveness. The concept of means substitution was first discussed by Stengel (1967), although he originally used the term *displacement hypothesis* to describe this issue. Although Stengel did not base his argument on any empirical evidence, the assumption of means substitution has nonetheless persisted over time, even in the face of more recent evidence that counters the concept. Several studies support significant effects of means restriction on suicide rate reductions, with no evidence of means substitution even when controlling for important critical variables that could also account for observed declines (Gunnell et al., 2007; Leenaars, Moksony, Lester, & Wenckstern, 2003; Nordentoft, Qin, Helweg-Larsen, & Juel, 2006). Furthermore, suicidal individuals tend to have a preference for a specific method of suicide and do not easily change methods. Based on an exhaustive literature review, Daigle (2005) therefore concluded that "studies as a whole indicate that many individuals prefer a particular means of suicide, if not a particular place for it" (p. 628). Thus, although means substitution cannot be completely ruled out in all cases, it does not appear to occur with sufficient frequency to undermine the overall effectiveness of means restriction.

The MI approach to means restriction counseling described in this chapter was specifically developed to address these common barriers to means restriction counseling, especially for patients who may be less motivated to follow through with a means restriction plan. Studies testing the effectiveness of means restriction counseling in primary care settings have not yet been conducted, however, and are needed to more definitely establish the utility of this approach. Furthermore, although two-thirds of parents of high-risk adolescents who are encouraged to secure or restrict access to lethal means, even firearms, by their clinicians take steps to comply with these recommendations (Kruesi et al., 1999), it is not yet known how many adults will willingly restrict access to potentially lethal means upon request, or if an MI-informed approach would improve upon such requests. Despite these limitations, means restriction counseling is especially well suited for primary care settings because of its brevity and considerable potential for positively impacting rates of suicide attempts and death by suicide among at-risk individuals.

References

American Psychiatric Association (2003). *Practice guideline for the assessment and treatment of patients with suicidal behavior.* Washington, DC: American Psychiatric Association.

Berman, A. L. (2006). Risk management with suicidal patients. *Journal of Clinical Psychology, 62,* 171–184.

Britton, P. C., Conner, K. R., & Maisto, S. A. (2012). An open trial of motivational interviewing to address suicidal ideation with hospitalized veterans. *Journal of Clinical Psychology, 68,* 961–971.

Britton, P. C., Williams, G. C., & Conner, K. R. (2008). Self-determination theory, motivational interviewing, and the treatment of clients with acute suicidal ideation. *Journal of Clinical Psychology, 64,* 52–66.

Brown, G. K., TenHave, T., Henriques, G. R., Xie, S. X., Hollander, J. E., & Beck, A. T. (2005). Cognitive therapy for the prevention of suicide attempts: A randomized controlled trial. *JAMA, 294,* 563–570.

Bruce, M. L., Ten Have, R. T., Reynolds, C. F., Katz, I. I., Schulberg, H. C., Mulsant, B. H., Brown, G. K., McAvay, G. J., Pearson, J. L., & Alexopoulos, G. S. (2004). Reducing suicidal ideation and depressive symptoms in depressed older primary care patients: A randomized controlled trial. *JAMA, 291,* 1081–1091.

Bryan, C. J., Corso, K. A., Neal-Walden, T. A., & Rudd, M. D. (2009). Managing suicide risk in primary care: Practice recommendations for behavioral health consultants. *Professional Psychology: Research and Practice, 40,* 148–155.

Bryan, C. J., Corso, K. A., Rudd, M. D., & Cordero, L. (2008). Improving identification of suicidal patients in primary care through routine screening. *Primary Care and Community Psychiatry, 13,* 143–147.

Bryan, C. J., & Rudd, M. D. (2010). *Managing suicide risk in primary care.* New York, NY: Springer Publishing.

Bryan, C. J., Stone, S. L., & Rudd, M. D. (2011). A practical, evidence-based approach for means-restriction counseling with suicidal patients. *Professional Psychology: Research and Practice, 42,* 339–346.

Centers for Disease Control and Prevention (2010). *National Ambulatory Medical Care Survey: 2010 summary tables.* Retrieved from www.cdc.gov/nchs/data/ahcd/namcs_summary/2010_namcs_web_tables.pdf

Cooper-Patrick, L., Crum, R. M., & Ford, D. E. (1994). Identifying suicidal ideation in generam medical patients. *JAMA, 272,* 1757–1762.

Daigle, M. S. (2005). Suicide prevention through means restriction: Assessing the risk of substitution: A critical review and synthesis. *Accident Analysis and Prevention, 37,* 625–632.

Druss, B., & Pincus, H. (2000). Suicidal ideation and suicide attempts in general medical illnesses. *Archives of Internal Medicine, 160,* 1522–1526.

Gaynes, B. N., West, S. L., Ford, C. A., Frame, P., Klein, J., & Lohr, K. N. (2004). Screening for suicide risk in adults: A summary of the evidence for the U.S. Preventive Services Task Force. *Annals of Internal Medicine, 140,* 822–835.

Giggie, M. A., Olvera, R. L., & Joshi, M. N. (2007). Screening for risk factors associated with violence in pediatric patients presenting to a psychiatric emergency department. *Journal of Psychiatric Practice, 13,* 246–252.

Goldney, R. D., Fisher, L. J., Wilson, D. H., & Cheok, F. (2001). Suicidal ideation and health-related quality of life in the community. *Medical Journal of Australia, 175,* 546–549.

Grossman, J., Dontes, A., Kruesi, M., Pennington, J., & Fendrich, M. (2003). Emergency nurses' responses to a survey about means restriction: An adolescent suicide prevention strategy. *Journal of the American Psychiatric Nurses Association, 9,* 77–85.

Gunnell, D., Fernando, R., Hewagama, M., Priyangika, W. D., Konradsen, F., & Eddleston, M. (2007). The impact of pesticide regulations on suicide in Sri Lanka. *International Journal of Epidemiology, 36,* 1235–1242.

Hettema, J., Steele, J., & Miller, W. R. (2005). Motivational interviewing. *Annual Review of Clinical Psychology, 1,* 91–111.

Jobes, D. A. (2006). *Managing suicidal risk: A collaborative approach.* New York, NY: Guilford Press.

Jobes, D. A., & Mann, R. E. (1999). Reasons for living versus reasons for dying: Examining the internal debate of suicide. *Suicide and Life-Threatening Behavior, 29,* 97–104.

Juurlink, D. N., Herrmann, N., Szalai, J. P., Kopp, A., & Redelmeier, D. A. (2004). Medical illness and the risk of suicide in the elderly. *Archives of Internal Medicine, 164,* 1179–1184.

Kessler, R. C., Berglund, P., Borges, G., Nock, M., & Wang, P. S. (2005). Trends in suicide ideation, plans, gestures, and attempts in the United States, 1990–1992 to 2001–2003. *JAMA, 293,* 2487–2495.

Kovacs, M., & Beck, A. T. (1977). The wish to die and the wish to live in attempted suicides. *Journal of Clinical Psychology, 33,* 361–365.

Kruesi, M., Grossman, J., Pennington, J., Woodward, P., Duda, D., & Hirsch, J. (1999). Suicide and violence prevention: Parent education in the emergency department. *American Academy of Child and Adolescent Psychiatry, 38,* 250–255.

Leenaars, A. A., Moksony, F., Lester, D., & Wenckstern, S. (2003). The impact of gun control (Bill C-51) on suicide in Canada. *Death Studies, 27,* 103–124.

Luoma, J. B., Martin, C. E., & Pearson, J. L. (2002). Contact with mental health and primary care providers before suicide: A review of the evidence. *American Journal of Psychiatry, 159,* 909–916.

Martin, D. J., Garske, J. P., & Davis, M. K. (2000). Relation of the therapeutic alliance with outcome and other variables: A meta-analytic review. *Journal of Consulting and Clinical Psychology, 68,* 438–450.

McManus, B. L., Kruesl, M. J., Dontes, A. E., Defazio, C. R., Piotrowski, J. T., & Woodward, P. J. (1997). Child and adolescent suicide attempts: An opportunity for emergency departments to provide injury prevention education. *American Journal of Emergency Medicine, 15,* 357–360.

Miller, W. R., & Rollnick, S. (2012). *Motivational interviewing: Preparing people for change* (3rd ed.). New York: Guilford Press.

Nordentoft, M., Qin, P., Helweg-Larsen, K., & Juel, K. (2006). Time-trends in method-specific suicide rates compared with the availability of specific compounds. The Danish experience. *Nordic Journal of Psychiatry, 60,* 97–106.

O'Connor, E., Gaynes, B. N., Burda, B. U., Soh, C., & Whitlock, E. P. (2013). Screening for and treatment of suicide risk relevant to primary care: A systematic review for the U.S. Preventive Services Task Force. *Annals of Internal Medicine, 158,* 741–754.

Olfson, M., Shea, S., Feder, A., Fuentes, M., Nomura, Y., Gameroff, M., & Weissman, M. M. (2000). Prevalence of anxiety, depression, and substance use disorders in an urban general medicine practice. *Archives of Family Medicine, 9,* 876–883.

Olfson, M., Weissman, M. M., Leon, A. C., Sheehan, D. V., & Farber, L. (1996). Suicidal ideation in primary care. *Journal of General Internal Medicine, 11,* 447–453.

Pfaff, J. J., & Almeida, O. P. (2005). Detecting suicidal ideation in older patients: Identifying risk factors within the general practice setting. *British Journal of General Practice, 55,* 269–273.

Pirkis, J., & Burgess, P. (1998). Suicide and recency of health care contacts: A systematic review. *British Journal of Psychiatry, 36,* 29–35.

Price, J. H., Kinnison, A., Dake, J. A., Thompson, A. J., & Price, J. A. (2007). Psychiatrists' practices and perceptions regarding anticipatory guidance on firearms. *American Journal of Preventive Medicine, 33,* 370–373.

Regier, D. A., Narrow, W. E., Rae, D. S., Manderscheid, R. W., Locke, B. Z., & Goodwin, F. K. (1993). The de facto U.S. mental and addictive disorders service system: Epidemiologic Catchment Area prospective 1-year prevalence rates of disorders and services. *Archives of General Psychiatry, 50,* 85–94.

Rollnick, S., Butler, C. C., McCambridge, J., Kinnersley, P., Elwyn, G., & Resnicow, K. (2005). Consultations about changing behaviour. *BMJ, 331,* 961–963.

Rudd, M. D., Joiner, T. E., & Rajab, M. H. (2001). *Treating suicidal behavior: A time-limited approach.* New York, NY: The Guilford Press.

Stanley, B., & Brown, G. K. (2012). Safety planning intervention: A brief intervention to mitigate suicide risk. *Cognitive and Behavioral Practice, 19,* 256–264.

Stengel, E. (1967). *Suicide and attempted suicide.* London, UK: Penguin Books.

Sullivan, G. (2004). Assessment of firearm access. *Behavioral Emergencies Update, 1*(1). Retrieved from www.apa.org/divisions/div12/sections/section7/news/sp04/access.html

Trofimovich, L., Skopp, N. A., Luxton, D. D., & Reger, M. A. (2012). Health care experiences prior to suicide and self-inflicted injury, active component, U.S. Armed Forces, 2001–2010. *MSMR: Medical Surveillance Monthly Report, 19,* 2–6.

U.S. Department of Health and Human Services (HHS) Office of the Surgeon General and National Action Alliance for Suicide Prevention (2012). *2012 National Strategy for Suicide Prevention: Goals and objectives for action.* Washington, DC: HHS.

U.S. Public Health Service (1999). *The Surgeon General's call to action to prevent suicide.* Washington, DC: U.S. Government.

Verger, P., Brabis, P., Kovess, V., Lovell, A., Sebbah, R., Villani, P., Paraponaris, A., & Rouillon, F. (2007). Determinants of early identification of suicidal ideation in patients treated with antidepressants or anxiolytics in general practice: a multilevel analysis. *Journal of Affective Disorders, 99,* 253–257.

Wenzel, A., Brown, G. K., & Beck, A. T. (2009). *Cognitive therapy for suicidal patients: Scientific and clinical applications.* Washington, DC: American Psychological Association.

Zimmerman, M., Lish, J. D., Lush, D. T., Farber, N. J., Plescia, G., & Kuzma, M. A. (1995). Suicidal ideation among urban medical outpatients. *Journal of General Internal Medicine, 10,* 573–576.

Part IV
Special Issues

ten
Special Issues With Treating Suicidal Patients

Craig J. Bryan

NATIONAL CENTER FOR VETERANS STUDIES AND
THE UNIVERSITY OF UTAH

Traditional approaches for managing and treating self-directed violence have primarily adopted a psychiatric syndromal model that focuses on the classification and treatment of behaviors based on their topographical features, which typically include signs (i.e., what is directly observable, such as psychomotor agitation or repetitive behaviors) and symptoms (i.e., what is reported by the patient but not directly observable, such as depressed mood or worrying) of associated psychiatric disorders. From this perspective, suicidal ideation and suicide attempts are viewed as symptoms of an underlying psychiatric disorder (Jobes, 2006). Treatment of suicidal ideation and suicide attempts is therefore directed toward the resolution of the psychiatric condition that is presumed to underlie suicide risk (e.g., depression, borderline personality disorder). Unfortunately, this perspective has considerable limitations and has slowed our progress in understanding suicide, due in large part to the fact that suicidal ideation and suicide attempts are associated with *all* psychiatric disorders (Harris & Barraclough, 1997), suggesting there is no single psychiatric condition that serves as a core etiology for suicide. Furthermore, although psychiatric conditions serve as risk factors for suicide attempts, the vast majority of individuals with psychiatric conditions will not make suicide attempts or die by suicide, suggesting that psychiatric disorders are not particularly specific to understanding suicide risk. The fact that only some, but not all, individuals with psychiatric conditions engage in suicide attempts further suggests there must be other factors that more directly give rise to suicide attempts, regardless of an individual's specific diagnostic profile.

In contrast to the psychiatric syndromal model, a functional approach to understanding suicidal ideation and suicide attempts has been proposed by theorists and researchers (Bryan, Rudd, & Wertenberger, 2013; Hayes, Wilson, Gifford, Follete, & Strosahl, 1996; Nock & Prinstein, 2004). In the functional approach, suicide attempts are treated according to the underlying mechanisms that activate and sustain the behaviors over time. From this perspective, the environmental, contextual, and motivational factors that exist before *and* after the suicide attempt occurs are presumed to influence the emergence and recurrence of suicidal ideation and suicide attempts over time (Hayes et al., 1996). Most leading theories of suicide, for instance, propose that suicide attempts are best conceptualized as coping strategies to reduce emotional distress secondary to life stressors that are perceived as persistent and unsolvable (e.g., Joiner, 2005; Linehan, 1993; Rudd, 2006). The inability to effectively solve problems, tolerate emotional distress, and regulate emotions therefore gives rise to suicide attempts, whereas reductions in emotional distress and/or avoidance of life stressors after the suicide attempt has occurred serves to reinforce the behavior and increases the likelihood of recurrence in the future. Indeed, studies have confirmed that the attempt to avoid or alleviate emotional distress is the primary motivation for both suicidal and non-suicidal self-directed violence (e.g., Bryan, Rudd, & Wertenberger, 2013; Nock & Prinstein, 2004).

Avoidance of emotional distress is a common contributor to many psychiatric disorders, not just suicide attempts (Hayes et al., 1996). Substance use, for instance, is frequently used as a coping strategy to reduce emotional distress, whereas avoidance and suppression of intrusive memories of a traumatic event are primary drivers of posttraumatic stress disorder. In short, individuals who have difficulties regulating their distress tend to be more emotionally reactive and more likely to use avoidance and suppression as a coping strategy, which lends vulnerability to a range of psychiatric conditions and problematic behaviors that are frequently associated with suicide attempts (e.g., substance abuse, posttraumatic stress disorder, and personality disorders). Comorbidities therefore occur due to common underlying psychological processes, the most notable of which are avoidance-based coping and ineffective problem solving. By extension, treatments that target avoidance by teaching emotion regulation and problem-solving skills can not only reduce the risk for suicide attempts but also many of their most common co-occurring psychiatric and behavioral features.

Comorbid Substance Use Disorders

Substance use disorders are among the most common comorbidities of psychiatric disorders and are frequently associated with suicidal ideation and suicide attempts. Within the US general population, for instance, the 12-month prevalence rate of any substance use disorder is approximately 9%, of which the overwhelming majority (8.5%) is an alcohol use disorder (Grant et al., 2004). Grant et al. additionally reported that up to 20% of individuals with a substance use disorder of any kind also meet criteria for a mood or anxiety disorder, and around half (53%) who meet criteria for a substance *dependence* disorder have a comorbid mood or anxiety disorder. Thus, as the severity of substance use increases, so does the likelihood of a comorbid psychiatric condition. Alcohol and drug use of any severity level predicts subsequent suicide attempts even when controlling for demographic variables and comorbid psychiatric conditions (Borges, Walters, & Kessler, 2000), suggesting that substance use is a unique risk factor for suicide attempts and should be addressed in the treatment of suicidal patients regardless of its severity level. In combination with other psychiatric disorders, however, risk for suicide attempts is increased even further, with research suggesting that substance use and mood disorders, in particular, appear to contribute to suicide attempts with partial independence or additivity (Tondo et al., 1999).

For instance, individuals with comorbid substance use disorders and bipolar disorders are almost twice as likely to have made a suicide attempt during their lives as individuals with bipolar disorder alone (Dalton, Cate-Carter, Mundo, Parikh, & Kennedy, 2003). With respect to mood disorders, risk appears to be especially heightened with comorbid depressive or dysphoric mood disorders (e.g., major depressive disorder, bipolar II disorder, mixed depressive episodes) as compared to unipolar manic disorders (Tondo et al., 1999). The temporal relationship of depression and substance dependence may also influence risk for suicide attempts among individuals with comorbid depression and substance dependence. Specifically, depression that occurs before the onset of substance dependence is associated with more severe suicidal intent, but depression that occurs during periods of abstinence is associated with number of lifetime suicide attempts (Aharonovich, Liu, Nunes, & Hasin, 2002). Clinicians should therefore consider the relative timing of onset and remission of mood disturbance and substance use over time, as opposed to simply assessing for the presence or absence of each condition. Furthermore, clinicians should remain alert to periods of potentially elevated risk among patients with comorbid conditions, especially when depressive episodes occur during periods of abstinence, when both patient and clinician vigilance may be reduced.

Increased risk for suicide attempt is not limited to comorbid substance use and mood disorders, however. Comorbid substance use and anxiety disorders also have synergistic effects (Grant et al., 2004). Posttraumatic stress disorder (PTSD) in particular, which was previously classified as an anxiety disorder but was reclassified as a trauma- and stressor-related disorder in the recently-released *DSM-5*, has received considerable attention due to its high comorbidity with substance use disorders. Because individuals with comorbid PTSD and substance dependence may experience slower remission of suicidal ideation over time (Price, Risk, Haden, Lewis, & Spitznagel, 2004), clinicians may need to plan for increasing the intensity and/or duration of treatment over time. The persistence of suicidal ideation among individuals with comorbid substance dependence and PTSD may therefore require increased monitoring by clinicians, especially in light of evidence that increased risk for suicide attempts among patients with substance disorders is especially pronounced among individuals with a history of suicidal ideation (Borges et al., 2000). Furthermore, the presence of substance use among individuals with suicidal ideation significantly increases the likelihood of an "unplanned" or "impulsive" suicide attempt (Borges et al., 2000). Clinicians should be cautious about how they interpret this finding, however, as there are considerable misunderstandings about so-called unplanned or impulsive suicide attempts.

When considering the notion of an "unplanned" suicide attempt, for instance, many clinicians think of a suicide attempt that occurs "out of the blue," or with little or no forethought. Indeed, many suicide attempts often seem to emerge with little forewarning, planning, or contemplation and therefore *appear* to be unplanned or impulsive. However, it is important to keep in mind that the increased risk for these seemingly unplanned suicide attempts among individuals with substance use disorders occurs among those who also have a history of suicidal ideation. Suicide has therefore already been considered by the individual, suggesting that the suicide attempts may not be unplanned or impulsive after all. Instead, it appears that substance use (especially alcohol, inhalants, and heroin; Borges et al., 2000) reduces the threshold for suicidal action or shortens the length of time between the final decision to make a suicide attempt and the act itself among those individuals who have already contemplated suicide. This finding highlights an important consideration for clinical work with suicidal patients with comorbid substance use disorders: the presence of alcohol or drug use may narrow the window for intervention in a crisis. For this very reason, it is important for clinicians not to minimize or underestimate the severity or "seriousness" of suicide attempts that occur while a patient is intoxicated. Although some patients who make suicide attempts while intoxicated might later minimize the incident or insist that a suicide attempt was not a "real" suicide attempt (e.g., "I was just drunk and being stupid; I don't really want to kill myself"), clinicians should nonetheless treat these suicide attempts as serious events.

Because substance use facilitates suicide attempts, it can be conceptualized within the behavioral domain of the suicidal mode. Specifically, substance use often serves as a coping strategy for emotional distress, similar to the underlying function and purpose of suicide attempts, and should therefore be treated concurrently in brief cognitive behavior therapy. Indeed, concurrent treatment of substance use and suicidal ideation is associated with significantly decreased rates of suicidal ideation relative to treatment focused on substance abuse only (Esposito-Smythers et al., 2011). Substance use can be integrated into suicide-focused treatments with a fair amount of ease. For instance, crisis response plans might include alcohol or drug cravings as warning signs for a suicidal crisis, cognitive interventions might target faulty beliefs or assumptions about alcohol use (e.g., "I must have a drink now"; "I can't wait any longer"), and behavioral planning might include the awareness and avoidance of places or people associated with substance use. In short, when treating suicidal patients with comorbid substance use, the substance use must be targeted concurrent with other symptoms and drivers of suicide attempts, and alternative strategies for coping with emotional distress must be learned and reinforced.

Comorbid Posttraumatic Stress Disorder

Trauma has consistently been identified as a risk factor for suicidal ideation and suicide attempts, with research suggesting that the relationship is not confined to any particular type of traumatic experience; sexual assault, interpersonal violence, and combat exposure have all been implicated. However, studies suggest that the relationship between traumatic events and suicide is best explained by the occurrence of posttraumatic stress disorder (PTSD). For example, victims of assault are significantly more likely to make a suicide attempt than individuals who have never been assaulted, but only if they also meet criteria for PTSD (Wilcox, Storr, & Breslau, 2009); individuals who were exposed to traumatic events but who did not meet criteria for PTSD were not more likely to make a suicide attempt. Among US military personnel, Griffith (2012) has similarly reported that the relationship of combat exposure with post-deployment suicidal ideation occurs primarily through the symptoms of PTSD. Indeed, as trauma victims endorse more symptoms of PTSD, the likelihood of endorsing suicidal ideation increases (Marshall et al., 2008). Taken together, these findings suggest that it may not be traumatic experiences per se that contribute to increased risk for suicidal ideation and suicide attempts, but rather it is how the individual responds to or understands the event that contributes to increased risk.

The relationship of PTSD with suicide attempts is further magnified by comorbid depression (Panagioti, Gooding, & Tarrier, 2009). Gradus et al. (2010), for instance, reported that PTSD without depression was associated with a six-fold increase in the likelihood of death by suicide and depression without PTSD was associated with a 13-fold increase in risk, whereas comorbid PTSD and depression was associated with a 39-fold increase in the likelihood of suicide. The augmenting effect of depression on PTSD has also been noted in US military (Bryan, Clemans, Hernandez, & Rudd, 2013) and veteran (Rudd, Goulding, & Bryan, 2011) samples, suggesting that comorbid PTSD and depression may be an especially pernicious and risky combination of emotional distress.

Although the relationship of PTSD with suicide attempts is now well established, the exact mechanisms by which PTSD confers increased risk are not yet clear. Some studies suggest that the hyperarousal symptoms of PTSD are most strongly associated with suicidal ideation (Tarrier & Gregg, 2004), which may be due to the fact that insomnia and agitation, two prominent features of PTSD's hyperarousal cluster, are also independent risk factors for suicidal ideation and suicide attempts. Other studies have also implicated the reexperiencing symptom cluster of PTSD (Bell & Nye, 2007; Tarrier & Gregg, 2004), which may be due in large part to the prominence of nightmares, which are associated with suicidal ideation beyond the effects of depression and general insomnia (Bernert, Joiner, Cukrowicz, Schmidt, & Krakow, 2005). Others, however, have reported that emotional numbing symptoms, rather than reexperiencing or hyperarousal symptoms, are most strongly associated with increased severity of suicidal ideation (Guerra, Calhoun, & MIRECC, 2011), most likely because of the social isolation and depressive elements associated with this symptom cluster. It is also possible that other features of PTSD that are commonly experienced by trauma victims but that have not traditionally been included in the diagnostic criteria for PTSD, such as guilt, shame, and self-deprecation, may also be important mechanisms underlying the increased risk for suicidal ideation and suicide attempts in PTSD (Bryan, Morrow, Etienne, & Ray-Sannerud, 2013).

Treatment of suicidal victims of trauma therefore requires clinicians to target multiple facets of PTSD. Unfortunately, few studies to date have examined the implications of treating trauma patients who are also suicidal because patients who report suicidal ideation and suicide attempts are routinely excluded from PTSD studies. The absence of data on suicide-related outcomes among trauma victims receiving treatment has led to a widespread assumption that trauma-focused therapies are not safe with suicidal patients (Becker, Zayfert, & Anderson, 2004). Newer treatment studies that have *not* excluded suicidal patients suggest otherwise, however. Gradus et al. (2013) recently reported that the incidence of suicidal ideation actually decreases among sexual assault victims with PTSD who receive prolonged exposure (PE) and cognitive processing therapy (CPT)—two empirically supported treatments for PTSD—with reductions in risk persisting for at least 12 months post-treatment. Subsequent analyses indicated that the reductions in suicidal ideation were associated with the magnitude of improvement in overall PTSD symptomatology, indicating that patients with larger reductions in PTSD symptoms were significantly more likely to report improvement in suicidal ideation. Preliminary evidence from two separate studies conducted in US military populations—one focused on PE and the other on CPT—similarly suggest significant reductions in suicidal ideation across both treatments (Clemans et al., 2012; Morris et al., 2012). Furthermore, in contrast to the assumption that trauma-focused therapies may not be safe for individuals with PTSD, less than 5% of service members in these studies who started treatment with no suicidal ideation later reported "new" or emergent suicidal ideation. Research is underway to better understand why and how these various treatments work for both suicidal ideation and PTSD. Taken together, however, these newer studies suggest that suicidal ideation decreases among individuals with PTSD who receive empirically supported trauma-focused therapies, and PTSD severity improves among suicidal individuals treated with empirically supported suicide-focused therapies. From a practical standpoint, these findings suggest that clinicians can effectively use brief cognitive behavioral treatments for suicidal patients with PTSD.

Comorbid Personality Disorders

Of the many personality disorder diagnoses, borderline personality and antisocial personality disorders have been most consistently connected with increased risk for suicide attempts (American Psychiatric Association, 2003), which may be due to their prominent externalizing features (e.g., substance use, aggression), which have a much stronger association with suicidal ideation and suicide attempts than internalizing symptoms such as depression and anxiety (Verona, Sachs-Ericsson, & Joiner, 2004). Consistent with this possibility, a recent factor analysis of psychiatric disorders (Roysamb et al., 2011) suggests that antisocial and borderline personality disorders are the only two personality disorders with pronounced externalizing features. This study further suggests that borderline personality disorder is an especially unique disorder because it is the only psychiatric disorder that loads onto multiple factors of psychopathology associated with different subtypes of psychiatric diagnoses: externalizing symptoms (e.g., substance use disorders), internalizing symptoms (e.g., depressive and anxiety disorders), and cognitive relational disturbance (e.g., other personality disorders). The heterogeneous and multifaceted psychopathological features of borderline personality disorder therefore likely account for its very high comorbidity rates with other psychiatric conditions including mood disorders (94%), anxiety disorders (90%), and substance use disorders (79%; Linehan et al., 2006).

In addition to their complex clinical presentations, patients with borderline personality disorder can be especially challenging to treat due to the presence and recurrence of non-suicidal self-injury in addition to suicide attempts. Relative to other psychiatric disorders, non-suicidal self-injury occurs most frequently within the context of borderline personality disorder (Langbehn & Pfohl, 1993), typically as an emotion regulation or coping strategy. Although conceptually distinct from suicide attempts, non-suicidal self-injury is a very robust predictor of suicide attempts, especially among women (Klonsky, May, & Glenn, 2013). Comorbid PTSD and borderline personality disorder appears to augment risk for suicide attempts more so than other comorbid conditions, as this particular combination is associated with greater frequency of non-suicidal self-injury, higher rates of psychopathology, less emotion regulation, and fewer positive emotions (Harned, Rizvi, & Linehan, 2010), all of which confer greater risk for suicide attempts. Patients with borderline personality disorder who have engaged in non-suicidal self-injury and also made a suicide attempt present especially complex cases, as they report more severe depression, anxiety, and impulsivity, and tend to underestimate the lethality of their behavior (Stanley, Gameroff, Michalson, & Mann, 2001). This combination of emotional distress, rash decision making, and underestimation of lethality can create a particularly risky combination. Clinicians should therefore routinely assess for history of non-suicidal self-injury in addition to suicide attempts, and be careful not to underestimate potential suicide risk among those patients who report histories of both behaviors.

In terms of reducing risk for suicide attempts in patients with borderline personality disorder, most research to date has focused on dialectical behavior therapy (DBT; Linehan, 1993), which is a 12-month multimodal outpatient treatment that has consistently demonstrated significant reductions in suicide attempts relative to other active treatments (e.g., Linehan et al., 2006). It is not yet known if shorter, less intensive cognitive behavioral therapies are as effective as DBT for suicidal patients with borderline personality disorder, although a recent meta-analysis of 16 DBT trials suggests that the length of DBT (ranging from 12 to 52 weeks in duration) does not appear to influence the overall effectiveness of the treatment (Kliem, Kroger, & Kosfelder, 2010). Briefer cognitive behavioral therapies may therefore be as effective as DBT for reducing suicide attempts in patients with borderline personality disorder, although additional research is needed to determine sufficient "dose" levels of cognitive behavior therapy for these patients.

Integrating Cognitive Behavioral Therapy With Medication Treatments

Scientific evidence in support of pharmacologic interventions for suicide attempts is not as robust as the evidence in support of cognitive behavioral therapies. Based on an exhaustive review of scientific studies, the United Kingdom's National Institute for Health and Clinical Excellence (NICE; 2012) concluded that pharmacological treatments do not play a direct role in the management of suicide risk, although they have a significant role to play in the management of associated conditions such as depression and anxiety. In the United States, the Clinical Care and Intervention Task Force to the National Action Alliance for Suicide Prevention (NAASP, 2014) similarly concluded that there was limited evidence of the overall efficacy of pharmacotherapy-only treatment for suicidal ideation and the prevention of suicide attempts. Clinicians should keep in mind that these conclusions do not mean that medications should *never* be used with suicidal patients, but rather they should probably be used *concurrent with* empirically supported psychotherapies such as the cognitive behavioral treatments reviewed in this book.

It is also important to keep in mind that absence of evidence is not the same as evidence of absence. In other words, just because the effectiveness of pharmacologic treatments as stand-alone therapies are not yet well researched does not mean that we should conclude that they are not effective. One notable exception is clozapine, which has demonstrated preliminary effectiveness for reducing suicide attempts among individuals with psychotic disorders. Specifically, patients with schizophrenia who were treated with clozapine were approximately 50% less likely (7.7% vs. 13.8%) to make a suicide attempt during follow-up than patients treated with olanzapine, a different antipsychotic drug (Meltzer et al., 2003). Use of clozapine with patients with schizophrenia may therefore be an effective treatment strategy for suicide risk reduction in this particular population. Lithium has also received considerable attention as a medication that reduces suicide attempts and suicide deaths when used with patients with bipolar disorder (Cipriani et al., 2005). However, other researchers have noted that the "antisuicide effect" of lithium has largely been based on secondary analyses of randomized controlled trials, naturalistic studies, meta-analyses, and open-label medication trials, all of which could confound the decision-making processes of prescribing clinicians (Oquendo et al., 2011). For example, because lithium has a very high lethality profile when taken in excess, clinicians may be less likely to prescribe lithium to patients deemed to be at high risk for suicide. The apparent "antisuicide effect" could therefore be explained by physician decision making, as the patients most likely to receive lithium are the patients who are least likely to engage in suicide attempts. To address this concern, Oquendo et al. (2011) recently conducted a randomized controlled trial to test the suicide prevention properties of lithium relative to a newer generation mood stabilizer commonly used to treat bipolar disorder (i.e., valproate) that is not assumed to have the same effect. Results of this study suggested that patients with bipolar disorder who received lithium were just as likely as patients who received valproate to make a suicide attempt during follow-up, suggesting that lithium may not have a relatively stronger antisuicide effect than other pharmacologic agents for bipolar disorder.

Unfortunately, no studies have yet been conducted to determine if certain combinations of medications and cognitive behavioral therapy yield better outcomes than psychotherapy alone. Indeed, combined medication and cognitive behavioral therapy is arguably the most commonly used treatment package for suicidal patients. For instance, medication treatment was reported by 60% of patients who were actively engaged in cognitive therapy for the prevention of suicide attempts, and 33% continued to take medication of some sort 18 months later (Brown et al., 2005). Similarly, close to 90% of patients who receive dialectical behavior therapy report taking psychotropic medications at the beginning of treatment, and approximately 50% continue taking medication 1 year later (Linehan et al., 2006). Because medication use is not discussed in detail within the context of psychotherapy clinical trials, however, details about how and under what conditions medications are used effectively in conjunction with cognitive behavioral therapy remain relatively unknown. General consensus is that medications play an important role for the short-term stabilization of acute psychiatric symptoms that contribute to suicidal ideation and suicide attempts among patients engaged in cognitive behavioral therapy (e.g., hypnotics for insomnia, anxiolytics for agitation, and antidepressants and anticonvulsants for mood disturbance).

The FDA Black Box Warning Label for Antidepressants and Anticonvulsants

In 2004 the US Food and Drug Administration (FDA) placed a black box warning label targeting suicidal ideation and suicide attempts in children and adolescents up to the age of 18 years on all antidepressant drugs, to include selective serotonin reuptake inhibitors (SSRIs), the most widely prescribed psychotropic drug class in the United States. The warning label was subsequently updated in 2007 to extend the warning to all patients up to 24 years of age. The original intent of the warning label was to alert consumers and health care providers of a possible risk for increased suicidal ideation and suicide attempts (referred to as "suicidality" by the FDA) associated with antidepressant use, and it also included information about the benefits of antidepressants (i.e., *decreased* suicide rates) among older adults aged 65 years and older, although this latter piece of information is relatively unknown. In 2009, a similar warning label was issued for all antiepileptic drugs, more commonly referred to as "mood stabilizers" by mental health professionals.

Since the initial warning label for antidepressants appeared, there has been considerable discussion and debate in the scientific community and the general public about its potential impact on mental health treatment (see Rudd, Cordero, & Bryan, 2009, for a thorough review). Potentially lost to consumers and professionals alike is that *no deaths* occurred in any of the pediatric trials that prompted the original black box warning label for antidepressants. Indeed, 91% of primary care providers (PCPs) incorrectly believe that suicide deaths occurred in the pediatric trials, which is of particular concern given that 90% of these same providers indicate they routinely provide supplemental information about the risks associated with antidepressants (Cordero, Rudd, Bryan, & Corso, 2008). This suggests the vast majority of PCPs, the group of medical providers who prescribe the majority of psychotropic medications in the United States, may be providing patients and consumers with incorrect information about the risk associated with antidepressants. Although these studies focused on primary care medical providers, it is likely that mental health professionals would also demonstrate high rates of inaccuracies.

Misconceptions about medication-related risk for suicide attempts is also likely due to a failure to conceptualize suicide risk as a fluctuating construct over time, and to differentiate between chronic and acute dimensions of risk. For example, in a study of over 120,000 patients who received antidepressants over the course of 1 year in three difference clinical settings—primary care, outpatient psychotherapy, and outpatient psychiatry—the highest risk period for a suicide attempt was during the month *immediately before* starting antidepressant treatment, with declining risk in subsequent months after antidepressant initiation (Simon & Savarino, 2007). The first month after starting an antidepressant was therefore the highest-risk month for patients, but only if patients' risk level prior to starting the antidepressant was ignored. Contrary to the conclusion that antidepressants contribute to increased risk for suicide, this study suggests that antidepressants are typically started *after* a patient's highest-risk period, most likely as an intervention to reduce this risk. This same pattern has also been identified more recently among older patients treated with antiepileptic medications (Pugh et al., in press), although Pugh et al. additionally reported that patients who received antiepileptic drugs were more likely to make suicide attempts both before and after receiving antiepileptic drugs, suggesting that patients who are prescribed antiepileptics are at elevated risk for suicide attempts regardless of the medication they receive. Taken together, these findings suggest that antidepressants and antiepileptics probably do not *cause* suicide attempts; rather, those patients who are most likely to make suicide attempts are also more likely to be treated with psychotropic medications, probably because they tend to be more emotionally distressed.

When treating patients who are also treated with psychotropic medications, clinicians should be sure to regularly assess for and monitor agitation, physiological restlessness, psychomotor agitation, and racing thoughts, as these symptoms may be especially important indicators of increased suicide risk, especially when these agitated symptoms occur within the context of a depressive episode (i.e., a mixed depressive episode; Benazzi, 2005; Akiskal & Benazzi, 2005; Rihmer & Kiss, 2002; Rihmer & Pestality, 1999). Irritability and psychomotor agitation, in particular, are two symptoms that reliably differentiate a mixed depressive episode from a unipolar depressive episode, and may therefore serve as "red flags" for clinicians (Benazzi & Akiskal, 2006). Patients with depression who also manifest these symptoms should be evaluated for the possibility of unrecognized mixed or hypomanic episodes, which may require augmentation medication therapy with benzodiazepines, mood stabilizers, or antipsychotics (Rihmer & Akiskal, 2006). In all cases, clinicians should continue to monitor patient risk for suicide and clinical status over time and emphasize medication adherence.

Summary

Suicidal patients often present with complex clinical profiles characterized by high rates of comorbidity, which can present considerable challenges for treatment. Encouragingly, preliminary results from clinical trials suggest that clinicians do not need to dramatically alter treatment plans or protocols with complex cases. By developing a treatment plan that is based on a functional model of psychiatric and behavioral disorders, clinicians can simplify the treatment process and effectively "treat two birds with one stone." Because the majority of suicidal patients who receive cognitive behavioral therapy will also be treated with psychotropic medications, clinicians should plan to coordinate care with prescribing providers and incorporate medication interventions and side effect monitoring into their overall treatment plans.

References

Aharonovich, E., Liu, X., Nunes, E., & Hasin, D. S. (2002). Suicide attempts in substance abusers: Effects of major depression in relation to substance use disorders. *The American Journal of Psychiatry, 159*, 1600–1602.

Akiskal, H. S., & Benazzi, F. (2005). Psychopathologic correlates of suicidal ideation in major depressive outpatients: Is it all due to unrecognized (bipolar) depressive mixed states? *Psychopathology, 38*, 273–280.

American Psychiatric Association (2003). Practice guideline for the assessment and treatment of patients with suicidal behaviors. *The American Journal of Psychiatry, 160(Suppl. 11)*, 1–60.

Becker, C. B., Zayfert, C., & Anderson, E. (2004). A survey of psychologists' attitudes towards and utilization of exposure therapy for PTSD. *Behavior Research and Therapy, 42*, 277–292.

Bell, J. B., & Nye, E. C. (2007). Specific symptoms predict suicidal ideation in Vietnam combat veterans with chronic post-traumatic stress disorder. *Military Medicine, 172*, 1144–1147.

Benazzi, F. (2005). Suicidal ideation and bipolar-II depression symptoms. *Human Psychopharmacology, 20*, 27–32.

Benazzi, F., & Akiskal, H. S. (2006). Psychometric delineation of the most discriminant symptoms of depressive mixed states. *Psychiatry Research, 141*, 81–88.

Bernert, R. A., Joiner, T. E., Cukrowicz, K. C., Schmidt, N. B., & Krakow, B. (2005). Suicidality and sleep disturbances. *SLEEP, 28*, 1135–1141.

Borges, G., Walters, E. E., & Kessler, R. C. (2000). Associations of substance use, abuse, and dependence with subsequent suicidal behavior. *American Journal of Epidemiology, 151*, 781–789.

Brown, G. K., Have, T. T., Henriques, G. R., Xie, S. X., Hollander, J. E., & Beck, A. T. (2005). Cognitive therapy for the prevention of suicide attempts: A randomized controlled trial. *JAMA: Journal of the American Medical Association, 294*, 563–570.

Bryan, C. J., Clemans, T. A., Hernandez, A. M., & Rudd, M. D. (2013). Loss of consciousness, depression, posttraumatic stress disorder, and suicide risk among deployed military personnel with mild traumatic brain injury (mTBI). *Journal of Head Trauma Rehabilitation, 28*, 13–20.

Bryan, C. J., Morrow, C. E., Etienne, N., & Ray-Sannerud, B. (2013). Guilt, shame, and suicidal ideation in a military outpatient clinical sample. *Depression and Anxiety, 30*, 55–60.

Bryan, C. J., Rudd, M. D., & Wertenberger, E. (2013). Reasons for suicide attempts among active duty soldiers: A functional approach. *Journal of Affective Disorders, 144*, 148–152.

Cipriani, A., Pretty, H., Hawton, K. et al. (2005). Lithium in the prevention of suicidal behavior and all-cause mortality in patients with mood disorders: A systematic review of randomized trials. *American Journal of Psychiatry, 162*, 1805–1819.

Clemans, T. A., Bryan, C. J., Resick, P. A., Mintz, J., Evans, B. B., Young-McCaughan, S., . . . & the STRONG STAR Consortium. (2012, November). *Impact of cognitive processing therapy on trauma-related guilt and suicidality.* Symposium conducted at the annual convention of the Association for Behavioral and Cognitive Therapies, National Harbor, MD.

Cordero, L., Rudd, M. D., Bryan, C. J., & Corso, K. A. (2008). Accuracy of primary care medical providers' understanding of the FDA blackbox warning label for antidepressants. *Primary Care and Community Psychiatry, 13*, 109–114.

Dalton, E. J., Cate-Carter, T. D., Mundo, E., Parikh, S. V., & Kennedy, J. L. (2003). Suicide risk in bipolar patients: The role of co-morbid substance use disorders. *Bipolar Disorders, 5*, 58–61.

Esposito-Smythers, C., Spirito, A., Kahler, C. W., Hunt, J., & Monti, P. (2011). Treatment of co-occurring substance abuse and suicidality among adolescents: A randomized trial. *Journal of Consulting and Clinical Psychology, 79*, 728–739.

Gradus, J. L., Qin, P., Lincoln, A. K., Miller, M., Lawler, E., Sorensen, H. T., & Lash, T. L. (2010). Posttraumatic stress disorder and completed suicide. *American Journal of Epidemiology, 171*, 721–727.

Gradus, J. L., Suvak, M. K., Wisco, B. E., Marx, B. P., & Resick, P. A. (2013). Treatment of posttraumatic stress disorder reduces suicidal ideation. *Depression and Anxiety, 30*, 1046–1053.

Grant, B. F., Stinson, F. S., Dawson, D. A., Chou, P., Dufour, M. C., Compton, W., . . . & Kaplan, K. (2004). Prevalence and co-occurrence of substance use disorders and independent mood and anxiety disorders: Results from the National Epidemiological Survey on Alcohol and Related Conditions. *Archives of General Psychiatry, 61*, 807–816.

Griffith, J. (2012). Suicide and war: The mediating effects of negative mood, posttraumatic stress disorder symptoms, and social support among Army National Guard soldiers. *Suicide and Life-Threatening Behavior, 42*, 453–469.

Guerra, V. S., Calhoun, P. S., & the Mid-Atlantic Mental Illness Research, Education, and Clinical Center Workgroup (MIRECC) (2011). Examining the relation between posttraumatic stress disorder and suicidal ideation in an OEF/OIF veteran sample. *Journal of Anxiety Disorders, 25*, 12–18.

Harned, M. S., Rizvi, S. L., & Linehan, M. M. (2010). Impact of co-occurring posttraumatic stress disorder on suicidal women with borderline personality disorder. *American Journal of Psychiatry, 167*, 1210–1217.

Harris, E. C., & Barraclough, B. (1997). Suicide as an outcome for mental disorders: A meta-analysis. *British Journal of Psychiatry, 170*, 205–228.

Hayes, S. C., Wilson, K. G., Gifford, E. V., Follete, V. M., & Strosahl, K. (1996). Experiential avoidance and behavioral disorders: A functional dimensional approach to diagnosis and treatment. *Journal of Consulting and Clinical Psychology, 64*, 1152–1168.

Jobes, D. A. (2006). *Managing suicidal risk: A collaborative approach.* New York, NY: Guilford Press.

Joiner, T. E. (2005). *Why people die by suicide.* Cambridge: Harvard University Press.

Kliem, S., Kroger, C., & Kosfelder, J. (2010). Dialectical behavior therapy for borderline personality disorder: A meta-analysis using mixed-effects modeling. *Journal of Consulting and Clinical Psychology, 78*, 936–951.

Klonsky, D., May, A. M., & Glenn, C. R. (2013). Relationship between nonsuicidal self-injury and attempted suicide: Converging evidence from four samples. *Journal of Abnormal Psychology, 122*, 231–237.

Langbehn, D. R., & Pfohl, B. (1993). Clinical correlates of self-mutilation among psychiatric inpatients. *Annals of Clinical Psychiatry, 5*, 45–51.

Linehan, M. M. (1993). *Cognitive-behavioral treatment of borderline personality disorder.* New York City, NY: Guilford Press.

Linehan, M. M., Comtois, K. A., Murray, A. M., Brown, M. Z., Gallop, R. J., Heard, H. L., . . . & Lindeboim, N. (2006). Two-year randomized controlled trial and follow-up of dialectical behavior therapy vs therapy by experts for suicidal behaviors and borderline personality disorder. *Archives of General Psychiatry, 63*, 757–766.

Marshall, R. D., Olfson, M., Hellman, F., Blanco, C., Guardino, M., & Struning, E. L. (2008). Comorbidity, impairment, and suicidality in subthreshold PTSD. *American Journal of Psychiatry, 158*, 1467–1473.

Meltzer, H. Y., Alphs, L., Green, A. L., Altamura, C., Anand, R., Bertoldt, A., . . . & Potkin, S. for the InterSePT Study Group (2003). Clozapine treatment for suicidality in schizophrenia: International Suicide Prevention Trial (InterSePT). *Archives of General Psychiatry, 60*, 82–91.

Morris, S., Kitsmiller, E., McLean, C. P., Foa, E. B., Litz, B. T., Stein, N. R., . . . & the STRONG STAR Consortium. (2012, November). *Predictors of suicidal ideation in active duty soldiers: The role of PTSD, depression, and trauma-related guilt.* Poster presented at the annual meeting of the Association of Behavioral and Cognitive Therapies, National Harbor, MD.

National Action Alliance for Suicide Prevention: Research Prioritization Task Force (2014). *A Prioritized Research Agenda for Suicide Prevention: An Action Plan to Save Lives.* Rockville, MD: National Institute of Mental Health and the Research Prioritization Task Force.

National Institute for Health & Clinical Excellence (2012). *Self-harm: The NICE guideline on longer-term management.* London, UK: The British Psychological Society & the Royal College of Psychiatrists.

Nock, M. K., & Prinstein, M. J. (2004). A functional approach to the assessment of self-mutilative behavior. *Journal of Consulting and Clinical Psychology, 72*, 885–890.

Oquendo, M. A., Galfalvy, H. C., Currier, D., Grunebaum, M. F., Sher, L., Sullivan, G. M., . . . & Mann, J. J. (2011). Treatment of suicide attempters with bipolar disorder: A randomized clinical trial comparing lithium and valproate in the prevention of suicidal behavior. *American Journal of Psychiatry, 168,* 1050–1056.

Panagioti, M., Gooding, P., & Tarrier, N. (2009). Posttraumatic stress disorder and suicidal behavior: A narrative review. *Clinical Psychology Review, 29,* 471–482.

Price, R. K., Risk, N. K., Haden, A. H., Lewis, C. E., & Spitznagel, E. L. (2004). Posttraumatic stress disorder, drug dependence, and suicidality among male Vietnam veterans with a history of heavy drug use. *Drug and Alcohol Dependence, 76S,* S31–S43.

Pugh, M. J. V., Hesdorffer, D., Wang, C., Amuan, M. E., Tabares, J., Finley, E. P., . . . & Bryan, C. J. (in press). Temporal trends in new exposure to seizure medication monotherapy and suicide-related behavior. *Neurology.*

Rihmer, Z., & Akiskal, H. S. (2006). Do antidepressants t(h)reat(en) depressives? Toward a clinically judicious formulation of the antidepressant-suicidality FDA advisory in light of declining national suicide statistics from many countries. *Journal of Affective Disorders, 94,* 3–13.

Rihmer, Z., & Kiss, K. (2002). Bipolar disorders and suicidal behaviour. *Bipolar Disorders, 4,* 21–25.

Rihmer, Z., & Pestality, P. (1999). Bipolar II disorder and suicidal behavior. *Psychiatric Clinics of North America, 22,* 667–673.

Roysamb, E., Kendler, K. S., Tambs, K., Orstavik, R. E., Neale, M. C., Aggen, S. H., Torgersen, S., & Reichborn-Kjennerud, T. (2011). The joint structure of DSM-IV Axis I and Axis II disorders. *Journal of Abnormal Psychology, 120,* 198–209.

Rudd, M. D. (2006). Fluid vulnerability theory: A cognitive approach to understanding the process of acute and chronic risk. In T. E. Ellis (Ed.), *Cognition and suicide: Theory, research, and therapy* (pp. 355–367). Washington, DC: American Psychological Association.

Rudd, M. D., Cordero, L., & Bryan, C. J. (2009). What every psychologist should know about the FDA blackbox warning label for antidepressants. *Professional Psychology: Research and Practice, 40,* 321–326.

Rudd, M. D., Goulding, J., & Bryan, C. J. (2011). Student veterans: A national survey exploring psychological symptoms and suicide risk. *Professional Psychology: Research and Practice, 42,* 354–360.

Simon, G. E., & Savarino, J. (2007). Suicide attempts among patients starting depression treatment with medications or psychotherapy. *American Journal of Psychiatry, 164,* 1029–1034.

Stanley, B., Gameroff, M. J., Michalson, V., & Mann, J. J. (2001). Are suicide attempters who self-mutilate a unique population? *American Journal of Psychiatry, 158,* 427–432.

Tarrier, N., & Gregg, L. (2004). Suicide risk in civilian PTSD patients—predictors of suicidal ideation, planning and attempts. *Social Psychology and Psychiatric Epidemiology, 39,* 655–661.

Tondo, L., Baldessarini, R. J., Hennen, J., Minnai, G. P., Salis, P., Scamonatti, L., . . . & Mannu, P. (1999). Suicide attempts in major affective disorder patients with comorbid substance use disorders. *Journal of Clinical Psychiatry, 60,* 63–69.

Verona, E., Sachs-Ericsson, N., & Joiner, T. E. (2004). Suicide attempts associated with externalizing psychopathology in an epidemiological study. *American Journal of Psychiatry, 161,* 444–451.

Wilcox, H. C., Storr, C. L., & Breslau, N. (2009). Posttraumatic stress disorder and suicide attempts in a community sample of urban American young adults. *Archives of General Psychiatry, 66,* 305–311.

Index

Made in the USA
Las Vegas, NV
02 December 2023

81932103R10108